THE DIE-HARD FAN'S

Guide to

LONGHORN
FOOTBALL

THE DIE-HARD FAN'S
Guide to
LONGHORN
FOOTBALL

GEOFF KETCHUM

Since 1947
REGNERY
PUBLISHING, INC.
An Eagle Publishing Company • Washington, DC

Cataloging-in-Publication Data on file with the Library of Congress

ISBN 978-1-59698-531-5

Published in the United States by
Regnery Publishing, Inc.
One Massachusetts Avenue, NW
Washington, DC 20001
www.regnery.com

Manufactured in the United States of America

10 9 8 7 6 5 4 3 2 1

Books are available in quantity for promotional or premium use. Write to Director of Special Sales, Regnery Publishing, Inc., One Massachusetts Avenue NW, Washington, DC 20001, for information on discounts and terms or call (202) 216-0600.

To the three women who made me the person I am today—
my mom, Alice Ketchum; my grandmother, Mary Paris;
and my great-grandmother, Lillie Bishop Hellums. In particular,
this book is dedicated to my mom, who not only raised me without
a lot of help, but taught me the lessons of hard work and integrity,
while insuring that my mind, heart, and soul would always
be open to everything that is good.

CONTENTS

Foreword

It wasn't too long ago, maybe a little over a decade, but I remember it like it was yesterday. I woke up in tears, but they were tears of joy. I had been dreaming that I'd just been given a football scholarship. I remember in the dream looking out at a stadium with my dad and Spike Dykes. That's right, I was in tears over a dream of an offer to play ball not at the University of Texas, but at Texas Tech, located in a little place in west Texas where they throw tortillas and wear red and black. It was my childhood dream ever since I can remember.

Since my early years in Lubbock, when my dad was coaching at the university, I dreamed of wearing the Double T. When I was no older than two or three, I was featured on a poster promoting walk-on at Tech. It showed me on the field dragging a helmet about as big as I was. In bold letters the poster read, "Some people just can't wait to walk on at Tech."

That wasn't too long ago at all, but oh, how things have changed. All of us 'Horns bleed orange. Some of us were born with it and some chose it, while a very few got it not by a twist of fate, but through destiny. I'm one of the lucky ones in that last category.

On a warm fall afternoon in 1998, I attended my first game at DKR Memorial Stadium. I would bet that most 'Horn fans remember that day, and not positively. On that afternoon I watched Texas get throttled by UCLA. I can't say I was upset, because I hadn't quite been converted yet.

Then I began attending games in College Station, which was only an hour from home. My first game there was much different than the one I saw in Austin—I watched the Aggies hand the No. 2-ranked Nebraska Cornhuskers a convincing loss. I remember walking out of the stadium at dusk on a nice evening and telling my dad, "I think I could really enjoy this place." I went on to attend a lot more games and even the summer camp at A&M, and I thought I had made up my mind. At one point, I indicated to some of the football coaching staff that I intended to play there.

It seemed that the chips where stacked high against the 'Horns, but like I said, it was destiny. I received a call one evening from Tim Brewster. For whatever reason, mainly because "no" wasn't an option, I agreed to make just one trip to Austin. And that trip would change my life.

I wasn't in Austin for long before I began to feel some strong emotions. I visited with the coaching staff, met many players, and held the Heisman trophy. It was great—I immediately felt that there was something unique about UT. Before we left, I asked Coach Brown to recommend a place to eat. He named a spot that was a bit outside of town, but promised it would be well worth the trip. I took his advice and headed west. It wasn't two minutes after we were seated on the deck at the Oasis, looking out over Lake Travis, when I realized I was home. This was it, there would be no more looking. I didn't even wait until I got home to let the Texas coaches know—I couldn't. I was like a child with a big surprise who just can't wait to tell you what it is.

It was a decision that changed my life in so many ways, and one that I would make again in a second if I had the chance. I was given the opportunity to be part of history, to be part of something great, something bigger than all of us. By coming to the University of Texas, I was able to meet some of the best friends any person could ever have. Unfortunately, we lost one of my closest friends, Cole Pittman, but I got to be part of a game that we dedicated to him. In that game we took a knee to preserve forty-four points on the scoreboard to reflect Cole's jersey number. That's the kind of stuff movie writers couldn't make up.

I was able to play with countless great players and for a coach who forgets more about the game of football than most people will ever know. I had the opportunity to substitute in for Chris Sims on his last play in DKR Memorial Stadium; I was able to hit B. J. Johnson in the corner of the end zone to give us a win against Texas Tech, a play that will likely define my time at the University of Texas; and I was part of Texas's first-ever Rose Bowl victory. I was part of some great things—sometimes I feel like I'm in the movie *Big Fish*. The things I've been a part of, the people I've met, and the opportunities afforded to me by this great university are unmatched anywhere. It's the stuff daddies tell their little boys and girls at night. It's what many people dream about. But I got to live the dream.

I will always be the ultimate optimist about the university that I truly love. Coming here to UT, "it" gets in your blood and you can't get it out—there is no denying that. True, my timing wasn't great, and most people will only remember me as a back-up. But as I always jokingly say, "Vince Young, one of the greatest to ever put on the pads, was MY back-up for six games!"

Yes, I was close to leaving school and finishing my playing somewhere else; it probably would have been the best thing for my NFL career. But I couldn't. I couldn't leave the fans that I had grown to love, having seen them hold the horns up high when "The Eyes of Texas" played. I couldn't leave a group of coaches and players with whom I had laughed, cried, bled, and celebrated. I couldn't leave because every time I see the sun set to a burnt orange sky, it confirms the same sentiment you get from reading this book: that God truly is a Longhorn.

—Chance Mock, '04

Introduction

November 25, 1989: If you're looking for a memorable date in the history of the Texas football program, this one likely qualifies—in the worst possible way.

In what certainly can be considered one of the lowest moments in the history of the proudest college football program in the country, a paltry 49,081 fans showed up to watch an unranked Baylor squad thrash an uninspired Longhorn team to the tune of 50–7.

When Baylor linebacker James Francis wasn't sacking a Longhorn quarterback that day, Bears defensive back Robert Blackmon was intercepting him. It was a contest between two teams that were simply playing out the string in a disappointing season for both clubs. The glory days of the Southwest Conference were a distant memory on this afternoon.

It was on this day, however, that I was truly introduced to the Longhorn Nation. As a thirteen-year-old kid from Waco, I had grown up as a huge Bears fan, even if I had moved to Austin at the age of ten. As just about every current resident of Austin might say, "I wasn't born here, but I got here as fast as I could."

With a 50-yard-line ticket that I bought for five dollars just before the game, I attended the first of what would eventually become an endless stream of contests at Memorial Stadium.

After the game, I made my way down to the field and finagled autographs from Francis, Blackmon, and a host of other Baylor players. As Francis and a group of Bears enjoyed the final moments of a 5–6 season, an older gentleman wearing a Longhorn shirt and hat walked up to the Baylor faithful and said something that I've never forgotten.

"The difference between our school and your school is that this will probably be one of the greatest moments in Baylor history, and you'll be talking about this game in fifty years," the man said. "By that time we'll have won more national championships, and you'll still be Baylor," he added.

The crowd of Baylor fans and players began responding excitedly, but the man simply turned his back on them and walked away.

The remark lacked sportsmanship, even in the aftermath of a 43-point loss, but it opened my eyes to the amazingly high bar that the Longhorn football program had established for itself. In no uncertain terms, UT fans, players, and coaches expect greatness at all times. And even during the lean years, the standard never changes.

Perhaps it's both a blessing and a curse.

As the seasons have passed since that day, a lot has changed. Instead of putting on green and gold in college, I opted to stay in Austin and wear burnt orange.

Over the years, I've been on hand at Memorial Stadium for a number of transcendent moments. I was standing on the field in 1998 when Ricky Williams broke the NCAA rushing record, and I nearly caught Phil Dawson's 1995 game-winning field goal against Virginia as the ball slowly fell from the sky, just past the southern end zone goalpost.

After covering the team for fourteen years, I consider myself privileged to have built relationships with some of the greatest names of Longhorn lore.

Along the way, the remark made by the frustrated Longhorn fan on that late November day has always stood out in mind.

If there's one thing that I've learned about everyone who calls himself a Longhorn, it's that there are always expectations to excel in everything. Whether it's in business or an athletic contest, Longhorns don't expect greatness—they demand it. It's that kind of supreme confidence that erases the thin line between confidence and arrogance, and it makes Texas both the most loved and most hated school in the Lone Star State.

The names and faces might change yearly, but expectations that Longhorns will excel in every endeavor, from sports to academics, never change. That's what I learned on my first trip to Memorial Stadium.

The old man's comment was often on my mind as I covered the 2005 national championship season. In the final days leading up to the big showdown against USC, I'll never forget the fierce look in Vince Young's eyes when he was asked if the Longhorns would be able to keep pace with the favored Trojans.

You could tell that the possibility of losing had never crossed Young's mind. Perhaps the prospect of failure occurs to mortal men, but that wasn't the case with this player or with this Longhorn team.

I imagine that the determined look on Young's face that day was similar to the one that Tommy Nobis might have had the day the Longhorns squared off against Navy's Roger Staubach in the 1964 Cotton Bowl, or the one that James Street had during the final minutes of the "Big Shootout" in 1969.

The Die-Hard Fan's Guide to Longhorn Football seeks to convey this passion to succeed, which has driven the Longhorns to so many incredible accomplishments. It's an inside look at some of the great players and thrilling moments that have defined more than a hundred years of Texas football. From the very first Longhorn game in 1893 to Mack Brown's national champions, this book recalls the triumphs and the grandeur that characterize one of the greatest programs in the history of college sports.

Chapter One

GENESIS

THE LONGHORN NATION COMES TO LIFE

I t's there, in an 1893 issue of what was then called the *Austin Daily Statesman*, tucked between an ad for a play at Millett's Opera House and news items like the man who found his own missing brother's body while on a trip to town. It's short, but it's there—a report on UT's first football game.

Football, only a few years old, was not yet the national obsession it would later become. Texas, which will always be young—and big—was both, of course, in those days. It was a frontier so vast, several entire ecosystems were identified in the state.

But football was born that year in the Great State, and the University of Texas bulled its way to four wins in its inaugural season. (Interestingly, "No Coach" is listed as the squad's general. Imagine what they would have accomplished with one!)

The game summaries from those "Genesis" days make for some fun reading, as the sun has risen on Texas football glory in the century since. It is clear that Texans of all stripes were whipped up to a fever pitch as they readied to

field a football team—something that would give them equality with the staid and regal states back East. The *Statesman* had this account of the hullabaloo before UT's first game:

The Crack "Varsity" Team
Plays With Dallas Friday

Never before in the history of the university has there been such enthusiasm manifested in any one game as is shown in that coming national sport of football. Yesterday afternoon the sole topic of conversation at the university was the game which is to be played with Dallas today. For several weeks, in rain and sunshine, the boys have practiced incessantly, and are now in the very pink of condition for what promises to be one of the hardest fought contests that has ever taken place in this state. The Dallas boys have a crack team which has so far never met defeat, but if there is not a surprise in store for them in the "Varsity" boys then indications count for naught. The two teams are very evenly matched, the combined weight of the "Varsity" team being 1780 pounds while Dallas foots up 1786. The game is to be played on the Dallas exposition grounds and with excursions from Fort Worth and surrounding cities, will attract very much attention. The following men compose the Austin team and that they will strive to uphold the name of their institution as long as a breath remains or a bone is unbroken, will be but in keeping with the reputation of our Varsity boys.

The Team.

McLane, right end; Morrison, right tackle; Richardson, right guard; Meyer, center; Philp, left guard; Le Roy, left tackle; McLane P., left end; McLean, quarter back; Furman, right half; Jacks, left half; Day, full back.

Substitutes—Graves, Clark, Andrews.

Umpire and Referee—Fred F., Shelley.

The boys left on the 11:30 train last night with every student who could beg or borrow the necessary funds on board as well as a considerable number of Austin citizens who enjoy the lively sport of football. As the train rolled out the boys were rehearsing the University yell, which for the benefit of those who have heard the string of demoniacal yells but could not distinguish the separate sounds, is here given:

Halla-ba-loo, Hooray, Hooray.

Halla-ba-loo, Hooray, Hooray,

Hooray, Hooray.

Varsity, Varsity, U.T.A.

The Texas "elevens," as football squads were known back then, were ready for their first-ever game. By contrast, Oklahoma, two years later, dropped its first, 34-0, to the Oklahoma City *high school* team.

Unlike UT, Dallas University had an experienced team that, in fact, had never given up a touchdown. It didn't matter.

Varsity Club Wins
Defeats The Dallas Club By
Eighteen To Sixteen
Victory Was Won by Hard Work Against the Vigorous Dallas
Elevens—Two Thousand Spectators Highly Entertained.

Special to the Statesman

DALLAS, NOV. 30—The University of Texas Football team wiped up the earth this evening with the Dallas eleven. This is the first time that the latter club has ever been scored against, much less defeated. Both clubs were in the pink of condition and a great game was anticipated by the enthusiastic crowd of fully 2000 people. The "Varsity" club won the toss and scored a touchdown in three minutes, and Day promptly kicked a goal. Then Dallas scored six points. At the close of the first half the score stood Dallas 10, Varsity 12.

The second half was characterized by sharp and close playing, each team scoring six points and when time was called by the referee the score stood 18 to 16, and the Varsity team was declared the champion eleven of Texas. The features of the game were runs by Day, the tackling of Paul McLane, and the interference of Morrison and Ray McLane.

A few weeks later, the Longhorns continued their path to inaugural season greatness by beating San Antonio at home. The *Statesman*'s coverage of the game proved at least one thing: today's sensationalist newspaper writers are rank amateurs compared to their predecessors in the old days. (However, perhaps an article from 1973 could compete with the earlier muckrakers. After Roosevelt Leaks ran for 342 yards against SMU, a headline read: "Roosevelt Leaks All Over the Field.") In the article, underneath the bland headline "The Football Game," there appeared this fantastic sub-head: *They Literally and Figuratively Wiped Up the Face of the Earth with the Visitors from Tamaleville—How the Boys Did It.*

Moving past the image of the Texas team "literally" using the bodies of San Antonio college boys to clean the streets from Austin to Beijing, let's take a look at the pregame atmosphere:

> Well, football fever has struck Austin at last. For months have our people been reading of the doings of the football fiends and university cranks in the cities of the North and East, and yesterday they were treated to a specimen of what can take place when 22 gladiators have lined up on the gridiron and victory has perched on the banners of the home team.
>
> With the rising of the sun the enthusiasts in all sections of the city began to file down their vocal organs and get them in shape for

THE VERY FIRST
UT-A&M game, 1902

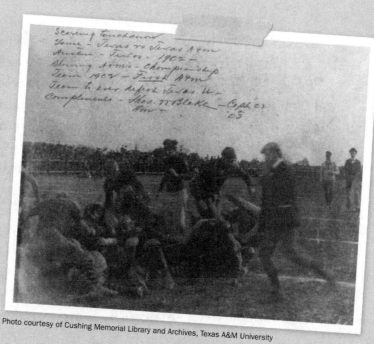

Photo courtesy of Cushing Memorial Library and Archives, Texas A&M University

❝It was their first opportunity to witness a game which is fast seizing upon the first spot in the hearts of the sports-loving American people.❞

the unearthly and indescribable volley of sounds which, later in the day, they fired so unmercifully into the atmosphere, tearing great rents in it and almost paralyzing the ear drums of the quiet and inoffensive citizens. The man, woman, or child who did not sport the yaller and white of the Varsity was not in it. The streets were a changing flash of those colors, the bright ribbons being stuck on the anatomies of those who yelled the "Hullabaloo" in the most conspicuous manner possible. Every student of the university was decorated and hundreds of the people of Austin out of loyalty for the U.T.A. wore the colors. The dear girls showed by their excited and knowing talk the interest that they felt in the event and on whose brawn and staying qualities they placed their faith.

Before The Game.

The university boys were full of confidence before the battle. Their opponents had only come in from San Antonio in the morning and were looked upon as unknown quantities. The Varsity boys were still puffed up with the thought that "they were the people," memories of the glorious Thanksgiving victory over Dallas still filled their minds. The San Antonio rooters kept pretty much to themselves and what they thought and felt they also kept to themselves.

The scene of the battle and what turned out to be such a Waterloo was Zoo Park, at the dam, and to that direction people began to wend their way about 2 o'clock. When the game opened there were 500 or 600 standing around the gridiron eager and anxious for the fray to open up. In the crowd were people who knew it all and people who knew nothing at all about it. The last class was in a large majority. It was their first opportunity to witness a game which is fast seizing upon the first spot in the hearts of the sports-loving American people. The college yell of

Hallabaloo, hooray, hooray,
Hallabaloo, hooray, hooray,
Hooray, hooray;
Varsity, Varsity, U.T.A.

shot out from all sections of the field to die away and give place to
the ungodly snort of the asthmatic tin horn. The last named instru-
ment of aural torture was used so much that the din and racket
became almost unbearable. It was a grievous wrong to convince the
reporter and Governor Hogg, who occupied a seat on a high spring
wagon, that the rosebud lips that were so prettily pucked over the
damp, cold extremities of those tin tormentors were capable of having any earthy connection with sounds so horrible. The way some of
those girls did blow was a caution. With cheeks puffed out and eyes
staring they tooted and tooted at the same time putting unlimited
confidence in the garments which so tightly fitted their trim figures.
How the strain was stood in several instances is a mystery to the mas-
culine mind.

The writer seems captivated by the colorful scene accompanying the strange,
new phenomenon of UT football. If he was so put off by the girls blowing tin
horns, one wonders about his reaction if he'd lived to see the Dallas Cowboy
cheerleaders.

And he was no less intrigued by the game itself:

After the necessary preliminaries which the dignity of the occasion
demanded, the 22 heroes of the day took their places while the spectators knowingly waited and watched for developments. Two pretty
men with clothes on [*what was this reporter smoking?*] and sticks in

their hands were also in sight. They allowed that they were the referees. The players didn't wear clothes. They were inside of an assortment of things which made them look like Egyptian mummies. From different portions of their persons knots protended which were found to be pads. Some of them wore their hair a la chrysanthemum. That was done to make a good soft mat to be used in butting and also to furnish a handle for somebody. Finally all was ready and at the word the mummies mixed. Running like mad for a brief space of time the man with the ball would suddenly clasp it to his breast and drop on it. If the wind was knocked out of him by the drop it was soon shoved into him again, for before he could think twice 21 men would be sitting or standing on top of him.

And thus the thing kept going. A man, after running like chain lightning for a number of yards, had someone spear him and thus about the time his chrysanthemum head in trying to bury itself in the earth to have two or three men sit on his neck and another brace of them plant their feet in the pit of his stomach.

Whenever a good play was made by the Austin boys, or whenever a gain was accomplished or a touchdown secured the noise was almost deafening, and in fact it was almost a continual roar throughout the game.

Technically Described

The game was called at 3 o'clock. San Antonio won the toss and took the ball and led off with a wedge; gained 13 yards. Tobin of San Antonio got the ball and made a brilliant run, which would have resulted in a touchdown had he not been tackled by Day on the 25th yard line. Varsity then got the ball and worked slowly but surely down the field and made a touchdown.

Furman made the first score and was ably aided by the interference of Paul and Ray McLane. San Antonio led off with a wedge for 10 yards, but could get no farther, and Varsity got the ball after three downs, but lost it by a fumble. Meyer soon recovered it, and Morrison made the second touchdown for the Varsity team. After a few more downs time was called on the first half, the score being 12 to 0 in favor of the Varsity.

The Second Half.

Austin had the ball and gained 16 yards on a wedge and by steady work carried it to within a few feet of the Antonio's goal line. Here occurred another fumble, and San Antonio made a safety. They then brought the ball to their 25 yard line, but Varsity stopped them in their tracks and got the ball on downs. Varsity here bucked the center three times and Day made the third touchdown, but failed to kick a goal. San Antonio repeated her wedge play from the center of the field. But it was the same old story. Varsity quickly got the ball and started it the other way. Here Ray McLane made a splendid end run for 45 yards, but lost the ball after crossing the goal line and Jacks dropped on it, making another safety. Austin again blocked them on their 35 yard line for three downs, and Lee made a great run and was stopped only a foot short of the goal line. Day bucked the line at left tackle and made the fourth touchdown but again failed to kick goal. Austin made her next touchdown in short order. Morrison carried the ball to the 15 yard line and Brackenridge followed suit and made a touchdown. Day kicked a goal and time was soon called with the ball in the center of the field.

Varsity made five touchdowns and kicked three goals from them, and San Antonio made two safeties, making a total of 30 to San Antonio's 0.

The teams lined up as follows:

San Antonio	Position	Varsity
Hamilton, V.E.	left end	McLane, P.
Buttler	left tackle	Ray
Rogers	left guard	Philp
Johnson	center	Meyer
Merritt	right guard	Moore
Van Riper	right tackle	Morrison
Phillips	right end	McLane, R.
Pitts	quarter back	Mclane
Hamilton	left half back	Lee
Tobin	right half back	Furman/ Brackenridge
Robards	fullback	Day

Referee, Mr. Fred Shellie.

Umpire, Mr. J.W. Tobin

Notes On The Game.

Only 15 minute halves were played. What would the score have been if regulation halves of 30 minutes had been played?

Day, who kicked every goal at Dallas, missed two yesterday.

Morrison was hurt pretty badly near the end of the game.

The disgraceful slugging in the first half was the result of a misunderstanding between two of the players.

Ray distinguished himself in several instances by his tackling.

The San Antonio boys got a chance to avenge the 30–0 blowout in early 1894 at home. Once again, one sees the great respect the *Statesman* writers had for their neighbors to the west, beginning with their now-standard headline:

The Varsity Team Wipes Up the Earth
With the Tamale Eaters

SAN ANTONIO, FEB. 3—About 500 people witnessed the first football game of Rugby football ever played in San Antonio this afternoon between the University of Texas and San Antonio. It was a fine enthusiastic crowd and was a very fair game. Austin's team were heavier and more experienced and better drilled players, but they were not pluckier than the San Antonio boys. The game was called at 4:15 p.m. and from the beginning Austin had the San Antonio boys practically at their mercy. The best plays on Austin's side were made by Morrison, Day, McLean, Moore, Brackenridge, and Furman, while San Antonio showed up best with C. and J. Gobin, Pitts, King, Walton, Johnson, Sharpe, and Maverick. The crowd that witnessed the game was composed of San Antonio's most aristocratic and social element, who showed that they enjoyed the occasional brilliant plays by cheering and displaying colors. The game lasted one hour and 15 minutes, the final score being, Austin 34, San Antonio 0. Umpire, Mr. Caldwell of San Antonio; referee, Mr. Smith of Austin.

Texas wrapped up its unbeaten season with another rematch, this time against Dallas on a cold day in Austin. It appears that in those days reporters weren't actually sent to away games, so their coverage of home games was much more extensive. The article begins with a recap of the previous UT victory over Dallas, which the writer downgrades from UT "wiping the earth" with Dallas to a mere scalping:

Varsity Wins

The Score Is Sixteen To Nothing

In Favor Of Our Boys

The Spectators Stand Around

Camp Fires And Freeze While

The Game Waxes Hotter

And Hotter For The

Ball Players

Some Very Brilliant Playing

The Dallas boys stack up well on the

Field and play great ball, but our

Varsity boys are too much for
Them, and they were very
Easily whitewashed

Yesterday was a day among days. It was the anniversary of our George Washington. It was Arbor day, it was the 22nd of February, it was a legal holiday, but greater than all these, it was the day for the great football game between the University boys and the Dallas team.

On last Thanksgiving day the University boys went up to Dallas and when they returned that night they had not only succeeded in beating the Dallas team clear off the gridiron; they had not only succeeded in getting large and luxuriant fists full of the auburn, brown and black hair of the Dallas team but they triumphantly bore back the entire scalplock of the aforesaid victims. The Dallas boys are like the cat possessed of the nine lives, however, and after a long wait and mature deliberations, they came once more to meet the foe. Their scalplocks and the pardner hairs that go to make up the beautiful doormat known as the chrysanthemum head had all grown back to their natural place.

The Dallas team came in yesterday looking fat and saucy. The steel like expression of their eyes bespoke ere lips gave utterance to the thought, that they were here for business. Time heals all things said the poet, but that poet was dead off his base if he intended that expression to be applicable to a defeated football team. No sir. That Dallas football team have been thinking since last Thanksgiving day. The Statesman's sporting reporter doesn't mean to insinuate that the gentlemen never thought before, but what he does mean to insinuate is that the Dallas boys have been nursing their wrath. They have been thinking and chaffing over their defeat by the Varsity team and when they rolled into Austin it was with a purpose. That purpose was

> **❝ The Dallas team came in yesterday looking fat and saucy. ❞**

to roll the Varsity boys with such force as they had never been rolled before.

Next comes an extravagant description of the players:

They were doomed to disappointment again, however. The Dallas boys were certainly a brawny set of men. They showed up well on the field, but not one whit behind them in imposing appearance was our own Varsity team. The two teams were rigged out in the regulation uniform, the trousers being all alike and decidedly of the zouave pattern, very full and loose all over and gathered about the knee. If such a thing be possible these trousers are made with the soft side inside, like unto the famous coat of Brian O'Linn.

It is a thing destructive of poetry and delusion to witness a game of football, says one fair maid, and about right is she.

The dear boys, certainly do not look like the gods that one would think them when gazing on their picture. The hopeless mixture of legs, the sudden uplifting of a no. 12 shoe which moves frantically in the air while the other end of the boy known as his head is making frantic endeavors to join the bones of his ancestors in the graves of early days, all combines to dispel with terrific emphasis the definition of "the poem of motion." We are often told that there are few localities on earth that fairly typify the former conditions through which our planet has passed on the way to its present development. It would be a vain effect to attempt to tax the mind to conceive of the slow cooling of an incandescent maze 8000 miles in diameter or to attempt to realize the long ages that were involved in these evolutionary changes.

It would be equally as vain an effort to in any way picture or describe understanding or elegantly at least the warmth that is experienced by the man "at the bottom of the pile." The exact definition of this term can only be understood by the man that has "experienced" it. To the onlooker his lot is certainly a hard one, but to the close observer it is little short of wonderful how he survives the ordeal at all. With the unpleasant contact of an enormous foot in the pit of your stomach and the close proximity of its mate to the windpipe in your throat, the assertion may safely be ventured that the average society dude would prefer his mamma. In addition to the unpleasant contact of these nineteenth century products the additional weight of some fifteen or twenty strong athletic weights is well calculated to be attended with a longing for a lodge in some vast wilderness. Physicians watching the game last afternoon looked with feelings of envy upon the strength of the limbs that bore so much. It was remarkable, the endurance of the man at the bottom. A hydraulic press was as nothing compared to the force that was mashed down upon the pile. It was all in the game though, and had to go whether or no.

The reporter also vividly describes the "ladies" and "dudes" in the crowd. They arrived in vehicles not entirely conducive to tailgating:

The crowd was on their foot, they were there on the street cars, they were there in buggies, in carriages, in coaches and tours, on horseback and in everything but balloons. They sat around the gridiron, in chairs, they stood up in buggies and carriages, they walked from place to place on the grounds. Far away in the distance the presence of a number of small boys, perched on the high board fence, bespoke the presence of the old times at the sport.

A faint but emphatic yell from this quarter every once in a while would give assurance that the game was going to their liking. Any particular prominent case of "pile on" met with the heartiest of welcome from these faraway Moses. Distance, however, did not prevent locating every good play that was made, and the enthusiasm with which they received such was quite frequently attended by a general "falling off" of the aforesaid patrons from their rather dangerous perch on the top of the fence.

Positions were quickly regained, however and while they grew more careful of future tumbles they never ceased one iota in giving the Comanche reception to all meritorious work. The ladies, excited as they were by the interest of the occasion, clapped their fair hands with the greatest vigor and gave utterance to merry laughter or heaved deep sighs of corresponding despondency when their favorite won or lost a point.

While they were all in the game from the start, what of the generous present? They were like everybody else—enthusiastic not withstanding the weather, even. The list embraced all kinds of gentlemanlike attire, the dude with more pretensions and less money, the sport, the would-be sport, the university boy, town boy, the big boy and the little boy, the banker and the merchant, the clerk and the not clerk, the loafer and the gentleman of leisure were all there, and they all enjoyed the game from start to finish.

In front of a thousand people, Austin took a 10–0 lead at the half and went on to wipe out the Dallas boys, 34–0. The curtain was brought down on a cold night in Austin, as the Longhorns celebrated their first unbeaten season.

FIRST WIN OVER THE GOONERS

It took eight seasons before the Longhorns took on the good folks north of the Red River. Oklahoma, starting off slow in football, had an 8–2 record after six seasons coming into the new century. Most of the wins came under Vernon L. Parrington, the first real coach the Sooners had.

UT's

INAUGURAL SEASON

1893-94

Coach: None

Season: 4–0–0

SWC:—

Nov. 30 Dallas W 18–16

Dec. 16 San Antonio W 30–0

Feb. 3 San Antonio W 34–0

Feb. 22 Dallas W 16–0

The teams met on October 10 in Austin. The match-up had been hotly anticipated by the residents of both Austin and Norman. Texas already had statehood, and University of Oklahoma students looked longingly for the same legitimacy. (It would be seven more years before "Indian Territory" became known officially as Oklahoma.)

The *Statesman*, in its Wednesday sports section, previewed the upcoming inaugural game in a match-up that would later blossom into one of college football's most notorious rivalries:

Oklahoma Football Team
The red football warriors
arrive in this city this
morning to play this
afternoon

The University of Oklahoma football team will meet the Varsity this afternoon on the University athletic field. The Oklahoma men have several Indians among them, two of whom are said to be the fastest half backs in the south. It has been impossible to obtain the line up of the team, as the game was only arranged this week. The Oklahoma men have been endeavoring to meet the Varsity on the gridiron for several seasons and their persistent efforts coupled with the reputation that the team has for putting up a stiff game, together with the fact that Coach Thompson wished to try the metal of his men on a good team before Saturday's big game [against Vanderbilt, which the Longhorns won, 22–0], led the Varsity management to agree to bring the Oklahoma men down here.

The Varsity team is crippled by the temporary loss of Hart, who had been confined to his bed for the last two days with malaria. He is still unwell and will not be in the game today. Bewley will occupy his place at full back. Leslie's broken thumb still bothers him, but he will play this afternoon at right half back.

Today's game, aside from the fact that it promises to be a well played contest will be of unusual interest because it will show clearly what may be expected of the Varsity in Saturday's game with Vanderbilt at Dallas. Coach Thompson will probably give all the promising candidates a trial today and the showing that they make will determine the composition of the team that will go against Vanderbilt at Dallas.

Another circumstance that tends to make today's game interesting is that the Oklahoma men are a heavy team and the Varsity big men will have to handle large opponents. The Varsity team this year is the heaviest that ever represented the University, and it will be interesting to see how the big men handle themselves against big opponents. Vanderbilt is also a team of heavy weights and still has the veteran guard, Crutchfield, who weighs two hundred and forty pounds and who will play against Sam in the big game Saturday.

> **Men, we have to face the fact that our coach is incompetent. . . . He should be taking lessons from us, rather than we from him.**
>
> —Longhorn guard Lucian Parrish, on Texas Coach Henry Schenker, 1906. Parrish later became a U.S. congressman.

In regard to Saturday's game, the University faculty have decided to grant the students' petition and to suspend University exercises from Friday at noon until Monday morning in order that all the students may go to Dallas for Saturday's game. The excursion train leaves this city at 12 Friday and will return Saturday night at 12.

UT students who made the trek to Dallas got to watch their boys hammer Oklahoma, 28–2. In one of the first collective insults against Sooner football by UT partisans, the *Statesman* headlined its account of the game, "Practice Game Yesterday." It was noted that the Sooners distinguished themselves by holding Texas to one touchdown in the second half, and actually drove to the Longhorn 3 at one point. Still, it was a 28–2 shellacking (mistakenly recorded as a 29–2 win in the newspaper).

It was reported that Oklahoma did not play all that badly, but the team had some key weaknesses—tackle and end—that were exploited by the Texas backs. The Longhorn backs, in turn, were criticized for failing to heed Coach Thompson's instructions to run low and fast at the line of scrimmage. The Sooners' interior line was beefy and fairly quick, and it took Texas some time to adjust to this and begin beating Oklahoma with end runs.

THE UNBEATEN LONGHORNS OF 1914

Aside from the 4–0 record of 1893, the early Longhorns had a few other unbeaten seasons. But the team really turned the corner in 1914, a perfect season in which the Longhorns scored over fifty points in three of their eight games. Only three teams scored on the UT squad for a combined total of twenty-one points. Texas's offense put up 338 points, while the defense posted five shutouts. The team was coached by Dave Allerdice, who had compiled a 19–4 record going into his fourth year at Texas.

The 1914 Longhorns featured phenom Louis Jordan. Considered the greatest lineman of his era, Jordan would become Texas's first all-American. He was born in Fredericksburg, Texas, in 1890 and also starred for the Longhorn track team. Sadly, he was killed in action in France during World War I. The Texas teams he played on compiled a stellar record of 27–4.

Seasons in those days started a bit later than they do today, with UT opening the 1914 season on Saturday, October 3. Against Trinity, Texas effectively used end runs, line plunges, and the "forward pass." Texas came at Trinity from all directions, right from the start, and overwhelmed the visitors to Clark Field. According to the *Statesman,*

Photo courtesy of Texassports.com

THE FIRST

Longhorn All-American, Louis Jordan, 1914

Twenty two hundred fans watched the University of Texas defeat Trinity, 30 to 0, yesterday afternoon in the opening game of the season at Clark Field. The game was Texas' from the time the Longhorns first gained possession of the ball. They outclassed their opponents in every department of the game with the possible exception of kicking.

Although Texas could grind it out on the ground, it was a pass play that thrilled the crowd:

> The most sensational play of the afternoon came when Turner at left end received a forward pass of eighteen yards from Littlefield and then ran the remaining forty-two yards for a touchdown. He had two men to get by. One he stiff-armed and threw off, the other he succeeded in dodging.

Allerdice substituted freely, bringing in the second team by the second half. It was noted that a new star was discovered, fullback Walker, who carried sixteen times for 120 yards.

The next victim was Baylor. "The Baptists," as the *Statesman* called them, were outmanned across the board, being outweighed twenty pounds per man. They also lost one of their better players—permanently—when he was tackled after a reception and broke his neck. Another suffered a bruised spinal cord, and still another went "out of his head" for several minutes after getting hit in the head and kidneys.

Texas threw twenty-one times against Baylor, but completed only five. That handful of completions, however, netted 124 yards, even though a forty-yarder was called back for holding.

Rice was next. "The Institute" put up a good fight; their sure tackling and great conditioning helped the visitors play Texas virtually even in the first half, with the Longhorns taking a mere 7–0 lead into halftime. The key play of this drive, coming halfway through the first quarter, was a "basket ball"

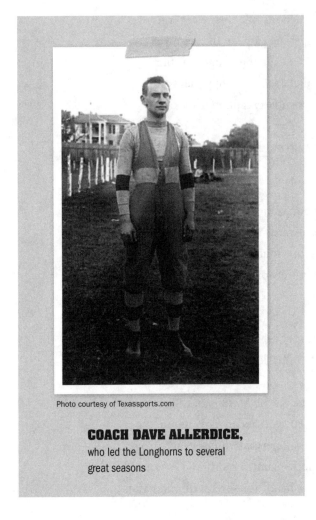

Photo courtesy of Texassports.com

COACH DAVE ALLERDICE,
who led the Longhorns to several
great seasons

pass from Barrell to Littlefield that netted seven yards.

In the second half, Texas' superior size began to wear down Rice, as Barrell intercepted four Rice passes.

Texas added three touchdowns in the third quarter, then mopped up with reserves in the fourth. The Longhorns won 41–0, their third straight shutout.

In the following game, the Longhorns took on their budding rivals at Oklahoma. Texas held an 8–5–1 record against OU coming into 1914. A tie in 1903 was the Sooners' main accomplishment against UT until a strange game in 1905, when Oklahoma scored a safety at the end of the game to win by the awkward score of 2–0.

In 1914, however, the Sooners were no pushovers; they had a powerful team that would go unbeaten the following year with a record of 10–0.

The *Statesman* reported that on October 24 in Dallas, 7,500 people witnessed "the most spectacular and hardest fought game ever seen in Texas." UT employed "smashing bucks," "perfect passes," and "a spectacular run" in the game, while Lincoln Beachy made his "dare-devil loop-the-loop over Gaston Park." Every Longhorn starter played the whole way this day.

Sooner Forrest Geyer scored first with an 85-yard kickoff return in the opening quarter. Soon afterward, Texas quarterback Littlefield scored on a 1-yard run. The point-after was no good, leaving OU with a 7–6 lead. OU kept the Longhorns out of the end zone for the entire first half, at one point stopping Texas on the 12.

But Longhorn quarterback Clyde Littlefield came alive in the third quarter. He tossed a 40-yard touchdown pass early in the quarter, then hit another, a 25-yarder, later. A 5-yard run pushed UT's lead to 20–7. After a few more scores, including a final, 33-yard touchdown pass from Littlefield, the Longhorns left the field with a 32–7 victory that clinched them the Southwestern championship.

Two weeks later, Texas played its closest game of the season, against Haskell. Founded in 1894 in Lawrence, Kansas, as the United States Indian Industrial Training School, Haskell had a reputation in the those days for fielding top-quality football teams.

Haskell scored first, on a 60-yard fumble return. But after that, it was all Texas. Longhorn Len Barrell kicked a field goal, and later ran back an interception sixty yards for a touchdown. Twice in the third quarter, Texas stopped Haskell at the 10-yard line. A crowd of 5,300 saw the Longhorns' defense put in another dominating performance as UT earned a 23–7 win.

A.M. Vanne, director of athletics, paid the Longhorns the ultimate compliment after the game:

> The Texas team is the best that we have played. The Texans surpass Notre Dame in the open play, and have a much better line. In fact, Texas has a much better team than Notre Dame all the way around. We did something against Notre Dame that we could not do against Texas: carry the ball seventy yards on line bucks for a touchdown without losing possession. The Texas players are a clean set of men, and I hope that we will be able to play them again next year.

The Longhorns wrapped up the 1914 season with wins over Mississippi (66–7) and Wabash (39–0 on Thanksgiving Day), going a perfect 8–0 for the season.

THE 1914 LONGHORNS

Coach: Dave Allerdice

Season: 8–0–0

SWC:—

Oct. 3 Trinity W 30–0

Oct. 10 Baylor W 57–0

Oct. 17 Rice W 41–0

Oct. 24 Oklahoma W 32–7

Oct. 31 Southwestern W 70–0

Nov. 7 Haskell W 23–7

Nov. 17 Mississippi W 66–7

Nov. 26, Wabash W 39–0

AUSTIN AMERICAN: SUNDAY MORN

Football--Prizefights--Races

TEXAS SWAMPS OKLAHOMA—13 TO 7
YALE CONQUERED—13 TO 7
PENN STATE TIES HARVARD

SMASHING BUCKS, PERFECT PASSES, SPECTACULAR RUN BEAT OKLAHOMANS 32 TO 7

Coming From Behind in Second Half Longhorns Play Greatest Uphill Game of Their Career, Battering Sooners Down to Defeat While 7500 Frantic Texans Cheer and Aviator Loops-the-Loop Over Dallas Field — Littlefield, Edmond, Turner, Barrell, Ditmar, Wimmer, Jordan, Berry, All Star.

(By Julien E. Gillespie.)

DALLAS, Texas, Oct. 24.—With Lincoln Beachy making his dare-devil loop-the-loop over Gaston Park, 7500 people watched the Texas Longhorns defeat Oklahoma, 32 to 7, in the most spectacular and hardest fought game ever seen in Texas.

By winning this game, the Texas Longhorns won their fourth game of the season and clinched the Southwestern championship.

The game was filled with thrills from start to finish, and will never be forgotten by Texas football lovers. Both teams were very nervous for the first few minutes of play. After that they settled down and played football, the like of which may never be equalled in Texas.

WISCONSIN WINS BY 7-6 SCORE OVER OHIO IN A CLOSE CONTEST

COLUMBUS, Ohio, Oct. 24.—Wisconsin won today's Western conference football game with Ohio State, 7 to 6. Captain Graf failed to make his team's total 7 by missing an easy try for a goal. All the counting was done in the second quarter.

NOTRE DAME EASILY BEATS SOUTH DAKOTA, 33-0; PASSES BEAUT

SIOUX FALLS, S. D., Oct. 24.—By its defeat today of South Dakota, 33 to 0, Notre Dame has maintained its record of almost unbroken victories.

Line up:

Notre Dame	Position	South Dakota
Elward	Left end	Coll
Jones (Capt.)	Left tackle	Will
Keefe	Left guard	Po
Fitzgerald	Center	Mans
Bachman	Right guard	Horn
Lathrop	Right tackle	McCormi
Baugan	Right end	Parlin
Berman	Quarterback	Her
Finnegan	Fullback	Ferguson (C
Cofall	Left half	
Larkin	Right half	

It was the early twentieth century, and the Longhorn program was off and running. The success of the team's first two decades offered a tantalizing taste of the UT dynasties yet to come.

Chapter Two

DARRELL
LONGHORN ROYALTY

Darrell K. Royal is an icon in a state full of them. Personifying the innovation, daring, and toughness of Texans, Royal was the Longhorns head coach for twenty years beginning from December 1956. In that time, Texas won three national championships and a staggering eleven Southwest Conference Championships. (Royal's close friend, Arkansas coach Frank Broyles, took the Razorbacks to seven SWC titles in the same timeframe, underscoring the stranglehold these two men had on one of the proudest conferences in college football.) As a former coaching rival said of Royal: "He was a tough son-of-a-gun to beat."

In the spring of 2008, the Die-Hard Fan sat down with the Legend.

DF: Coach, tell us about the circumstances surrounding your hiring at Texas.

ROYAL: I was hoping that they would call. I knew that they had only won one game and they were going to possibly change coaches. I was hoping that I could get in for that interview.

I don't remember how long the interview took, but the athletic council offered me the job and someone said, "Wait a minute. Hadn't we better check with the board of regents and president before we offer it to him?" Well, I had already interviewed with them. They called them and they said they approved. That's the way I got hired. It went pretty quick.

They gave me a $500 raise. I had been paid $15,000 at the University of Washington. They raised me $500. Boy, have times changed!"

DF: Why were you eager to take the job?

ROYAL: Those down years that were just before I came, I think they were abnormal. I didn't think there was any way that would continue.

DARRELL ROYAL
works his magic at the
1970 Cotton Bowl

Photo courtesy of Dave Campbell's 40 years of Texas Football

DF: It must have been a big deal, given your association with Oklahoma. What kind of reception did you get from the UT fans?

ROYAL: I imagine some of them thought, "Who is this kid they've hired?" I was only thirty-two years old.

DF: Did it all surpass even your expectations?

ROYAL: I envisioned myself going to work. That's all. Let the chips fall where they may.

DF: Was the scrutiny at Texas then tougher than at other places?

ROYAL: No. They had won one game the year before. What the hell? If I won two, that's a 100 percent increase.

I think it changed after they started winning. We had a fairly good season. That helped us recruit the next year and we started building the basis for our future.

DF: Do you miss it? If you could coach in today's environment, would you?

ROYAL: If I were thirty-two years old again, yes I'd like to coach.

DF: What made you decide to retire when you did?

ROYAL: Well, I had been a head coach for a long time. I was head coach up at Edmonton, Alberta. I moved from there to Mississippi State. Then I went to North Carolina State, the University of Tulsa, then back to Mississippi State as head coach. And then I was at Washington for a year.

You just feel like that's the time. That's the way I felt. I quit pretty early. I was fifty-two at the time.

DF: Do you regret retiring "early"?

ROYAL: I felt like it was a fairly good time to hang 'em up. Everything's turned out okay, I guess.

DF: You were innovative away from the field, too. Tell us about your commitment to academics at Texas.

ROYAL: When I came to the University of Texas, I talked about their academics and found that there were very, very few freshmen becoming sophomores. I said, "Well, I don't need to hire a new coach,

I need to hire a new brain coach." So I hired Lan Hewlett as our academic counselor. He wasn't interested in a coaching job. He was in the high school system in Texas. He had no ambitions to be a football coach. He had an ambition to do just what he did—handle academics. We were the first ones in the nation to do that and nearly every other one followed.

DF: What do you feel is your greatest accomplishment at Texas?

ROYAL: Lasting long enough to retire [laughs]. I never felt any pressure. But that's pretty good when you can stay at one place until you can retire.

DF: How about the decision to go to the Wishbone?

ROYAL: An assistant coach, Emory Bellard, brought that idea to me. I liked it. There were a lot of aspects of it that related to the Split-T and that appealed to me. I learned from Coach Wilkinson at Oklahoma. He deserves more credit than he gets. I never coached anything but option football.

I thought, "Let's give it a try." That was Bellard's idea. I bought it."

DF: Were you nervous the first time you rolled out the Wishbone?

ROYAL: Hell, I was nervous every time we rolled it out.

DF: What was it like standing on that sideline so many years?

ROYAL: It's impossible to describe. It changes from first down to first down, from a blocked punt or something like that. Hell, you run through everything on the sidelines. But that's what I wanted to do.

DF: Do you have any regrets or disappointments?

ROYAL: I'm sure I made some mistakes that I'd like to go back and correct, but I can't think what they were. But I'm sure I didn't have 100 percent satisfaction with everything we did.

DF: How much involvement do you have with the program today?

ROYAL: None. Oh, I'm welcome to come to practice. Coach Brown has been exceptionally nice to me. I feel free to walk right out there and walk into a practice session. Or I feel free to go by the office and see them but I don't overdo it.

DF: What was it like having the stadium named after you?

ROYAL: I'm very proud of it. They called me and asked me what I thought about it. I thought they were calling to fire me or something. They called and asked me what I thought about naming the stadium after me. I said, "My goodness, you think you have to call me to get my approval on that?" They said, "Yes, we have to have your approval. Do you approve?" And I said, "Yes, I do," right then and there.

DF: What is your view of Mack Brown?

ROYAL: He's done a great job. He does a great job with alumni. He does a great job with the high school coaching association to recruit. And he and his staff do an exceptional job of instructing them after they get here.

I was on that selection panel and I think we could still be looking and not find a better fit for the University of Texas.

DF: Describe for us the selection process that ended with Brown coming to UT.

ROYAL: There was one question asked. Someone said, "What do you think?" Everyone started shaking their head yes. That was pretty easy to understand. It was unanimous.

He has an engaging personality. He's great with the microphone when he travels around the state and meets with alumni. He's an outstanding on-the-field coach. I don't know what else you could expect.

DF: Nineteen sixty-three was your first national championship. What was that feeling like?

ROYAL: Any time you have a championship year, whether it's for the conference or for the national championship, you certainly remember those national championships and you'd rather talk about those than those other seasons.

DF: What is your biggest memory from that season?

ROYAL: Probably the game against Navy.

DF: Longhorn fans remember the comments from the writer Myron Cope before the game. Cope said, "Tune in your television to the Cotton Bowl and you'll laugh yourself silly. . . . Texas is the biggest fraud ever perpetrated on the football public." Then Navy's coach, Wayne Hardin, offered a negative opinion, too.

ROYAL: They were number two, we were number one. Hardin said when number two plays number one, and number two beats number one, they are then the national champions. That's what he said out at midfield. I replied, "We're ready." What else can you say? We're ready, we accept the challenge. Then, fortunately, we went out and beat them pretty good.

DF: Another special season followed in 1969.

ROYAL: I didn't have quite as many things as I did in '63, in terms of the satisfaction of the season. But any time you can sit on the throne as number one, how much better can it get than that?

I don't lay awake every night before I go to bed and think about that stuff. We've got new folks in town now. We've got new coaches, a new approach. I stand behind them 100 percent and that stuff is in the past.

DF: It must be pretty special running into your former players.

ROYAL: It's great any time I run into them. That's kind of what it's all about. If a coach is not thrilled about that, he shouldn't have been in the profession.

DF: The Shootout with Arkansas remains a classic.

ROYAL: My stomach wasn't in knots, but I knew we were behind 14–0, and it was about time we cracked up and did something. When you're behind 14–0, a lot of doubts creep into your mind. You wonder if it's going to be twenty-one. But that doesn't mean you gave up.

DARRELL ROYAL*
UT HEAD COACH 1957-76

LIFETIME RECORD AT TEXAS: 167-47-5

D. X. Bible's legacy as Texas's football coach may have ended in the 1940s, but he continued to exert a dramatic impact as athletics director in the 1950s. For it was Bible, more than any single person, who fashioned the hiring in December 1956 of Darrell Royal, a young, thirty-two-year-old former Oklahoma football star, as the next Longhorn football coach.

Born in Hollis, OK, Royal had played his college ball at the University of Oklahoma and served as an assistant coach at North Carolina State, Tulsa, and Mississippi State. He coached the Edmonton Eskimos of the Canadian League, and in 1955, he returned to Mississippi State for his first collegiate head coaching job. He spent the next season at the University of Washington and was there when Bible called him to interview for the Texas job.

Royal was an immediate success at Texas, leading the Longhorns—who posted their worst record ever (1–9) in 1956—to a 6–4–1 record, a No. 11 national ranking, and a berth in the Sugar Bowl in his first season. He would never suffer a losing season in twenty years at Texas, led the Long-horns to their first National Championship in 1963, and followed that with national titles in 1969 and 1970.

Royal posted an astonishing 167–47–5 career record at Texas, which included a 109–27–2 mark in SWC games. He claimed a league-record eleven SWC Championships, led UT to sixteen bowl games, and nine times finished the year ranked among the nation's top five.

In 1968, Royal was the first to install the famed Wishbone formation backfield. His teams would eventually spend thirty weeks ranked No. 1 in the nation and post an astonishing thirty-game winning streak (forty-two straight wins at home) from 1968–70. From 1968–73, Royal's squads claimed six straight SWC titles and six con-secutive Cotton Bowl berths. He coached seventy-seven All-SWC players and twenty-six All-Americans.

Still at the top of his game in 1976, Royal retired and continued in the role of athletics director at Texas—a position he had main-tained since taking over the dual role of coach and AD in 1962. His overall coaching record was 184–60–5.

*Reprinted with permission, *Mack Brown Texas Football*

DF: Tell us about the fourth-down pass.

ROYAL: It was called because we hadn't moved the ball consistently all day. Time was running out. If we tried to drive it on down and score, we'd have used up a lot of clock. That was a call to have time left on the clock.

DF: What do you think the odds are that the play would work again if you were calling it today?

ROYAL: I don't know. It worked once, so I don't have to answer that.

DF: In 1970, you won it all back-to-back. That's pretty rare.

ROYAL: Any time you have a bang-up season like that, it's a lot of fun. It's exhilarating for the coaching staff and exhilarating for the players and exhilarating for the fans. If you can get all of those folks happy, you're doing pretty good.

DF: The loss to Notre Dame in the Cotton Bowl was tough.

ROYAL: It took a little bit away from it, yeah. Anytime you lose, it takes a little luster off.

DF: How do you sum up James Street?

GAMEDAY HAUNTS

Best place to eat enchiladas after the game—**Matt's El Rancho**—2613 South Lamar Boulevard, (512) 462-9333

Best place to hang out before and after the game—**Scholz Beer Garten**—1607 San Jacinto, (512) 474-1958

Best place to eat a greasy burger around the stadium—**The Posse East**—2900 Duval St, (512) 477-2111

Best place on The Drag to eat a greasy burger—**Dirty Martin's**—2808 Guadalupe Street, (512) 477-3173

ROYAL: He started twenty games and won twenty games, period. If you start twenty and win twenty, I'd say you're a winner. He was just a great competitor.

DF: Earl Campbell.

ROYAL: He had great size, speed, and determination. There aren't many Earl Campbells that come around. He was in a class of his own.

DF: Tommy Nobis.

ROYAL: Tommy Nobis was one of the best tacklers that I remember coaching. They didn't go very far after "Red" got to them. We had some methods and the way we went about it. Not everybody did it that way, but Tommy did. He was the best tackler I've seen.

DF: Steve Worster, the first Wishbone fullback.

ROYAL: He was a powerful runner. He was a great runner. He made a lot of yards for us. He was a great player.

DF: Some of those guys, like Worster, had reputations away from the field for having a lot of fun.

ROYAL: Well, I don't recall anybody having a lot of fun when we were practicing. That's all I can tell you.

DF: Thank you for sharing some great memories with us, coach.

ROYAL: You're welcome.

A ROYAL HISTORY

Royal is a legend at UT, but certain other schools try to "claim" him as well. Nevertheless, the following article, from *Sooners Illustrated*, offers a fine tribute to the full breadth of Royal's storied career: *

The University of Oklahoma football team was entering a new era after the war. The five-year tenure of Head Coach Dewey Luster had just been ushered out and the new regime of Jim Tatum and his

*Reprinted with permission, *Sooners Illustrated*

THE WIT AND WISDOM OF

★★★

DARRELL ROYAL

Royal has always been known for his colorful expressions. Here's a selection of some of his more memorable quips.*

» On the rest of a tough schedule after beating a couple of soft opponents: "All the white meat is gone. There's nothin' but necks on the platter."

» On a Baylor tight end: "That guy is a big ol' cuss...look at him rumblin' down the field...looks like a grizzly bear haulin' a walnut."

» "Football doesn't build character. It eliminates the weak ones."

» "Breaks balance out. The sun don't shine on the same ol' dog's rear end every day."

» "Luck is what happens when preparation meets opportunity."

» "A boy shows how much he wants to play in the spring, when it's tough, and during two a days, when it's hot and tough. I don't count on the boy who waits till October, when it's cool and fun, then decides he wants to play. Maybe he's better than three guys ahead of him, but I know those three won't change their minds in the fourth quarter."

» Royal on losing a game in the last minute: "It was like having a big ol' lollipop in your mouth and the first thing you know all you have is the stick."

» When asked if the abnormal number of Longhorn injuries that season resulted from poor physical conditioning: "One player was lost because he broke his nose. How do you go about getting a nose in condition for football?"

» "When you get to the end zone, act like you've been there before."

» "Every coach likes those players who, like trained pigs, will grin and jump right in the slop."

*Reproduced from www.hornsfans.com

assistant, Bud Wilkinson, had just come in. Wilkinson and Tatum had coached at Iowa Pre-Flight and they brought Don Faurot's Split-T offense with them to Norman. Wilkinson was in charge of implementing that offense while Tatum concentrated on defense.

"Coach Wilkinson was my coach for the four years I was there, even when he was an assistant under Tatum," said Royal. "Tatum worked more with the defense. He pretty much gave Coach Wilkinson free rein. He and I were very, very close. When Coach Wilkinson passed away I gave his eulogy. It was the hardest thing I ever had to do."

Royal played halfback in 1947 and 1948. "General" Jack Mitchell led OU behind center during those seasons. The Sooners went 7–2–1 in 1947, which was Bud Wilkinson's first year as head coach after Jim Tatum's resignation. Oklahoma started 1947 by winning their first two games, 24–20 against Detroit, and 26–14 against Texas A&M. And then things went sour in Dallas. Heavily favored Texas led Oklahoma 7–0, but with three minutes left in the first half, Jack Mitchell scrambled three yards for the equalizing touchdown and after Royal's conversion, the score was knotted at seven apiece. Just before halftime, with time running out and the score still tied, an incident reared its head which is still talked about today.

Texas had the ball on the Oklahoma 2 yard line with 20 seconds remaining. Texas tried two successive running plays, and as the clock expired, an official by the name of Jack Sisco rushed to the scrum and signaled a Texas touchdown. When it became clear that Texas had, indeed, not scored, he reversed his call to 'Texas timeout,' and one second was put back on the clock. Texas, behind Bobby Layne, scored on the next play. The 'Horns went on to win the game going away, 34–14, but Oklahoma fans have never forgotten Jack Sisco and his creative game watch.

"I just remember that there was a big controversy on the field over a play that was called by Jack Sisco. You mention Jack Sisco to a lot of people from Oklahoma today and they'll bristle, but it happened such a long time ago that most of 'em probably don't even know why they dislike him," chuckled Royal.

The Sooners opened 1948 with a 20–17 loss to Santa Clara, but completed the year winning their final ten contests. Royal contributed heavily with his running, blocking, halfback passing, defense, and punting.

With the graduation of Jack Mitchell, Darrell Royal took over the quarterbacking duties in 1949. Much has been written of the Sooners' 1949 season. OU encountered little real competition as they defeated nine of their eleven opponents by an average score of 39–6. The other two, Texas and Nebraska, were the only teams to play Oklahoma closely, with Texas falling 20–14, and Nebraska by a score of 28–21. The Sooners wrapped up their undefeated year with a 35–0 Orange Bowl drubbing of LSU, 35–0.

When Darrell Royal left Norman, he held two career records that still stand today: he intercepted 17 passes, and he had the longest punt return, 96 yards. He made All-American "in certain polls," he said with a chuckle. He also passed a twenty-one game winning streak on to the 1950 Sooners.

"That was a big thrill, the winning streak. We went from the second game in '48 all the way through to graduation after '49 without losing a game," said Royal.

The Sooners also finished 1949 ranked second nationally in the Associated Press poll, behind Notre Dame. "Somebody's got to beat Notre Dame for anyone else to be number one," continued Royal. "If they go undefeated, they're going to be number one. And they were undefeated in 1949. But so were we."

After Darrell Royal left college, he accepted assistant coaching positions at North Carolina State (1950), Tulsa (1951), and Mississippi State (1952). While Royal had been negotiating with coach Buddy Brothers for the position of assistant coach at the University of Tulsa, he was unaware that Bud Wilkinson had been trying to contact him to offer him an assistant coaching position at Oklahoma. After Royal accepted the Tulsa job, he learned of Wilkinson's offer. Not being the kind of man to renege on a commitment, Royal went back to Brothers and asked to be released. But Brothers refused and Royal spent a beneficial season in Tulsa.

"We had a good year in Tulsa (the Hurricane posted a 9–1 record) and I got a lot of valuable experience. But coach Brothers knew Oklahoma was calling before I committed and he didn't tell me about it. But it all worked out for the best."

After his stint as assistant coach at Mississippi State in 1952, Royal was interviewed by the Edmonton Eskimos of the Canadian Football League and, at 28 years of age, became the youngest head coach in the history of the CFL. "Canada is where Claude (former OU quarterback Claude Arnold) and I became close friends," continued Royal. "I also coached Billy Vessels and Leon Manley up there. Manley and I have had quite a career together. We played high school football together, we played college football together, and then I coached him up in Canada after being teammates all this time. Later, I hired him on our coaching staff at Texas and he was still there when I retired. So, that's pretty unusual, to have that long an association with someone. He still lives here in Austin and we stay in touch."

The Eskimos fell one game short of going to the Grey Cup (the CFL's Super Bowl) in '53, and soon afterwards Mississippi State offered Royal its head coaching position. Edmonton, although unhappy about losing their successful coach after only one season,

DID YOU KNOW?

When Darrell K. Royal Texas Memorial Stadium first opened in 1923, it was called Memorial Stadium and had been dedicated to the 198,520 Texans who fought in World War I, including the 5,280 who lost their lives. The stadium was later rededicated to honor all former UT alumni who had lost their lives while fighting in American wars.

finally agreed to an amicable split and Royal departed for Starkville.

"I left Edmonton when I got a chance to be a head coach at Mississippi State. If you look around up in Canada, there aren't a heck of a lot of jobs; if you lose one, you might have a problem finding another. So you'd better make it there or you're out of coaching. Plus, I had always wanted to head a major college football team. So I'd have some opportunities I wouldn't have in Canada. Up there," stated Royal, "it was do or die."

After two successive 6–4 seasons in Starkville, Royal was lured to the University of Washington in 1956. Royal led the Huskies to a 5-5 record that year but more importantly, defeated Washington's instate rival, Washington State.

And then Royal got the call he wanted but hadn't expected. Texas Athletic Director and storied coach Dana X. Bible summoned Royal to Austin to discuss their head coaching vacancy. After one interview, Royal was offered the job on the spot and proceeded to move his growing family to Texas.

Royal's tenure at the University of Texas is the stuff of which legends are made. From 1957 through 1976, Darrell K. Royal owned the 1960s with his 'flip-flop' Split-T and his 'Wishbone' offenses. During his career in Austin, Royal led the Steers to...

» A 167–47–5 record
» Three national championships (1963, 1969, and 1970)
» A top-five national finish nine times
» 11 Southwest Conference Championships (a league record), and
» 16 Bowl games.

Additionally, Darrell Royal...
» Coached 26 All-Americans

- » Coached 77 All SWC players
- » Was named Coach of the Year in 1961 and 1963, and
- » Was named Coach of the Decade for the 1960s by ABC.

Darrell Royal was indeed a Longhorn coach for the ages.

NINETEEN SIXTY-THREE

In the tumultuous year of 1963, the nation mourned the loss of a president and celebrated a national football championship from the great state of Texas—the very definition of the American pioneering and persevering spirit.

In Darrell Royal's seventh season, the Longhorns were chasing perfection, having gone 9–1–1 the season before.

During fall practice, Royal fretted over injuries. Despite the long tradition of coaches lowering expectations before going on to great success, he seemed genuinely concerned that Texas might drop its opener for only the sixth time since the program started in 1893.

Tulane offered a challenge, and Royal worried the week of the game that the team's weak practices were indicative of what was to come. "We don't look good," he said simply.

However, there was some cause for optimism. Sportswriter Lou Maysel noted that the injury situation had improved, and he pointed out "the impressive performances of two rookies, guard Tommy Nobis and wingback Phil Harris." Duke Carlisle at quarterback, Maysel reported, looked "satisfactory."

Overall, worries about the team seemed exaggerated in light of their No. 1 ranking in the preseason. And that turned out to be the precursor of a historic perfect season for the Longhorns, perhaps to Royal's own surprise. Here's how it went down:

SEPTEMBER 20 AT TULANE

Royal had worked his players hard in practice, and it paid off in the season opener. UT ran for 282 yards, threw for eighty-six, and grabbed three turnovers. The Green Wave ran into that buzzsaw Longhorn defense and totaled only 138 yards and eight first downs.

The Longhorn offense, however, was also shut down through much of the game, mustering just two field goals until the fourth quarter. Then Texas really came alive, scoring fifteen points. Phil Harris scored twice on 1-yard runs and grabbed a two-point conversion pass. For the game, Ernie Koy and Carlisle ran for sixty-one yards each, while Tommy Ford added fifty-seven as Texas blanked Tulane, 21–0.

SEPTEMBER 28, TEXAS TECH

In its biggest point total since a 56–7 win over Idaho in 1949, Royal's Longhorns clobbered the Red Raiders, 49–7, in Austin.

The brutal Texas defense continued its scorched-earth style, yielding only 142 yards to Tech. The Longhorns rolled up 383 yard of total offense, and Royal played everyone after gaining a 28–0 halftime lead. The starters didn't play very much, as Tommy Ford, with forty-six yards on eight carries, was the only starter to reach double figures.

OCTOBER 5, OKLAHOMA STATE

The "other" team from Oklahoma traveled to Austin and didn't fare any better than UT's previous two victims.

The Longhorns were a bit shocked at the outset, by a native son, no less. Lewisville's Walt Garrison, the third-team fullback for OSU, took a handoff eight minutes into the game and ran forty-eight yards down the sideline for a touchdown. But that would be the high-water mark of the night for the visitors; Garrison would gain only fifteen yards the rest of the game.

The Longhorns shut down another Texan transplant that day. OSU punter Jerome Bell, a great prospect from Houston Wheatley High School, had one punt blocked, while two others traveled only fifteen and four yards, respectively.

GENERATIONS:
Royal (right) talks
things over with
Mack Brown

It was said that Texas's total of 353 yards was directed "with a maestro's effort" by Duke Carlisle. The Longhorns gained 150 yards of offense in the third quarter alone.

The 34–7 win moved Texas up the charts to No. 2, behind Oklahoma. It would be the last time Texas would be ranked so low all season.

OCTOBER 12 VS. OKLAHOMA

The Sooners crossed the Red River in what would be Bud Wilkinson's last shootout with Texas. Fans on both sides were white-hot for a slugfest between the two top-ranked teams.

The Sooners had dominated football in the 1950s. By the early sixties they had lost some of their firepower, but they still had an intimidating roster in 1963.

They didn't seem to impress Texas, though.

The Sooners the week before had shocked Southern Cal in the Coliseum, but super quarterback prospect Mike Ringer backed into an electric fan and mangled his elbow.

For his part, Royal unleashed a spruced-up version of the old Split-T offense at his former boss. Texas used straight handoffs, power sweeps, and option keepers by Carlisle to exhaust the Sooners.

> **66 It is no place for the timid. 99**
> —Darrell Royal on Texas-Oklahoma

Still, OU didn't go down without a fight. Losing 21–7 going into the fourth quarter, the Sooners recovered a fumble and set up at Texas's 30. Scott Appleton, Nobis, and David McWilliams led a strong defensive stand that turned back OU.

With just under a minute left, the Longhorns put their finishing touch on the game, with third-stringer Marvin Kristynik hitting George Sauer, Jr. with a 14-yard TD pass.

OCTOBER 19 AT ARKANSAS

The games between these teams had become tough scraps in recent years. This one was no different.

Fullback Harold Philipp ran for 135 yards on twenty carries, as Texas piled up a 17–0 lead late in the second quarter. Then, the Razorbacks decided to make a game of it.

Less than a minute remained before the half when Jackie Brasuell took Crosby's kickoff on his five, faked a handoff, and ran eighty-nine yards before being brought down by Jim Hudson. Quarterback Jon Brittenum then threw a TD pass to Stan Sparks to narrow the score to 17–7.

In the fourth, Brittenum took the Razorbacks on a grueling, twenty-play drive, going ninety yards for a touchdown. But Texas held on, winning 17–13.

The Longhorns churned out 247 yards on the ground and 301 yards total, while Arkansas totaled 162.

OCTOBER 26, RICE

By now, the bull's-eye on the Longhorns' back made for a tempting target every week for ambitious opponents.

The Owls ran for only thirty-nine yards on the night, but they threw for 216, and that kept them in it.

All the scoring came in the first half. Tommy Ford ran thirty-three yards for a touchdown. Rice used a 19-yard pass from quarterback Walter McReynolds to Jerry Kelley to pull within one late in the first quarter. But Tommy Nobis blocked the point-after try, preserving UT's lead. Later, Tony Crosby tacked on a 22-yard field goal for Texas.

The 10–6 win kept the Longhorns on the path to football glory.

NOVEMBER 2 AT SMU

The Methodists were not in a charitable mood when the Longhorns came calling.

For the first time all year Texas was out-gained, with SMU totaling 291 yards—despite losing four turnovers—against 265 for the Longhorns.

It all started so beautifully for Texas, which built up a a 14–0 lead thanks to Tommy Ford, who ran for 107 in the first half, including a 50-yard dash that set up Phil Harris's TD run. SMU scored in the second quarter on a

FIRST WIN OVER OKLAHOMA

Darrell Royal was only a few years younger than his old OU coach, Bud Wilkinson, when he took over at Texas in late 1956. The move by Texas to hire the bright young coach may have been one of the things that provoked Wilkinson to give up coaching a few years later and run for the U.S. Senate.

Bud beat his protégé, 21–7, in 1957, the same year Notre Dame stopped OU's 47-game winning streak. But times were changing, and Oklahoma was slowly getting left behind.

In the UT-OU series, more than one Texas quarterback has come from obscurity to lead his team to victory. These improbable heroes have as their inspiration one Vince Matthews.

Matthews, a junior in 1958, had been buried on the depth chart. With the Sooners riding a 6-game win streak in the series, it looked as if they would continue. In the second quarter, Matthews passed thirty yards to Kleo Halm to put Texas on the OU 3. A tough stand by the Oklahoma defense kept Texas out of the endzone, but the drive gave the Longhorns some confidence that they could take on Oklahoma and win.

Texas found itself "down there" again a bit later in the game. This time, they made it count. Halfback Rene Ramirez hit George Blanch with a 10-yard scoring pass on fourth and four, and the Longhorns were on their way.

Late in the third quarter, Texas was clinging to an 8–6 lead when a fumble was returned twenty-four yards by OU's Jim Davis. For a while, it looked like OU's 14–8 lead would hold in the tight defensive game. But this is where Texas simply refused to lose.

With a little over six minutes left in the game, OU stalled on a drive and punted. That set Texas up at its own 26. OU fans licked their lips.

But an unsung hero answered the call. Matthews hit Ramirez and Bob Bryant with three consecutive passes totaling twenty-seven yards. After an 8-yard loss, Matthews passed Texas to the OU 19. Backing up to defend against the passing attack, OU didn't count on Longhorn fullback Mike Dowdle, who ripped off a 14-yard run down to the 5. Royal then crossed-up the Sooners again by sending in alternate quarterback Bobby Lackey. He fired a quick pass over the middle to Bryant, who scored untouched.

Serving only to tantalize Sooner fans, a late run by quarterback Bobby Boyd almost went the distance. On fourth and five, Boyd got around left end from his 30 and went twenty-six yards before getting stopped by the last man. Lackey picked off a desperation pass as the game ended.

Ecstatic Longhorn fans went crazy, celebrating the one-point win. Royal considered that a last-minute drive earlier in the season to beat Georgia, 13-8, was key to the victory. "It sure gives you confidence maybe you can do it again. You do it a few times and you've got a tradition started," he said.

Wilkinson called Texas's final drive "as fine a finish" as he'd ever seen. Boyd was even more blunt:

"Sure they earned it, or they wouldn't have got it. They came seventy-four yards. If you can't stop'em in seventy-four yards, you don't deserve to win."

For the junior from Garland, Texas, that last point was poignant indeed.

touchdown pass to cut the lead to 146. Tony Crosby, who missed two field goals on the day, then kicked a 34-yarder with a second left in the half to extend UT's lead to 17–6.

After going most of the second half without a score by either team, with under four minutes remaining, SMU hit another scoring pass, but couldn't convert on the two-point try. Texas escaped a close one, winning 17–12.

NOVEMBER 9, BAYLOR

The Bears couldn't get their offense going, but their defense limited the Longhorns to just seven points. Turns out, that wasn't good enough.

Baylor's Don Trull took a dramatic last stab at tying the game with twenty-two seconds left, but his pass was picked off by Carlisle in the Longhorn end zone.

NOVEMBER 16, TCU

After the Horned Frogs' upset of then No. 1 ranked Texas in 1961, Royal offered one of his trademark colorful opinions.

"TCU is like a cockroach. It isn't what he eats or carries off, but what he falls into and messes up."

This time, Royal's team was well-prepared for the bug. Phil Harris scored around left end a minute into the second quarter, giving Texas a 7–0 lead. A few minutes later, Crosby kicked his eighth field goal of the year to boost the lead to 10–0. Sub fullback Tommy Stockton scored the final Longhorn points on a 3-yard run to cap a 7-play, 63-yard drive and seal a 17–0 win for Texas.

NOVEMBER 28 AT TEXAS A&M

Anticipation of this big match-up quickly dissipated due to the devastating events in Dallas the week before—on November 22, Lee Harvey Oswald gunned down President Kennedy.

The assassination plunged the football world into a funk. Some games were called off completely, while others, including the UT-A&M showdown, were rescheduled.

When the two teams finally squared off, the atmosphere was still strained. Tommy Wade, a third-string Longhorn quarterback, took Texas most of the way on an 80-yard, last-minute drive in a 12-point fourth quarter. Carlisle returned from injury to dive over the final yard with seventy-nine seconds left. Texas walked away with a close, 15–13 win.

A Texas writer, perhaps as rocked by Kennedy's murder as anyone else, penned this strange description of the game:

> Tommy Wade, as anonymous as a secret service agent this season, stepped in and foiled an assassination plot that almost took the life of another of America's No. 1 citizens, The University of Texas football team, here Tuesday.

UT coach Darrell Royal felt the pressure of the moment. Taking a phone call from "Nellie" Connally, wife of the Texas governor wounded during Kennedy's shooting, Royal smiled, then buried his face in his hands. "I can't get my breath," he whispered.

The dramatic win in an emotional week left Texas on the doorstep of a national championship.

JANUARY 1 VS. NAVY

The circumstances of this game made it difficult to forget the tragic fate that had recently befallen America's former president.

Texas's opponent in the Cotton Bowl was Navy, which was the academy where JFK had distinguished himself. Texas Governor John Connally had been Secretary of the Navy under Kennedy, and this biggest of games would, of course, be played in Dallas.

The Longhorns tried to put their grief aside and focus on their formidable opponent. The Midshipmen were led by Heisman Trophy winner Roger Staubach, who would go on to star for some other Texas team later in the decade.

Eastern writers had a field day disparaging the unbeaten Longhorns. But that didn't seem to bother Darrell Royal, who concentrated on directing his team's emotions toward the game.

Perhaps foreshadowing a great bowl day by another Texas quarterback many years later, Carlisle silenced his critics who laughed at his passing ability. Against Navy, he threw for 213 yards while running for fifty-four. He overshadowed Staubach and broke the Cotton Bowl record for total offense. As a team, Texas totaled 400 yards.

> **"I've never seen a team which deserved to be No. 1 more than Texas."**
> —Navy coach Wayne Hardin

Throughout the game, Navy throttled Texas's great rushing game, to the tune of forty-one yards. But Carlisle dropped bomb after bomb on Navy, hitting Phil Harris with touchdown passes of fifty-eight and sixty-three yards. Carlisle also ran nine yards for a TD, as Texas pounded Navy into submission, winning 28–6.

Texas finished its legendary perfect season with a highly deserved No. 1 ranking.

SHOOTOUT IN ARKANSAS

After a season-defining win over Oklahoma in October 1969, the Longhorns reeled-off five straight SWC blowouts. The team was so loaded with all-star players that no one could keep up with them.

Until Fayetteville.

The mountains of northwest Arkansas are beautiful any time of year. In the winter, they seem more mysterious; the ever-present smoke curling from chimneys points to a populace that "hibernates" for a time. And in 1969, it was simply hard to get there, with very few accessible roads. So when the Longhorns came through, nearly the whole town shut down to enjoy the marquee match.

Early in the year, Arkansas coach Frank Broyles agreed to move the game to December because ABC wanted a marquee match-up. It was a decision he still ponders.

Texas won 15–14, in a game that is still talked about today. James Street's dramatic fourth-down pass is well known to Longhorn fans. What is less known is the long-term impact the loss had on Arkansas.

"It was so crushing to me and to everybody that I just don't talk about it," Broyles remembers. Arkansas fans still lament the defeat, with some even citing it as the cause of some of the program's problems to this day. That last point is debatable, but the game, especially the fourth quarter, was epic.

The Razorbacks had almost as many great players as Texas had. Outstanding players like end Chuck Dicus, quarterback Bill Montgomery, tailback Bill Burnett, end Bruce James, and linebacker Cliff Powell helped make the Razorbacks a formidable No. 2 in the country.

Both teams came in 9–0.

Associated Press writer Harry King earned his pay a couple days before the game with a discerning comment, predicting that "Texas and Arkansas

ROYAL (left) with former OU head coach Bud Wilkinson

Photo courtesy of Mack Royal, licensed under the creative commons licensing terms

may produce the ultimate Saturday in what has become a series of heart-stoppers."

Austin sportswriter Jack Agness, in that colorful way journalists of the day described titanic clashes, wrote the week of the game, "With the tension of the Arkansas game crawling up his back like a cheap undershirt, Texas Coach Darrell Royal came scrambling down from his 30-foot tower at practice and pointed an accusing finger at a scout team member. The boy wasn't doing his job against the first-teamers and Royal wanted everything letter perfect during Arkansas week."

Games were traditionally tight between the two clubs. In the previous ten years, only one game had seen a winning margin of more than ten points. Seven times, the game had been decided by less than a touchdown. The match came at a time when Royal and Broyles dominated the South—over the course of their careers, the two combined to win eighteen of twenty Southwest Conference championship

> 66 **I've never played in a game like this—one that meant so much to so many people.** 99
> —Glen Halsell, on the 1969 UT-Arkansas game

THE LINEUPS—TWO-DEEP

ARKANSAS

Pos.	No.	Offense
SE	20	Chuck Dicus (172)
		William Powell
LT	78	Mike Kelson (230)
		Dewitt Smith
LG	74	Jerry Dossey (235)
		Jim Mullins
C	57	Rodney Brand (226)
		Terry Hopkins

TEXAS

Pos.	No.	Offense
TE	40	Randy Peschel (200)
		Jay Cormier
LT	50	Bobby Wuensch (225)
		Chris Young
LG	74	Randy Stout (250)
		Bobby Mitchell
C	52	Forrest Wiegand (205)
		Jim Achilles

ARKANSAS

Pos.	No.	Offense
RG	70	Rodney Hammers (230)
		Ronnie Bennett
RT	75	Bob Stankovich (237)
		Tom Mabry
TE	88	Pat Morrison (220)
		Bob Nichols
QB	10	Bill Montgomery (180)
		John Eichler
TB	33	Bill Burnett (189)
		Russell Cody
FL	25	John Rees (174)
		David Cox
FB	34	Bruce Maxwell (214)
		Russ Garber

Pos.	No.	Defense
LE	85	Bruce James (221)
		Tommy Dew
LT	72	Rick Kersey (200)
		Don Wunderly
RT	61	Dick Bumpas (225)
		Gary Parson
RE	71	Gordon McNulty (215)
		Roger Harnish

TEXAS

Pos.	No.	Offense
RG	66	Mike Dean (205)
		Sid Keasler
RT	62	Bob McKay (245)
		Charles Crawford
SE	88	Charles Speyrer
		Ken Ehrig
QB	16	James Street (175)
		Eddie Phillips
LH	35	Jim Bertelsen (192)
		Billy Dale
RH	24	Ted Koy (212)
		Terry Collins
FB	30	Steve Worster (210)
		Bobby Callison

Pos.	No.	Defense
LE	77	Bill Atessis (257)
		Jim Williamson
LT	31	Greg Ploetz (205)
		Scott Palmer
RT	70	Carl White (226)
		George Cobb
RE	89	David Arledge (195)
		Stan Mauldin

ARKANSAS			TEXAS		

Defense

Pos.	No.	Defense	Pos.	No.	Defense
LB	64	Cliff Powell (215)	LB	80	Bill Zapalac (215)
		Robert Lewis			Stan Mauldin
LB	53	Lynn Garner (205)	LB	86	Mike Campbell (190)
		Ronnie Jones			Mack McKinney
LB	59	Mike Boschetti (195)	LB	67	Glen Halsell (202)
		Richard Coleman			Larry Webb
M	19	Bobby Field (175)	LB	61	Scott Henderson (217)
		Steve Birdwell			David Richardson
LH	24	Terry Stewart (191)	LH	84	Tom Campbell (190)
		David Hogue			Paul Kristynik
RH	18	Jerry Moore (198)	RH	23	Danny Lester (180)
		Robert Dew			Jimmy Gunn
S	36	Dennis Berner	S	28	Fred Steinmark (168)
		Gus Rusher			Rick Nabors

The game opened in dramatic fashion. Arkansas struck after just ninety seconds, with Burnett going over from a yard out. Neither team gained any more points until the third, when Montgomery used his own 18-yard run to set up a 29-yard scoring strike to Dicus. Earlier, a 26-yard touchdown by the pair was wiped out by a penalty.

Down 14–0 with a loud crowd of Hog-hat-wearing fans, there was not much to suggest that Texas would pull this one out.

But the Longhorns finally got their ground game going. Moving steadily from their 20 to the Hog 42, Texas's James Street looked over the defense and called his own number. Popping through the tight defensive line, Street cut to his right and scored. A pall began to settle over Arkansas.

I'D SOONER BE A LONGHORN

★★★

LEON MANLEY

Tiny Hollis, Oklahoma produced a handful of key players in Oklahoma's resurgence under Bud Wilkinson. Its most famous son, of course, is Darrell Royal. But according to former Sooner quarterback Claude Arnold, who backed up Royal on the undefeated team of 1949, Leon Manley was at least as good a lineman as his more celebrated teammates.

"I remember players who couldn't carry Leon Manley's jock," Arnold remembers today.

Manley took his talent to the coaching ranks in the days of small pro contracts. The emphasis in those days was not on long playing careers in the NFL. College players either concentrated on their degrees or planned for a career in coaching. Manley did both, earning a degree at OU, then bypassing an NFL career (despite being drafted by the Packers) and entering the coaching field.

After a stint playing in Canada (many American players obtained better contracts in our northern neighbor), Manley worked as a grad assistant at OU under Bud Wilkinson. He then left to go to Northeast Louisiana,

> **❝ I remember players who couldn't carry Leon Manley's jock. ❞**
>
> —Claude Arnold

and later settled on a two-decade career with Royal at Texas.

Beginning as an offensive line coach before becoming offensive coordinator, Manley enjoyed his time at Texas immensely; in fact, he still lives there. Interestingly, Texas went 3-1 against OU while Manley was OC. And before that, as offensive line coach, he felt at home with Emory Bellard's Wishbone, as he and Royal had played in the Split-T under Wilkinson.

Still, it's hard for some fans to understand how a Sooner could wind up a Longhorn! The Red River Rivalry is perhaps the nation's most ferocious. How does Manley straddle that fence?

"People don't understand the difference between coaching and playing," Manley says today. "You play with people you know and become close. Then when you're coaching, you become a team with the players you're coaching. But it's hard for people to understand how you can be loyal when you're playing, then loyal coaching for another team." As for Longhorn fans, they're just glad another Sooner crossed the Red River to stay.

This key run occurred on the first play of the fourth quarter. It is but one play among many that place Street in the pantheon of great Texas players. "Slick," "Rat," or whatever you want to call him, the guy's blood was as cold as the rain in Arkansas on December 6, 1969.

In the fourth quarter, Arkansas was driving for a knockout score. Up 14-8 after Street's 42-yard touchdown run, Broyles' bunch got down close. The head coach had to decide whether to go for a field goal or the hammer. He chose to try to drive a spike in Texas's hopes. But at the end of a truly great day, Montgomery threw an interception in the end zone.

Texas was still alive.

The play that remains etched in everyone's mind—Right 53 Veer Pass—was set up like this:

Arkansas tackle Gordon McNulty pounced on a Ted Koy fumble at the Arkansas 42, but the Razorbacks couldn't do anything with it. The Longhorns had held.

A 28-yard punt didn't help Arkansas, and Texas set up on their own 36. Three straight running plays were stopped and the Longhorns were faced with a fourth down and a bit less than three yards for a first.

Timeout was called and Street jogged to the sideline.

"I remember that we were in a helluva jam, going into the late part of that game," Darrell Royal recalled nearly four decades later.

Royal consulted with his coaches, including Emory Bellard. Although Royal is often eager to downplay his own contributions, he quickly answers the question of who called the pass:

"I did."

Street got the call to go long, turned to the huddle, then stopped to come back. He wanted to make sure he'd heard correctly. Royal laughs at the memory. "He jogged out to midfield and got about to the huddle, when he came back and said, 'Coach, let me get this straight. . . .'" The legendary DKR adds, "I think the press box was a little stunned!"

After all, Texas had Worster, Koy, and Jim Bertelsen in the backfield. Further, wasn't it Royal himself who observed that three things can happen when you pass and two of them are bad?

TEAM STATISTICS FROM THE '69 SHOOTOUT

	TEXAS	ARKANSAS
First downs	19	18
By rushing	14	7
By passing	5	10
By penalty	0	1
Yards rushing	244	103
Yards passing	124	205
Passes	6-10-2	14-22-2
Punts, average	2-36.5	7-31.7
Return yardage	47	-2
Fumbles lost	4	0
Penalties	2—30	6—40
Number of rushing attempts	60	44
Total yards rushing	249	162
Yards lost rushing	5	59
Total offense yardage (net)	368	308
Punt return yardage	2—27	0—0
Kick-off return yardage	2—56	0—0
Interception return yardage	2—20	2—2

INDIVIDUAL STATISTICS

Texas Rushing	TC	Yds	Avg.
Street	8	73	9.1
Bertelsen	10	29	2.9
Koy	3	28	2.1
Worster	25	94	3.8
Callison	3	6	2.0
Speyrer	1	14	14.0

Passing	C-A	Int.	Yds
Street	6-10	2	124

Receiving	No.	Yds	
Speyrer	4	65	
Peschel	2	59	

Punting	No.	Yds	Avg
Monzingo	2	73	36.5

Arkansas Rushing	TC	Yds	Avg
Montgomery	15	-2	0
Burnett	19	82	4.3
Maxwell	10	23	2.3

Passing	C-A	Int.	Yds
Montgomery	14-22	2	205

Receiving	No.	Yds	
Dicus	9	146	
Rees	2	33	
Burnet	3	26	

Punting	No.	Yds	Avg
Stockdell	6	222	37.0

But he called it long, and he stuck with it.

Street bent under the center and barked the signals. He took the snap, looked downfield, and saw Randy Peschel, who had previously reported to Royal that he was not being covered on deep patterns.

The ball dropped right over his head and into his waiting hands. It was as if the entire stadium was now a barbecue spit, and Hog was ready to be served.

Texas went crazy, sensing victory. The Razorbacks went limp on the sidelines, but to the credit of their defense, the team didn't lay down.

From a new set of downs at the Razorback 13, Koy ran for eleven yards on a play that is often overlooked in light of the huge pass that preceded it. Bertelsen then scored, and Happy Feller "kicked goal" with 3:30 left. Arkansas managed to punch it out to Texas's 39, but another interception killed off any hopes of some last-minute heroics.

Texas received the national championship trophy from President Richard Nixon, who was in attendance.

"It was a great game," said President Nixon afterward. "It was worthy of the championship game of the one-hundredth year of football. That says a lot."

Other American royalty were at the stadium, too: Billy Graham had given the invocation, and Bud Wilkinson was there for ABC.

They saw an unforgettable game.

Chapter Three

IT'S OURS

TEXAS INVENTED THE WISHBONE

In 1968, Darrell Royal had to do something. Football is king in Texas, and the King of Texas football would not accept mediocrity. Shoot, having a "good" team wasn't even enough for him. Leave that to other schools.

The Longhorns had already won a national championship under Royal. Texas had followed up the 1963 title year with a 10–1 record in 1964, including blowout wins over rivals Oklahoma and Texas A&M.

In 1965, the Longhorns shut out the Sooners, but cracks were showing in the team. Narrow, back-to-back losses to Arkansas and Rice were followed by larger margins of defeat against SMU and TCU. A 6–4 final record didn't sit well with a fierce competitor like Royal or his staff.

All sorts of things go into a championship football team: schemes, players, coaching, Lady Luck. Texas didn't have all these in the mid-60s, and in typical blunt fashion, Royal took full responsibility. DKR admitted he had spent too much time on the lecture circuit, living off the accolades for 1963, and he hadn't devoted enough time to what he was hired to do: coach to win.

Texas ended 1966 at 7–4, in a season featuring its first loss to Oklahoma in a decade. The mediocre record and defeat by OU coincided with Royal's decision to move from the option to the I-formation. Royal began thinking about bringing back the option in some new form.

The following year was even more frustrating, as an opening loss to No. 7 Southern Cal on the road signaled that problems encountered in the previous two seasons hadn't been resolved. Texas finished the year with a disappointing 6–4 record. There were some narrow losses which, if a few key plays went the other way, could have been victories. But then again, there were close wins over SMU and Oklahoma that could have ended worse.

A 9–7 victory over eventual Orange Bowl champion OU that year showed how tantalizingly close Royal was to turning it around. But something wasn't quite right. Texas still had good players. The coaching staff, as good as any in the country, had refocused. What was the problem?

Enter a former Single-Wing tailback, one of those hardscrabble boys from the tough Texas badlands. Royal had spotted him coaching in the high school ranks and thought this fellow just might be the ticket to rejuvenating the Longhorns. Emory Bellard signed on as an assistant after that 1967 season, and Darrell was fixin' to set things right.

A UT player himself in the 1940s, Bellard had been hired by Royal to coach freshman linebackers—basically get his feet wet in the whirlpool of college coaching. His coaching style already bordered on the legendary at places like Breckenridge and San Angelo. Royal wasn't afraid to take a chance on this high school coach.

Bellard was an innovator, and his tinkering with an offensive formation intrigued Royal. For some time, Bellard had been experimenting with an offensive scheme that looked something like the Split-T that he and Royal had experience running. After all, during his unfortunate stint as a Sooner, Royal himself had run it to perfection during OU's unbeaten season of 1949. OU head coach Bud Wilkinson taught Royal option football so well that Royal would use it for the rest of his own coaching career.

And it didn't hurt that Royal watched A&M use option football to beat Bear Bryant and Alabama in the Cotton Bowl. (The game also had a deep impact on Bryant, who adopted the option himself in 1971.)

A decision in 1968 to go back to some sort of "T" formation still didn't quite cut it. So one day, Bellard brought Royal the outlines of a new offense, one that would take the best of the Split-T and add more of a passing threat. As folks got their first look at the new formation in practice, somebody called it the "pulley bone." But legend has it that *Houston Post* writer Mickey Herskowitz devised the name for the formation that eventually stuck—the Wishbone.

Then offensive line coach Leon Manley remembers how the formation was born at Texas. After introducing it against Houston in the 1968 opener, it became clear that something was wrong in the backfield. "Darrell told Bellard he didn't want to run the option without a lead blocker," Manley recalls. "They moved [fullback Steve] Worster back a little from the quarterback, and that helped. We moved him back a little to lead that first lineman. That's what made our blocking easier." Moving Worster was one of those small things that, in the end, really turned out to be a big thing.

Manley also credits coach Willie Zapalac with implementing zone-blocking, which simplified the linemen's responsibilities.

Today, from his Austin home, Manley can guess what visiting writers really want to ask: Would the Wishbone work today?

"I think it would. You'd have to put in more of a passing attack, but yes, I think it'd work. But I'm partial."

Royal, who remains close to old friends and assistants like Manley, also remembers a key detail that elevated the Wishbone into a more lethal offense than the option had been: "We read the defensive end. We didn't read the handoff."

DID YOU KNOW?

Dell Computers founder and CEO Michael Dell dropped out of UT at nineteen after starting a computer company called PC's Limited in his room at Dobie Center. That company later became Dell Computer Corporation and ultimately Dell Inc.

Suddenly, in that 1968 season, Texas had what it wanted on offense: a full-house backfield, along with the blocking Royal knew from his days with the Split-T at Oklahoma.

Texas coaches had running backs Ted Koy and Chris Gilbert line up with new fullback Steve Worster. The formation was led by quarterback "Super" Bill Bradley, a smart, gifted athlete.

The team's new direction looked promising to Bellard and Royal, although Royal also worried that the blocking wouldn't come around in time. His suspicions were confirmed in that first game with Houston, when Texas struggled early and went on to tie, 20–20.

Then came Texas Tech. The *Galveston Daily News* on September 27 reported:

> Tech will be the second test for Royal's new offense, which he calls a "wish-bone T," with fullback Steve Worster up a step behind the quarterback. Royal said he was generally pleased with the new look but the Longhorns needed better execution.

He was right. Tech pulled out a 31–22 win.

During the game, the coaches saw that something still wasn't quite right with the team. They thought it might be a problem with the quarterback. Scanning the roster, they thought the back-up QB might have that something, that intangible winning quality that you just can't coach into someone. He had a marquee confidence to go with a marquee name.

So the head Horns decided to give James Street a try. Although his play wasn't enough to turn the Tech game around, it seemed promising to Royal, who gave Street the starting slot.

In those days of "yes, sir" and "no, sir," there was perhaps more of a tendency than today for players to subordinate their personal concerns to the cause of victory. It was all about the team and all about unity.

The selfless attitude displayed by Bill Bradley when informed of the change still stands out forty years later. Bradley reportedly stood up in a team meeting, announced that James Street was now leading the offense, and declared that everyone had better rally behind him.

That heroic little speech set the stage for the success that was to come to the Longhorns later that season, notwithstanding Street's own outstanding talents. The team seemed infused with real purpose after seeing Bradley's sacrifice. The next week, Texas defeated Oklahoma State by four touchdowns.

After the massacre at Oklahoma State, a showdown with OU loomed. The Land Thieves came to Dallas with a super tailback in Steve Owens and an excellent passer in Bobby Warmack. They also had some fine defensive talent. Many fans predicted the game would be a real brawl.

In fact, that's exactly what it was. With just under three minutes to go, Texas was down, 20–19. And that's when the legend of James Street was born.

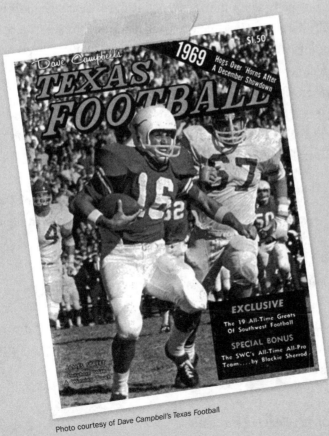

THE PEERLESS
James Street

Photo courtesy of Dave Campbell's Texas Football

He led the Longhorns eighty-five yards to the winning touchdown. And after that, for the rest of his days at Texas, he never lost a game that he started.

None other than Barry Switzer has attributed OU's three-season-long downturn of 1981–83 to the lack of a quarterback who could make the formation great. Plenty of quarterbacks can technically run it, but it really needs a QB whose natural talents, primarily the split-second decision-making reading the defense, fit the formation. When the Sooners had a Jack Mildren or Thomas Lott, the formation ran smoothly. When they didn't, well, the Sun Bowl was a nice consolation.

For the Longhorns, James Street proved to be the ideal director of the Wishbone. With Street at the helm, Texas would not lose again that season—or for the next thirty-one games.

A *New York Times* story at the end of the season described Texas's killer new formation:

"Gilbert is the heart of the Texas backfield, which aligns itself in the 'Y' or so-called 'Wishbone T' formation. The sophomore fullback, Steve Worster, in a four-point stance, places himself directly behind the quarterback, James Street, who either gives the ball to Worster for a quick pop up the middle or pitches out to Gilbert or Ted Koy."

Going 9–1–1 in 1968, the Longhorns closed out the season with a 36–13 dismantling of Tennessee in the Cotton Bowl. As the *Washington Post* reported several months later:

Coach Darrell Royal's Wishbone-T attack at the University of Texas produced a ground game second only to Houston's nationally. Named for the split alignment of the set backs, the Wishbone is gaining many followers too, especially from those dazzled by the Longhorns' deft 36–13 Cotton Bowl execution of Tennessee.

As the 1969 season approached, anticipation ran high. As it played out, Texas had only three close games that season: Oklahoma, Arkansas, and Notre Dame in the Cotton Bowl. The Longhorns won them all.

Their other opponents weren't so lucky; Texas won in blowouts, shutouts, and everything in between. Over the next few years, the Wishbone produced seven conference titles and two national championships.

One of the key features of the Wishbone was that it led to high-scoring games—sometimes outrageously so. Before the Wishbone, even Texas's best teams sometimes struggled to put up points in the tough Southwest Conference. But during the decade spent running the Wishbone, the Longhorns put up 49 on Texas Tech, 56 on Baylor, 69 on TCU, and so on. The huge margins of victory instilled even more confidence in the players.

In the national championship year of 1970, Texas destroyed TCU, A&M, and Arkansas on consecutive weekends. Oklahoma was clobbered by thirty-two points in October.

Texas was back in a big way.

THE MEN OF THE WISHBONE

The Wishbone teams produced numerous All-Americans, including Chris Gilbert, Bob McKay, Happy Feller and Cotton Speyrer. In fact, Speyer proved with back-to-back AA honors in 1969–70 that a split end could catch enough balls to be noticed in the run-oriented Wishbone.

Amidst the flood of high-water marks in those years, there is this: against SMU in 1969, Texas ran for more than 600 yards, with four backs going over a hundred: Worster and Jim Bertelsen had 137 each, followed by Street at 121 and Koy with 111. It is rare for any offense to produce two backs who run for the century mark in a single game. Four is just insane.

Texas was also fortunate to have the quarterbacks to run it. Street has his place in football lore, as the first. (Arguably, he was also the best. OU's Jack Mildren may have given him a run for his money but, it should be noted, even Mildren was a Texas boy from Abilene.) After Street's time was up, Eddie Phillips served as a pretty darned good replacement in 1970–71. And Alan Lowrey put together an outstanding season in 1972 culminating in a Cotton Bowl win over Alabama (which had started running the Wishbone a year

Photo courtesy of the
Arkansas Democrat-Gazette

« COTTON SPEYRER, a two-time All-American split end on a UT Wishbone team

⌄ TEXAS STAR and later NFL great Earl Campbell

Photo courtesy of Lex Gillean

earlier). In that game, Lowrey ran for 117 yards and two touchdowns to help subdue the Tide.

And we can't forget Marty Akins, who won twenty-six games as a Longhorn quarterback and became Texas's only three-year starter at the position under Royal.

Texas also had great linemen in this era. Guys like Bob McKay and Bob Simmons, Jerry Sizemore, Bob Wuensch, and Bill Wyman all made All-American. They were supplemented by other supremely talented players, like David Studdard, Rick Ingraham, and Wes Hubert.

Ends such as Speyrer also continued a strong tradition at those positions, which included players like Alfred Jackson. In fact, Texas threw better out of the Wishbone than perhaps any other team that later ran it.

Of course, Royal and his assistants knew that any offense was limited if it didn't have high-octane athletes to run it. They recruited those big ol' rough linemen to block for athletes in the backfield. Texas was known for having strength at every position, but one stood out.

That was fullback. Texas was never without a great one. In fact, no other college team had such a run of talent at the position; Steve Worster, Roosevelt Leaks, and Earl Campbell all made All-America. Campbell, of course, won the Heisman Trophy in 1977 (ironically, the first year the Longhorns moved away from the Wishbone and installed an I-formation).

Worster, from Bridge City, was a big, rawboned runner (six-foot, 210 pounds) and made All-American twice, in 1969 and 1970. He was considered the prototype Wishbone fullback. At Texas, he ran for 2,353 yards and thirty-six touchdowns. More importantly, he joined a small, elite group that has won multiple championships in football. Three SWC titles and two national championships cemented Worster's status as a great fullback.

> 66 **This was a great experience for the kids. Twenty years from now these guys will be sitting in some bar in Idaho drinking beer and talking about the time they went down and played Texas.** 99
>
> —Utah State coach Phil Krueger, after getting clobbered by the Longhorns, 61–7, in 1975

Roosevelt Leaks, from Brenham, proved he wasn't just a memorable name. After making All-American (and running for a record 342 yards against SMU in 1973), Leaks played nine years in the NFL, with the Baltimore Colts and the Buffalo Bills.

Then there was Earl Campbell. He started for three years as a Wishbone fullback, then moved to tailback as a senior, when he won the Heisman.

In any program, players like Leaks and Worster would be placed on Mt. Rushmore. But Campbell was in a league of his own. Many fans old enough to remember The Tyler Rose call him the greatest football player of all time; Barry Switzer has repeatedly said that Campbell was the only player he ever saw who could have gone straight from high school to the NFL and been a star.

Teams were afraid of him. Defensive coordinators got migraines trying to plan out a way to stop him. With powerful legs, a confrontational running style (actually, he seemed more like a mad buffalo running through a prairie dog town), and greater speed than a man that big should have, Campbell brutalized Texas's opponents for four years. Then he repeated the performance in the NFL, first with the Houston Oilers, then with New Orleans.

Legend has it that a full-blown recruiting war erupted over Campbell. With an excellent staff at a university carrying a stellar reputation for football, Darrell Royal didn't have to get involved in the finer details of recruiting. Typically, Texas doesn't so much recruit as deign to offer a player a scholarship. But everybody wanted Campbell, and wanted him badly. Oklahoma in particular was keen to pick him up, and Switzer knew how to sweet talk recruits. So DKR decided to step in.

"Not only did I recruit him," Royal remembers, "but the coach who recruited that area got excited about Earl early on, and decided I needed to get involved, and I did. Most coaches didn't visit with his mother, but Mama was involved in it, too."

> **66 I don't know if Earl's in a class by himself, but it sure don't take long to call roll. 99**
>
> —Darrell Royal on Earl Campbell

In the end, Earl liked Texas, Mama liked Texas, and Texas liked both Earl and Mama. He signed in February 1974, becoming a starter at the moment the pen touched the paper on his letter of intent.

THE WISHBONE GOES NATIONAL

As teams began having success with option football, other teams felt pressured to adopt it in order to remain competitive. Tom Osborne acknowledged that the option rejuvenated his Nebraska program. "We switched to the option-I because of the athleticism of Oklahoma's quarterbacks," he said matter-of-factly. Simply put, he was tired of getting beat by his rival and decided to do something about it.

Texas started the Wishbone—Bellard was the technician, and Royal had the bravado to roll it out. Their success with the new formation made the Wishbone, like option football in general, seem very intriguing to a number of programs—in fact, many coaches found it irresistible. Each team that adopted the formation put its own stamp on the offense; Oklahoma was known for speed on the outside, while Texas A&M incorporated a bit more passing with a balanced backfield. Alternatively, Arkansas and Air Force under Ken Hatfield ran the "Flexbone," emphasizing more passing.

At A&M, the Wishbone was run by Bellard himself, who was hired as head coach there in 1972. Interestingly, the Longhorns continued to dominate A&M even after Bellard's transfer. The Aggies didn't defeat their rivals until the last two years of Royal's career, when Bellard had finally developed a defense to compliment his high-octane offense.

But the highlights of Texas's Wishbone years were the titanic battles against the Sooners. Both teams had incredible players and superior coaching. The spectacle of watching the two premier Wishbone offenses in the country go at it every year is something older fans remember to this day. Texas knocked the Sooners' collective helmet off for three straight years until 1971, when Jack Mildren led OU to a win. The next two years were tough for the Longhorns, but a three-year run beginning in 1974 saw some of the best games in the series' history.

Oklahoma might have made speed the feature element of their Wishbone, but Texas still had all the key ingredients: superior fullbacks, fast halfbacks like Ivy Suber and Johnny Jones, and crafty quarterbacks. In those days, OU coaches and players constantly debated how best to defend against Campbell and the passing ability of Akins.

In the 1974 Texas-OU match-up, OU kicked a late field goal to nip the Longhorns, 16–13. A year later, the Longhorns suffered from a couple key mistakes, and a late touchdown run by Navarro Junior College fullback Horace Ivory sealed it for the Sooners.

The 1976 Texas-OU game stands out for several reasons. It was the last year Texas would run its fabled formation; Royal must have already been planning to step down; and then there was the feud with Switzer, whose swashbuckler persona wore thin south of the Red River.

Texas came into that game without its own Wishbone wizard, Marty Akins, who'd graduated. But they still had Earl, as well as a sick defense that featured Brad Shearer, Tim Campbell, Ricky Churchman, and Glenn Blackwood.

And this amazing crew absolutely throttled the Sooners' famed offense. In fact, to this day, many OU fans consider the 1976 game against Texas to be the worst its offense has played in modern times.

Days before the game, Sooner quarterback Dean Blevins, more of a passer than a runner, came down with an illness. That opened the door for San Antonio sophomore Thomas Lott to debut.

It was a disaster. Lott would become a famed Wishbone operator in his own right, but on that day, Texas did more than merely bottle him up along with his backfield mates—the Longhorns trampled them. For the entire game, Oklahoma gained just 133 yards, with thirty coming on the final drive. Lott threw for thirty-eight yards while Elvis Peacock, Horace Ivory, and Kenny King managed a meager ninety-five yards on the ground.

» **"HAM" JONES** was the perfect halfback complement to "Lam"

⌄ **JOHNNY LAM JONES** began his career at UT as a Wishbone halfback, then made All-American at wide receiver

However, the Texas offense didn't fare much better, scoring only six points for the game on two Russell Erxleben field goals. Then, late in the game, a Texas fumble enabled OU to drive into the end zone. Standing so close to victory they could taste it, the Sooners blew it, with a bad snap leading to a missed extra point. Both teams walked away disappointed with a 6–6 tie.

The Wishbone was retired at Texas not long after that game against Oklahoma. The last Wishbone halfbacks at Texas, "Ham" and "Lam" Jones, were talented (Lam later made All-American), but Royal's successor, Fred Akers, wanted to "modernize" the offense.

In 1977, the Wishbone passed into history at Austin. Its final appearance came in the evening shadows in December when Texas bested Arkansas, 29–12.

EMORY BELLARD: FATHER OF THE WISHBONE

The famous Wishbone: winner of national championships. Do we need to list any other virtue? The genesis of this revolutionary offense is no secret—Darrell Royal, Frank Broyles, and even Barry Switzer, among many others, call Emory Bellard "the Father of the Wishbone."

The Die-Hard Fan sat down with Coach Bellard in the summer of 2007 at his home north of Austin. Looking out over a golf course, and with his ever-present graph paper by his chair—the better to sketch option plays for visitors—Bellard discussed how it all came about. Fit and tan at eighty, he looks as if he could line up at halfback.

DF: Coach, where did you go to college?

Bellard: I went to the University of Texas for my freshman year. At that time the freshmen were eligible, so I played on the varsity squad. But just before the A&M game that year I had a real severe break—I broke both bones in my leg and it never did heal up quite right, but anyhow, I played the next three years. Then during my sophomore year, all the guys came back out of the service right after '45 and '46, and you're talking about lots of folks coming back. I transferred at the end of my sophomore year and I played in '46, too, but I went to Texas State, which was called Southwest Texas State at the time. I played and graduated from there.

DF: And did you go directly into coaching?

Bellard: Yeah, all I ever wanted to do is coach. That's the reason I wanted to go play when I was living in Port Aransas—because I knew that's what I wanted to do. My older brothers, who were a good deal older than I was, both played football, and I used to hang around the dressing rooms with the players and, you know, I was always around. Somewhere in there I got it in my mind that I was gonna do that someday, that I was gonna coach football, and I did. I had a ball.

DF: When did you become a head coach?

Bellard: The first three years I served as assistant [high school] coach at Dallas. They were great years for learning and getting your feet on the ground, but I didn't want to be an assistant coach. I wanted to be a head coach. My first year was under a coach named Ox Emerson. It was really a great experience and a good starting point. I learned a lot of things about organization and priorities. Those three years were very important in developing my mind-set about what it takes to do things and do them right.

I applied for head coaching jobs, and I'd go in and the superintendent would ask me, usually, "How old are you?" because apparently

Photo courtesy of Texas A&M University

EMORY BELLARD, the Wishbone's creator

DEFENDING AGAINST THE WISHBONE

A key for Texas in remaining dominant once other teams "borrowed" the Wishbone was its defensive personnel. The Longhorns were never without smothering defenses, with elite players at every position. These included the likes of linemen Bill Acker, Steve McMichael, Doug English, and Brad Shearer; linebackers Lance Taylor, Glen Gaspard, and Bill Hamilton; and defensive backs Glenn Blackwood and Raymond Clayborn.

Photo courtesy of *Dave Campbell's Texas Football*

With this stand-out defense, Texas frustrated other teams that used the Wishbone against the Longhorns. Oklahoma offensive line coach Merv Johnson recognized that for years the Sooners were handicapped in blocking the Texas tackles. He told the Die-Hard Fan that Oklahoma began putting larger players at offensive guard in order to cope with the huge and mobile Longhorn tackles. In 1976–77, OU managed just one touchdown and two field goals in the Red River Shootout. From 1979–81, the Sooners were throttled again, scoring only thirty-four points. The defense alone made Texas hard to beat.

A case in point was safety Johnny Johnson. An All-American safety who practiced against the Wishbone, Johnson knew the formation well and how to slow it down. Though not a large player, Johnson was a headhunter; his hit on Thomas Lott sealed the Longhorns' 1977 win against OU. Outweighed by thirty pounds, Johnson hit Lott on fourth and one from the Texas 5, preserving a 13–6 Longhorn win.

JOHNNIE JOHNSON'S tackling ability at safety stopped OU's vaunted Wishbone several times

I looked a lot younger than I was. Of course, I wasn't very old either, I was in my early twenties—21, 22, and 23. But I knew I was out of a job just as soon as I was asked the question.

So I went to Ingleside, which is a peninsula right straight across the Corpus Christie Bay.

I had a great group of kids. My first year there we went 8–3, and we won the district championship. At that time to get into the state playoffs you had to win the district championship. Only the champions of each district had a playoff system, which is pretty strange now. But anyhow, we won that district championship and then we won the next twenty-four in a row over the next couple years.

DF: You also coached at Breckenridge, right?

Bellard: Yeah, I went from Ingleside to Breckenridge. I had opportunities at the end of that third year at Ingleside to go into college coaching. I was offered assistant coaching jobs at some Southwest Conference school every year after my third year as a head coach. But I didn't want to be an assistant coach. I wanted to coach my own stuff my own way. That wasn't egotistical, it was just what I wanted to do.

So I went to Breckenridge, where we won two state championships. I was there five years. There were four classifications in Texas at that time. 4A was the largest classification and Breckenridge was in 3A. It was the smallest 3A school in the state. Those kids loved to play football, though, and we won state championships in '58 and '59.

Then I went to San Angelo and that was probably the toughest football district in Texas. There were lots of areas in Texas that have numbers, but back then Abilene, San Angelo, Midland, and Odessa—those schools composed this district and nearly every year they were fighting for the state championship. When I was there, we won the district championship four times, and we won the state championship in '66.

Then I was offered the coaching job at the University of Texas. Darrell [Royal] had called and I knew that whole staff pretty well. I probably could have gone somewhere in the Southwest Conference ever since 1954, but I didn't want to. The University of Texas with Darrell was probably the only college situation I would have gone into. I thought I was gonna be working with a freshman football team there, and then the spring of that year [1967], I coached the linebackers.

DF: What kind of situation did you walk into? Texas had been pretty good, right?

Bellard: Texas has been down a little. They had been 6–4 for three consecutive years, including the '66 season. The first year I was at Texas I was sort of amazed that the personnel had dropped a little bit. At the end of spring training Darrell said to Mike [Campbell, the defensive coordinator], "Mike, I'd like to have you work in the press box with him."

So I remained coaching the linebackers that year and worked the press box with Mike Campbell. Mike was on the sideline and at the end of the season, right after the last game, which was against A&M, Darrell decided to reorganize the staff. He called after the game and wanted to know if I wanted to take over the offense. I had good offensive theories, good theories. They were real sound, and it wasn't a bunch of malarkey.

We went through spring training doing those things. We had good backs that were runners, and they weren't guys that you'd want to put out at the wingbacks or flankers or any of that bit, they were running backs. So they needed to be in, and I had been working for quite a while on an option concept. It was all about the triple option and the best of the linemen that I could come up with. That offense was eventually known as the Wishbone. I didn't even have a name for it, but a sportswriter, Mickey Herskowitz, I think, wanted to put the name Wishbone on it. But that's irrelevant as far as the offense was concerned.

DF: Where did this concept come from? In high school did you run some version of the Split-T or something like that?

Bellard: Yeah, I had always loved to run option football and always loved to run three- back offenses, which I had always done. Eventually that was the reason I felt like Darrell would okay this, because he had always been in those situations as a player and as a coach. He had always coached Split-T, except I think one year they ran a Wing-T, but not when I was there.

But anyhow, he liked those factors, too. And I had always felt like there are three optimums in football. One of them is if you get a body on a body and a ball carrier running behind it, that is one option. That is as good as you can hope for. You gotta assume that the other side has got some sense, but that is one optimum. The second optimum is to get a two-on-one situation with an option. That's a real advantage. That is as good as you can get it. You gotta handle all these other people adjacent to it, but still, if you can get it down to that, then you've got one of the optimums. And the third one is to get a one-on-one situation with a pass. You always had that going. Defenses, if you know defensive football, they've got to honor anybody going deep, whether it's the tight-end, split-end, or otherwise—you gotta honor that.

> 66 **So those are the principles under which it was based, and they're just as sound as a dollar.** 99
>
> —Emory Bellard

Then, if you know all that from a defensive standpoint, you know that that's a fact. And so your offense has gotta be designed by how the second man from that outside has gotta take the pitch, the third man has gotta take the quarterback, and where they play the fourth man dictates how you're gonna play against the inside thread. So those are the principles under which it was based, and they're just as sound as a dollar.

A DECADE OF DOMINANCE
TEXAS WITH THE WISHBONE

»1968

Season: 9–1–1
SWC: 61–0 (T1st)
Final Ranking: 3rd, AP; 5th, UPI

Sept. 21 (#4) 11 Houston T 20–20
Sept. 28 (#6) Texas Tech L 22–31
Oct. 5 Oklahoma St. W 31–3
Oct. 12 vs. Oklahoma W 26–20
Oct. 19 (#17) 9 Arkansas W 39–29
Oct. 26 (#13) Rice W 38–14
Nov. 2 (#11) 13 SMU W 38–7
Nov. 9 (#10) Baylor W 47–26
Nov. 16 (#8) TCU W 47–21
Nov. 28 (#6) Texas A&M W 35–14
Jan. 1 (#5) vs. 8 Tennessee W 36–13

»1969
NATIONAL CHAMPIONS

Season: 11–0–0
SWC: 7–0–0 (1st)
Final Ranking: 1st, AP; 1st UPI

Sept. 20 (#4) @ California W 17–0
Sept. 27 (#4) Texas Tech W 49–7
Oct. 4 (#2) Navy W 56–17
Oct. 11 (#2) vs. #8 Oklahoma W 27–17
Oct. 25 (#2) Rice W 31–0
Nov. 1 (#2) @ SMU W 45–14
Nov. 8 (#2) Baylor W 56–14
Nov. 15 (#2) TCU W 69–7
Nov. 27 (#1) @ Texas A&M W 49–12
Dec. 6 (#1) @ #2 Arkansas W 15–14
Jan. 1 (#1) vs. #9 Notre Dame W 21–17

»1970
NATIONAL CHAMPIONS

Season: 10–1–0
SWC: 7–0–0 (1st)
Final Ranking: 3rd, AP; 1st, UPI

Sept. 19 (#2) California W 56–15
Sept. 26 (#2) @ Texas Tech W 35–13
Oct. 3 (#2) #13 UCLA W 20–17
Oct. 10 (#2) vs. Oklahoma W 41–9
Oct. 24 (#2) @ Rice W 45–21
Oct. 31 (#1) SMU W 42–15
Nov. 7 (#1) @ Baylor W 21–14
Nov. 14 (#2) @ TCU W 58–0
Nov. 26 (#1) Texas A&M W 52–14
Dec. 5 (#1) #4 Arkansas W 42–7
Jan. 1 (#1) vs. #6 Notre Dame L 11–24

»1971

Season: 8–3–0
SWC: 6–1–0 (1st)
Final Ranking: 18th, AP; 12th, UPI

Sept. 18 (#3) @ UCLA W 28–10
Sept. 25 (#3) Texas Tech W 28–0
Oct. 2 (#3) Oregon W 35–7
Oct. 9 (#3) vs. #8 Oklahoma L 27–48
Oct. 16 (#10) @ #16 Arkansas L 7–31
Oct. 23 (#16) Rice W 39–10
Oct. 30 (#14) @ SMU W 22–18
Nov. 6 (#15) Baylor W 24–0
Nov. 13 (#13) TCU W 31–0
Nov. 25 (#12) @ Texas A&M W 34–14
Jan. 1 (#12) vs. #10 Penn State L 6–30

»1972

Season: 10–1–0
SWC: 7–0–0 (1st)
Final Ranking: 3rd, AP; 5th, UPI
Sept. 23 (#14) Miami W 23–10
Sept. 30 (#12) @ Texas Tech W 25–20
Oct. 7 (#9) Utah State W 27–12
Oct. 14 (#10) vs. #2 Oklahoma L 0–27
Oct. 21 (#14) #17 Arkansas W 35–15
Oct. 28 (#10) @ Rice W 45–9
Nov. 4 (#9) SMU W 17–9
Nov. 11 (#9) @ Baylor W 17–3
Nov. 18 (#7) @ TCU W 27–0
Nov. 23 (#7) Texas A&M W 38–3
Jan. 1 (#7) vs. #4 Alabama W 17–13

»1973

Season: 8–3–0
SWC: 7–0–0 (1st)
Final Ranking: 14th, AP; 8th, UPI
Sept. 21 @ Miami L 15–20
Sept. 29 Texas Tech W 28–12
Oct. 6 Wake Forest W 41–0
Oct. 13 vs. #6 Oklahoma L 13–52
Oct. 20 @ Arkansas W 34–6
Oct. 27 Rice W 55–13
Nov. 3 (#19) @ SMU W 42–14
Nov. 10 (#13) Baylor W 42–6
Nov. 17 (#11) TCU W 52–7
Nov. 22 (#11) @ Texas A&M W 42–13
Jan. 1 (#8) vs. #12 Nebraska L 3–19

»1974

Season: 8–4–0
SWC: 5–2–0 (T2nd)
Final Ranking: 17th–tie, AP
Sept. 14 (#10) @ Boston College W 42–19
Sept. 21 (#9) Wyoming W 34–7
Sept. 28 (#6) @ Texas Tech L 3–26
Oct. 5 (#19) Washington W 35–21
Oct. 12 (#17) vs. #2 Oklahoma L 13–16

Oct. 19 (#16) Arkansas W 38–7
Oct. 26 (#13) @ Rice W 27–6
Nov. 2 (#12) SMU W 35–15
Nov. 9 (#12) @ Baylor L 24–34
Nov. 16 @ TCU W 81–16
Nov. 29 (#17) #8 Texas A&M W 32–3
Dec. 30 (#11) vs. #6 Auburn L 3–27

»1975

Season: 10–2–0
SWC: 6–1–0 (T1st)
Final Ranking: 6th, AP; 7th, UPI
Sept. 13 (#12) Colorado St. W 46–0
Sept. 20 (#8) @ Washington W 28–10
Sept. 27 (#6) Texas Tech W 42–18
Oct. 4 (#7) Utah State W 61–7
Oct. 11 (#5) vs. #2 Oklahoma L 17–24
Oct. 18 (#8) @ #20 Ark W 24–18
Oct. 25 (#8) Rice W 41–9
Nov. 1 (#8) @ SMU W 30–22
Nov. 8 (#7) Baylor W 37–21
Nov. 15 (#7) TCU W 27–11
Nov. 28 (#5) @ #2 Texas A&M L 10–20
Dec. 27 (#9) vs. #10 Colorado W 38–21

»1976

Season: 5–5–1
SWC: 4–4–0 (5th)
Final Ranking: Unranked
Sept. 11 (#7) @ Boston College L 13–14
Sept. 18 (#19) North Texas W 17–14
Oct. 2 @ Rice W 42–15
Oct. 9 (#16) vs. #3 Oklahoma T 6–6
Oct. 23 (#13) SMU W 13–12
Oct. 30 (#15) @ #6 Texas Tech L 28–31
Nov. 6 (#20) #19 Houston L 0–30
Nov. 13 @ TCU W 34–7
Nov. 20 @ Baylor L 10–20
Nov. 25 #11 Texas A&M L 3–27
Dec. 4 Arkansas W 29–12

And they are sound today. If you get equal people, you're not gonna lose because the offense is not sound. You may get whipped somewhere in there, but that's the horse of a different color. You may get whipped on the other side of the ball too, you know, your defense may not be strong enough to stop the other guy. Nonetheless, I wasn't totally satisfied even though we had an excellent spring training that year. I had been working on this.

DF: Did you immediately install the Wishbone when you got to Texas?

Bellard: Yeah.

DF: And what offense had they run immediately before you got there?

Bellard: Well, they had been running I-formation and stuff; Gene Stallings was there. They didn't have that type of player [to run the option]. We were a very average football team, but we did beat Arkansas that year. That was the first game that we won, the Southwest Conference game against Arkansas.

DF: So your freshman class laid the foundation for the Wishbone there?

Bellard: Well, at first, we were running, but we couldn't do much. We couldn't do much of a whole lot of anything. But we got a little better as the season went on and like I say, we beat Arkansas and a couple of teams and things picked up a little bit. We were 3–8 the first year and then the next year 6–5, and then the next year it was 8–3, and then there was 10–2, 10–2, and so forth. And so, it got better and better as it went along.

DF: Is it a myth that you can't throw effectively from the Wishbone?

Bellard: Well, that's just what I was talking about. That tight-end, every time we ran the option, was always going into that deep third. And if that guy that was supposed to be covering the deep third didn't cover the deep third, the passer went behind him, caught the pass, and scored. Against Tennessee that first year we put it in. If you don't cover the ends, the safeties can be up there making tackles, but they can't cover the deep third. So it's one of those optimums I was talking about.

The biggest mistake I made in the passing game was assuming that we needed something short. We didn't—we just needed to throw deep. We did not need to throw short because everybody was coming up this way trying to stop the run. So as long as we kept out deep threats, post patterns, and the streak patterns—that's what we should have been placing the emphasis on.

But like I said, I had been working on that since 1954. My last year at Ingleside, if I'd have stayed there, I was going to go to this triple-option concept. The alignment of the backs wasn't exactly the same, but over the years, I had rarely pulled it in to make sure. There were three places I wanted that lead back to be able to block. In other words, I wanted him to be able to block number two in the structure, number three in the structure, and the first off-line support inside the structure. That was the combination of the options that we could run. His relationship to where the football was and where the pitchman was—all that dictated that unusual looking formation. It's a terrible alignment to do anything with unless you're gonna run the triple option, in which case that's the best way to align them.

DF: And so you pulled a fullback in from where they lined up in a Split-T?

Bellard: Well, the fullback was about on a level with the two halfbacks in the Split-T. The two halfbacks are really the ones that were deeper. The fullback, in fact, was up very, very close to start

> **❝I've been here five years and we've won five championships. [Travis] Roach and I are going to write a book. We're going to call it 'Five in a Row,' or 'Cab Driver, One More Time Around the Block.❞**
>
> —Linebacker Randy Braband, after UT defeated TCU, 27–0, in 1972 to earn Texas's fifth straight SWC title.

with. We moved him back just a little bit. His heels were at four yards and the halfbacks were at five yards deep so they had a little more depth than normal because most of their action was this way and this way, or counter-steps and then going back in and doing different things like that. But again, they were aligned in a relationship to where their relationship and the ball were all together whenever you run option football over to both sides.

In other words, your pitchman was way out in front of where the pitchman was in the Split-T. So the quarterback was making pitches this way and in the Split-T, he was making pitches back here [demonstrates]. So the speed with which he'd get to the corner was a lot faster.

I got my son and some kids, some high school friends of his, and looked at it, and then there were some kids that completed their eligibility that were in summer school at the University of Texas. I got them down to the stadium and I was going to see if I could make the reads. If I could make the reads, well, I knew I could teach a darn good athlete to make them. I ran it down there and we put it together and there were about three or four linemen that were there. They'd completed their eligibility and finished their school there and they were in summer school. So I got them and got sort of a half-line set up.

Then there was Andy White, who had completed his eligibility at Texas and was still finishing up that summer. He was in school, so I got him and I taught him, and he picked it up real quick. Then I wrote it up and presented it to Darrell. I remember him saying, "What the hell is this 1, 2, 3 business?" You know, I was telling him the concept, and of course it was all predicated on principles on which all defense is based. Like I said, if you know anything about defense, you've got to operate within those frameworks of defense. It was all predicated on the fact that you know that, so that's what the triple option has got to be. It's gotta take care of those situations.

So we talked, talked, talked, and talked daily for several days and then had him come down and I demonstrated it and then I'm just as certain of this as anything—he had always run option football and he had always run three-back offenses, so I knew that part was not going to be a factor for Darrell. Sure enough, he said, "Let's go with it."

So we put it in and we tied the first game and lost the second one and then we won the next thirty. And everybody in the country was looking to run the Wishbone. And it became the most winning formation in the history of the game of football for quite a while there.

DF: I know that today coaches consult with each other and go to spring practice and such. Did they consult with you at that time—coaches from Alabama and Oklahoma?

Bellard: I spent a week in a motel with the Alabama coaching staff because Darrell and Barry [Switzer] agreed. I went to Alabama and spoke at their high school clinic over there. During that week I was with the Alabama coaching staff when they put the Wishbone in—I was on the phone with Barry all the time. You can't imagine the number of colleges that were at our spring practice. We conducted a darn coaching clinic every day. It was the biggest mess I ever messed with. I got so tired of talking to people.

Pepper Rogers came down from UCLA and they had had a bad year. Mark Harmon, the young actor, was to be the quarterback and he ended up being a good one. But I spent about a week and I'd go back up to the office and talk with him at night and that jackass went back out and put the Wishbone in at UCLA and had a book published before Christmas. Boy, that takes a lot of gall there.

DF: But they didn't run it very long did they?

Bellard: They ran it the rest of the time he was there. He went to Georgia Tech soon after that. They had a real good year.

DF: And then Alabama put it in?

Bellard: They put it in just before Oklahoma played Southern Cal. Apparently Southern Cal didn't know they were gonna run it. I didn't see any of the players but I've always thought there were some players on campus at the time I was there, but I don't know that. That's just talk. But anyhow, they ran it and just beat the living hound out of Southern Cal. At one time I know that more national championships had been won with the Wishbone, and it was supposedly the most-winning formation in the history of football. I'm talking about a lot of national championships. Alabama and Oklahoma and the University of Texas and there were lots of them coming.

> ❝The personnel had dropped off and we just weren't real good for the University of Texas. For somebody else it might have been all right, but it wasn't for the University of Texas.❞

DF: And then you brought it out in '68 at Texas and Bill Bradley started out as quarterback?

Bellard: Bill was one of the best athletes that I've ever seen. He came to the University of Texas—Texas had been 6–4 a couple seasons and he was a freshman, and he was gonna solve all the problems. He played on very poor football teams for, I think, his first two years. I always had the feeling that he felt like he had to do whatever had to be done to bring the team to the forefront.

He played under such great pressure, which was unfair, because I'm just amazed at how poor a football team we were my first year there in a lot of ways. We didn't have great kickers. The first year I was there we recruited a great freshman class and we had all those great qualities in that great freshman class, but they weren't on the varsity. We weren't a good football team. The personnel had dropped off and we just weren't real good for the University of Texas. For somebody else it might have been all right, but it wasn't for the University of Texas. And I think Darrell would tell you that.

DF: Of the quarterbacks that you had in the Wishbone, can you name a few of them and give us their best attributes for running that offense?

Bellard: Well, James Street. James Street was a fierce competitor, and he had all the respect in the world for his teammates. They knew he was gonna make whatever play was necessary, and he did. He never lost a game. That's gotta instill a lot of confidence in a lot of folks. And then Eddie Phillips came after him and he was out of the same mold as James Street. Street wouldn't have gone into the pros with his arm, but he could throw deep as good as anybody, and so could Eddie. We worked on it awful hard. But he was a great deep passer. Cotton Speyer against Tennessee that first year. Street, he nailed him twice. Speyer beat that all-American corner.

DF: And you stayed at Texas through '71?

Bellard: Yeah.

DF: You spoke earlier about throwing out of the Wishbone formation. Some of Oklahoma's teams were not very effective throwing the ball, but you said as long as you had the element of surprise that the pass was a good weapon for your offenses?

Bellard: It's like most anything. At that particular point in time, it was during a different era as a starting point. In most instances, the leading passing teams in the nation invariably had losing records. Most offenses were very run-oriented and people say, every time you see a Wishbone, it was "a cloud of dust." People can say "three yards and a cloud of dust," but those runs are predicated on the principle that you put 'em back-to-back, you have a continued march toward the goal line. So there is some truth in it, I guess, but I used to not understand how people could make that statement. Like Oklahoma, with all the speed that they had and just flying up and down the field. I don't know how they could call that a cloud of dust.

DF: What was it like when you got to A&M, and had to play against Texas. Was that an odd feeling?

Bellard: It was tough.

DF: Just competition?

Bellard: Yeah. You know, just another football game. When you go into a job it is always a transition and you have to get things to the level that you're used to or you want to, and so that was no different. We had a lot of work to do. But we played Texas and we were higher than a kite. And we beat Texas. And we had to come back, I think it was in six days, and play Arkansas, and they were a good football team. Anyway, we had to play them without our quarterback, so it was sort of an afterthought-type thing.

DF: The Texas Wishbone was known for Worster and Street, while Oklahoma's was known primarily for the halfbacks. In your A&M teams, you seemed to incorporate everybody into it. The quarterback, fullback, and the halfbacks were all pretty equally involved. Is that right?

Bellard: The fullback and the quarterback are the principles on which the offense, the alignment, is based. They are as involved as the defense wants them to be, so to speak. And then there are certain things that are predetermined—fullbacks and halfbacks and stuff like that.

George Woodard was a great fullback. You know, going into his senior year, he was the leading ground-gainer in the United States that was coming back to play. He was a great one. He was never given the credit that he deserved, I didn't think, because everybody thought he was so big. And he was big, but he was a great athlete. Just as light on his feet. But in the early part of August just prior to the start of his senior year, he had a spiral break in the tibia of his right leg from slow-pitched softball and that ruined his career. It knocked the hound out of us. We had to reshuffle our whole backfield that had been playing together. Yeah, George could play.

DF: And then, back in those days, there was so much talent in Texas. I mean, you got Curtis Dickey.

Bellard: Of course, he was from Bryan, he was right there at College Station. He was a great player.

DF: Eventually, you left Texas A&M.

Bellard: Yes, I retired from coaching, and my wife and I we were living in Kingwood, which is out by Conroe. A bunch of kids came over to the house one night, when I'd been retired for a year, and they said, "Coach, come coach us." They needed a coach and they had never won anything. So I coached them, just told the superintendent and them that I'd work within all the frameworks and everything, but I didn't want a bunch of menial jobs around the school district. I just wanted to coach football. I did and we had a lot of fun and the kids won.

DF: Coach, thanks for visiting with us. It's an honor to talk to the Father of the Wishbone.

Bellard: My pleasure.

Chapter Four

JOHNNY LAM JONES

A LEGEND IS BORN AT DKR

The masses filed into Memorial Stadium on a hot Texas day in April 1977 with a single purpose.

With the sun beaming down heat that would normally suck the life out of a crowd of more than 15,000, people sensed that something historic was about to occur at the Texas Relays.

A track meet would not usually muster this much interest. But there was one participant who drew extraordinary attention that day.

John Wesley Jones.

Although he would eventually pick up the nickname "Lam," back then he was known simply as Johnny.

He was more than a mere nineteen-year-old freshman at the University of Texas. We're talking part Paul Bunyan and part Johnny Appleseed.

Jones might have been an aw-shucks country boy from the heart of Texas, but he was already a star freshman athlete for the Lone Star State's flagship university. In addition to playing running back on the UT football squad, he had achieved international renown running for the U.S. track team in the 1976 Summer Olympics in Montreal. His athleticism was spectacular enough to coax thousands of spectators into enduring a cooking Texas afternoon just to see him run.

The prospect that Jones might not win in the showcased 100 meters that day wasn't even a consideration. The crowd didn't turn out just to see Jones win. It wanted to see history get made.

Talk of a possible world record buzzed through the crowd until the muscular, six-foot, 175-pound phenom first appeared on the track. Then, a surge of excitement swept over the stadium.

With the beginning of the landmark race moments away, the noise from the crowd reached a small roar. American Jim Hines had set the current world record in the 100 meters at 9.95 seconds in 1968, and those in attendance felt sure the record wouldn't outlast the day.

Jones stepped into the spotlight that never seemed to blind him. He wasn't thinking about the excited crowd or any world record. Truth be told, he just wanted to run.

EARLY DAYS

The story of Jones's rise to athletic glory presents some delicious irony.

It almost didn't happen; it took a little luck, and if you listen to Jones tell the story, some divine intervention played a role as well.

A native of Lawton, Oklahoma, Jones grew up a fan of Barry Switzer's Sooners. He dreamed of suiting up one day and playing in a Wishbone offense that seemed tailor-made for his skills.

"In the neighborhood that I grew up in back in Lawton, we had a lot of great athletes," Jones recalls today. "We had a little sub-division in Lawton and we all went to a little school called Bishop Elementary School. It was this little country town and this little country school, but we won the city championship in the fourth, fifth, and sixth grades. Every school had their own team, and we won three city championships in a row. Most of the kids lived in the same neighborhood, and we played sports together every day. We played touch football or had little track meets around the corner. We were always in the parks or in the fields playing something. It was either football, baseball, or basketball, but we were always playing some sport."

In what some Texas fans might cite today as proof that God is a fan of the burnt orange, Jones headed south across the Red River in a move that would change every aspect of his life.

"I'd always go and visit my grandparents in Lampasas each summer, and one summer during the seventh grade I started living there. I moved down to Lampasas. It was an easy move because I already knew all the kids from my time down there in the summer. I moved in with my grandparents to help them out."

Ironically enough, Lampasas's future star athlete wasn't on everyone's must-have list when he first arrived there. Perhaps he had been a standout in

THE 1976 Lampasas High School mile relay team: Head Coach Scott Boyd is fourth from the left, Johnny Jones is on the far right

Photo courtesy of the *Lampasas Dispatch Record*

Lawton, but when he came to Texas in the early 1970s, Jones discovered that nothing would be handed to him on a silver platter.

"I remember the first time I moved down there and I started playing summer league softball," Jones says. "I remember that one of the coach's names was Coach Chaney. I played with his son, Bobby. Every small town has a coach that seems to have all the good players on his team, and Chaney was that guy. I showed up with a neighbor of mine who was a year younger than me. He still had some room for development as an athlete, and Coach Chaney seemed to think that I was going to be the same kind of athlete, so he wasn't really patient. He really didn't want to fool with me because I was the new kid in town and probably couldn't play anyway. He eventually put me on one of the other teams, and I ended up being a little better than he realized. I remember that next summer when I came down he was waiting for me at my grandparents' house, whereas before he didn't really have time for me."

After that summer, coaches always managed to find the time for Jones's unique blend of speed, quickness, and raw athleticism.

Over the course of an amazing prep career on the gridiron, Jones scored forty-five touchdowns and became one of the nation's most highly recruited running backs. In addition to his exploits on the football field, Jones became a state champion quarter-miler in track.

However, in February 1976, five months before he would compete in the Olympics, Jones had yet to run the race even once that would ultimately open so many doors for him. At the time, as a high school senior, the prospect of running the 100 meters in Montreal didn't even occur to him.

But, as fate would have it, Lady Luck would introduce herself to Jones in a big way during his senior track season.

"All through my high school career I had been a quarter-miler," Jones explains. "That's what I had run as a freshman, sophomore, and junior. Come my senior year at Lampasas, we didn't have a large track team. I had the record in the 440-yard dash, the 220-yard dash, and in the long jump. So early in my senior year, I started pestering my coach to let me run the 100-yard dash so that I could get the record."

That record at Lampasas was 9.90 seconds back then. Jones wasn't anticipating Olympic glory; he just wanted to get his name etched one more time in the athletics fieldhouse wall that marked the school track champions in each event.

"I kept pestering my coach, Scott Boyd, to let me run the 100-yard dash so I could see if I could break the record. He finally agreed to let me run it, but we had a track meet coming up—the Bluebonnet Relays that Saturday. Just to give me a little bit of a practice run he let me run it on Wednesday before the meet. So we go out there in practice and he marks off 100 yards on the track."

No sooner had Jones run his first 100 yards than his coach asked him to run it again.

"He wouldn't let me see what time I ran," Jones remembers with a laugh. "He just had this big smile on his face and he wouldn't let me look at the clock. I went up there to take a look, but he told me, 'That's okay. It's alright, but I want you to run another one.' He made me sit and wait awhile as he marked off the track again. Looking back on it now, I can see that he just wanted to make sure that he had the distance right. Then I ran the time again and he got this bigger smile on his face, but he still wouldn't let me see the time. He told me that I did okay, but that if I wanted to run the race on Saturday, I was still going to have to run the quarter and the 220. So that Saturday instead of just running my regular quarter-mile and the mile relay, I ended up running the 100, 200, the quarter, the mile relay, and the long jump."

Jones's life was about to take a sudden turn, even if he didn't see it coming.

"In the prelims of the 100-yard dash I ran a 9.25, and apparently that was the time that he wouldn't let me see on Wednesday. The college world record was 9.21. I ended up tying that later on in my freshman year at Texas."

Jones reached new milestones at each successive meet. At the district track meet in Round Rock, he ran a wind-aided 9.05 in the 100, which turned him into an overnight sensation in his home state.

While the rest of the state was wondering what record Jones would break next, his coach was trying to figure out how the team could most effectively use this supersonic weapon of speed. Even with the Olympics just four months away, Coach Boyd was still focused squarely on Texas.

"We came back in that next week from the meet and Coach Boyd—he was a math whiz," Jones observes. "He'd get all the times from around the state and he'd be in his office all the time with papers everywhere. He called me into his office and I thought I was in trouble. He said, 'You know, if I switch you from the quarter, and if you can win the 100 and the 220, and if we can win the mile relay, we can win the state meet from anywhere between two to four points.' At that point right then, I guess he came up with our goal that year. The Lampasas Badgers were going to win the state meet."

JONES crosses the finish line to capture the 1976 Class 3A mile relay title, clinching a team title for Lampasas

Photo courtesy of the *Lampasas Dispatch Record*

So the team set its sights on the state championship. The formula for success was a tricky one, however, with a number of dicey assumptions.

Having Jones pull out wins in the 100- and 220-yard dash was one thing. But winning gold in the mile relay would require not only talent, but a good deal of faith as well.

> **"Every week we'd either be twenty yards or forty yards behind, and every week we always ended up catching them."**

"Every week we'd either be twenty yards or forty yards behind, and every week we always ended up catching them," Jones recalls with evident pride. "Every week we knew exactly where we'd be because we ran the same positions every week. Everyone knew that everyone had to do their best in order for us to win, because if they didn't, I wouldn't be close enough to catch them. As long as they did their best and I did my best, it came out that we always had enough."

That strategy—relying on Jones to catch up and win in the relay's final leg—set the stage for one of the most memorable moments in the history of the Texas state track meet.

As expected, Jones won the gold in both sprints. But would his speed be enough to win the entire championship?

"When we went to the final event there were three teams that still had a chance to win state," Jones says. "Whichever team won the mile relay was going to win state. It came down to the last event and the last race. We were in seventh place because someone had dropped the stick."

Although Jones remembers being behind by "only" forty yards when he took the baton in that final race, the story has taken a life of its own over the years.

Whether he was down forty yards or by an entire lap, as local legend now has it, what happened next is undisputable: in a matter of seconds, Jones exploded back into contention, passing opponents in every lane in the blink of an eye. Before finishing his leg of the relay, he passed every competitor on the track, moving from seventh place to first in a flash.

And with that, Lampasas won the title.

"That's why everyone still talks about the state meet almost as much as they talk about the dang Olympics," Jones declares with a smile. "They think the state meet is the only time that it had happened. They thought it was only one race, but we did that every week."

To this day, Jones views that track championship as one of the most memorable athletic achievements of his career.

"It's special when people talk about our state meet," Jones avers. "When you say a defining moment in your career, when you ask what sticks out in your mind, winning our state meet is probably right up there at the top of all my experiences."

It was a Rocky story that people still talk about years later.

With Jones having wrapped up his high school career, Boyd put together a new plan for his star pupil, this time with much bigger aspirations than anything either had imagined when Jones first ran the 100 on the school's old dirt track.

"Coach Boyd told the school board that he felt I could qualify for the Olympic trials," Jones says. "And that became our goal."

GAMEDAY HAUNTS

Best place to eat BBQ around the stadium—**Willie's Bar-B-Que**—4501 E. MLK, (512) 9340

Best place to eat wings and find something incredibly strange on the menu (try the fried mac and cheese)—**Plucker's**—2222 Rio Grande, (512) 469-WING

Best place to get a cold chocolate shake—**Player's**—300 W Martin Luther King Jr Blvd., (512) 478-9299

Best place to get breakfast tacos before the game—**Juan in a Million**—2300 Cesar Chavez Street, (512) 472-3872

The whole town pitched in to try to get their boy to the big show in Montreal.

> We had to go all over the place and that's when the town of Lampasas raised money with fundraisers, bake sales, car washes, and everything else you could think of. Those efforts paid to send Coach Boyd and I to the Junior AAU meet in Tennessee. They paid and sent us to the Martin Luther King Games in Atlanta. Then they paid for us to go to the Steve Prefontaine Meet in Eugene, Oregon. By running in those meets I qualified for the 100, 200, and the 400. That doesn't mean you make the team, but it means you get to try in those events.

Jones sat down to strategize with Boyd. Although the quarter mile had typically been Jones's strongest race, both thought his best shot at the Olympic team was in the 100 meters and the 400 relay.

"Anything can happen in the 100," Jones maintains. "We both felt like that was my best chance at making the team. The 400 might have been my best event in high school, but those would be grown men running in that event, and they were just so much stronger than I was at the time."

In Eugene, Jones ran fourth in the 100 meters. This wasn't enough to earn him an Olypmic spot in that race, but it did place him on the relay team

At that point, Lady Luck stepped in once again. Jones's teammate Houston McTear, who finished second in the 100 meter trials, suffered a hamstring injury that prevented him from competing in Montreal. That opened up a spot for Jones in the 100 meter race.

"It happened so fast," Jones recalls. "Even in the trials, things were happening so quickly. I had no idea what was going on. I just knew that every time I ran, I needed to run fast."

And that was enough to earn eighteen-year-old Johnny Jones from Lampasas, Texas, a spot in two races on the United States Olympic team.

CANADA-BOUND

Slightly bewildered by his sudden change in fortune, Jones headed to Montreal. He found airtight security at the site of the first Olympics held since the Munich massacre of 1972. An air of uncertainty and angst hovered over the opening ceremonies.

Jones was overwhelmed by the entire experience.

"It's hard to walk people through something that feels like a dream to me," Jones claims. "Hell, I was there and it feels like a dream. For years it was like a blur. It's one of those experiences that is hard to explain because I was really too young to appreciate what was taking place. It was unbelievable for a kid from Lampasas. Up until that summer I had never run in a track meet outside of Texas, and now suddenly here I'm up in Canada? Now I'm traveling to Canada and representing the United States in the Olympics? It just blew me away."

With the relay finals scheduled for the last day of competition, Jones initially focused on the 100 meters. On the first day of qualifying, Jones won his preliminary heat with a time of 10.43. In his next qualifying race, Jones placed second at 10.46.

Jones finished the races like lightning, but he found himself struggling to overcome slow starts. "I had just started running that race a few months ago, so I wasn't as good technically as the guys that I was competing against. It wasn't that I was awful out of the blocks. I was actually pretty good, but the rest of the guys were the best in the world and they had been doing it longer than I had."

Having made the cut to the finals, Jones came eye-to-eye with some of the world's fastest runners. If he was going to compete with the likes of Halsey Crawford, Don Quarrie, and 1972 gold medal winner Valeriy Borzov, not to mention fellow Americans Harvey Glance and Steven Riddick, he'd have to put in the performance of a lifetime.

Wearing a red USA jersey and situated in lane three, Jones had a slow start out of the blocks, putting him in a deep hole twenty meters into the race. He ran faster than anyone over the final fifty meters, but the blazing finish wasn't enough to earn him better than sixth place.

His time of time of 10.27 was the best he had posted during the entire Olympics, but the competition in Montreal was a lot more intense than he was used to.

"It wasn't like I was some guy from Russia that was a great technician," Jones explains. "There were guys that could put everything on paper like it was scientific, but I was just a kid who was blessed with the ability to run and who had good coaches around me."

After the disappointing finish in the 100, Jones turned his attention to the relay.

Jones would run the second leg on the American squad, which also featured Glance, Riddick, and Millard Hampton. There were high hopes for the team. After underperforming for two weeks on the track, U.S. runners looked to the foursome to salvage a decent ending to the games.

Photo courtesy of Cathy Kuehne

JONES GETS CHOKED UP as his grandfather inspects his Olympic gold medal after his return from Montreal

As the climactic race got underway, the Americans appeared vulnerable early, after Glance got off to a slow start. Jones's debut was also imperfect due to an awkward baton exchange with Glance.

But Jones immediately settled in and did what he did best: he ran fast.

"This was a race that I felt very comfortable in," Jones declares. "I had earned the right to be there and I felt confident that I could compete with anyone."

Jones only ran for about ten seconds. But this was his moment, and he lived up to it. By the time he relinquished the baton, he'd gained the lead for the Americans. Hampton and Riddick kept up the blistering pace, giving the U.S. squad a decisive victory and a gold medal.

The native Texas son came home to Lampasas an Olympic champion.

ONE FOR THE RECORD BOOKS

So what did Johnny Jones do next? What life experience could possibly match a gold medal Olympic victory?

He became a Longhorn.

Jones played an unremarkable season of football during his freshman year at UT. After the season finished, he went over to the track team, looking to improve his performance in the 100-meters.

It was only his second year running that race, but expectations were high in light of his status as an Olympic gold medal winner. As the Texas Relays approached, Jones hoped to beat the time he'd posted in Montreal. The locals, however, hoped for more—they wanted to see a world record.

The competition was fierce as Jones approached the starting line on that clear Austin day. The finals featured fellow 1976 Olympian Dwayne Evans of Arizona, as well as Oklahoma's John Garrison, an All-American who had anchored the Sooner sprint relay team in the Texas Relay prelims earlier in the meet.

Crouched into a ball and hovering near the starter's line, Jones's white Longhorn uniform with block burnt orange letters stretched across his muscular frame. He settled into his stance and spread his fingers behind the starting line tape.

The entire crowd of 15,000-plus people was on its feet cheering. Then it quieted as it awaited the starting gun.

Bang!

Jones was known as a slow starter, but on this day he exploded out of the blocks like a bullet from a smoking gun.

The first twenty meters might have doomed him in Montreal, but this time they effectively marked the end of the race for everyone else. Your only chance at winning against Jones was to beat him out of the blocks and hope your lead could withstand his inevitable closing surge. With a start like this, no one else had a chance.

With each competitor several lengths behind him, Jones's legs pumped like a locomotive. Just like he had on that old dirt track in Lampasas, Jones closed his eyes down the homestretch and just ran.

Crossing the finish line, Jones didn't need to see the official time to know that he had done something special. The deafening roar of the crowd told him that.

The final time was 9.85. It was a new world record.

But a funny thing happened as he established a mark that would stand for nearly two decades. The electronic timing device, which was being used for the first time in the history of the Texas Relays, malfunctioned. Three different stopwatches all confirmed that Jones broke the world record, with one even clocking him at 9.80—a full .15 better than the previous record.

It didn't matter. Without the automatic timer, the mark would only register as an unofficial world record. Jones had beat his opponents and beat the record, but he couldn't beat faulty technology.

Yet, as the crowd roared with delight, the smile on Jones's face became as much of a lasting memory in Texas as the race itself.

Ultimately, Jones had never been driven by a desire for personal glory. Instead, he took—and still takes—immense pride in delivering a dream come true for the small Texas town of Lampasas. This was even more important to Jones than holding on to his Olympic gold medal, which he promptly gave to the Texas Special Olympics after returning home from Montreal.

All Jones had ever wanted to do was run, and on this day he had done it better than any person ever had. Jones had provided the Longhorn Nation with a collective memory that has now stood for thirty years.

On that day, a legend was born.

> 66 **Let them have their fun over there tonight. After we finish what we came here to do, this town will belong to us for the next three days.** 99
>
> —UT coach Blair Cherry to the Longhorns, in New Orleans, on New Year's Eve, 1947. The Horns beat Alabama the following day, 27–7.

ON THE GRIDIRON

The rest of the world might have known him as Johnny, but the Longhorn Nation called him something else: Lam Jones.

He was an American original, but in an ironic twist of fate, he was just one of several Johnny Jones's on the Texas football roster, alongside fellow running backs Johnny Jones of Hamlin, Texas and Johnny Jones of Youngstown, Ohio.

With three players sharing the same name and position, nicknames were a necessity.

So Jones of Lampasas became "Lam," Jones of Hamlin became "Ham," and Jones of Ohio became "Jam."

With a new moniker in the game program, Jones set about creating a football legacy to match the legendary status he'd achieved in track.

Of course, considering that he grew up cheering for the Sooners, it may seem unlikely that Jones would end up starring for OU's arch rival. But his journey to Austin was just another improbable twist of fate in a sports career marked by many similar surprises.

"Coming out in recruiting, I was leaning a little more toward the University of Oklahoma simply because back in those days they had the Wishbone," Jones relates. "At Lampasas High we ran the Wishbone, and they also ran the Wishbone at Texas, but Oklahoma had some Wishbone halfbacks that were just a little more flashier than the Texas running backs. Texas had Roosevelt Leaks and Earl Campbell. That's two of the best right there. If you were a Wishbone halfback, you'd lean a little more toward the Joe Washington and Greg Pruitt-type of running back. That's the type of back I was. I was considered more of the fast, quick, and shifty type of back. Those were the type of backs that had been going to the University of Oklahoma, so I was leaning heavily toward Oklahoma."

The Sooners might have had the offense that Jones coveted, but the in-state Longhorns had something that Switzer and Co. couldn't match.

Texas was family.

Jones recalls,

While Coach Royal and Coach [Ken] Dabbs were over visiting me at our house, we found out that there was a closer bond than we even realized. Coach Dabbs grew up in a little town called Freer, Texas, and his family owned a restaurant down there. Their cook's name was Lonnie MacPhall. Coach Dabbs didn't know my grandmother's maiden name was also MacPhall when he first started talking to her over at the house.

After finding out my grandmother's maiden name, he asked her if she knew a Lonnie MacPhall, and when he asked her that, she said, "Ken, is that you?"

I guess her brother had been talking about this Ken Dabbs for all these years. It turned out that my grandmother's older brother was the cook in Coach Dabbs' family's café. When Coach Dabbs was growing up, my grandmother's brother taught him how to drive. Once they found out that that connection was there, had I gone anywhere else they would have hung me. That's how I ended up at Texas.

> **" It also doesn't hurt when Coach Royal comes to your house and has dinner with your grandparents. "**

Jones also remarks that Royal's celebrity status in Lampasas didn't exactly damage Texas's chances of landing him: "It also doesn't hurt when Coach Royal comes to your house and has dinner with your grandparents. Your grandmother and grandfather are like rock stars in Lampasas to have Coach Royal sit in your home and have some of your homemade bread or homemade jelly. Not a lot of grandmothers could say that, and my grandmother was on top of the world for a long time after that."

Despite Jones's considerable star power, his career with the Longhorns didn't take off until Royal was replaced by Fred Akers following Jones's freshman season.

After years playing running back, Jones's new coach suggested a position change that would alter his career path forever. Many top athletes might have had some doubts about such a dramatic move.

Not Jones.

"We had some pretty good running backs," he says. "When Earl Campbell is playing at your position, it might be a good idea to find a better way to help the team. Why even question it? If the coach says, 'Go here,' you go there. That's just the way sports were in those days. You did what was good for the team, and the coach makes all the decisions. We trusted our coaches more than kids do today."

Or, to put it bluntly, "I was able to do a lot of great things by just keeping my ass out of the way and keeping my mouth shut."

Over the next few seasons, Jones proved to be one of the deadliest weapons in college football, earning All-America honors in 1978 and 1979.

In the process, he rewrote the Longhorn record book, setting new marks in career receptions (eighty-five), receiving yards (1,603), receiving yards in a game (198), touchdown receptions in a single season (seven), career touchdown receptions (fourteen), kickoff return average in a season (32.3), and longest kickoff return (100 yards).

He was a poster child for the speed that offenses were looking to showcase as the passing game evolved to further involve versatile players who could change the game on a dime.

Today, Jones recalls his Longhorn days with some nostalgia:

> Heck, if you look at what happened at Texas, what in the world could I complain about? I got to play under Coach Royal and Coach Akers. I got to play with Earl Campbell, Steve McMichael, Brad Shearer, Alfred Jackson, Raymond Clayborn, and all those guys. I got to play with so many teammates and I made so many friends. I got to play in Cotton Bowls and I was able to get my ass kicked by Joe Montana and crew. We kicked Maryland's butt. I got to run in some Texas Relays. I ended up being the No. 2 pick in the draft. What kind of knucklehead would I be if I sat here and complained about the way things turned out?

By the time his career on the Forty Acres had finished, Jones had emerged as one of the nation's top pro prospects. When the NFL held its draft in April 1980, the Jets traded two first round picks—numbers 13 and 20—to the

49ers in an effort to move up and select Jones with the No. 2 overall draft choice. At the time of his selection, only two Longhorns—Tommy Nobis in 1966 and Earl Campbell in 1978—had been selected higher.

THE FALL AND RISE OF LAM JONES

If Jones's college career had been the stuff of fairy tales, he quickly got to know the tough reality of the NFL.

In New York, Jones aimed to develop into a Hall of Fame player; anything less would be a disappointment. But a succession of injuries, along with a debilitating drug problem, kept him from rising to the level of the elite players. His performance over five seasons—138 receptions for 2,322 yards and thirteen touchdowns—was just a fraction of what the Jets expected from their million dollar recruit.

After the 1984 season, Jones was traded to San Francisco. But injuries kept him from ever suiting up for another NFL game.

"I never reached my full potential in the NFL and that is the one thing that is a hard pill for me to swallow," Jones states sullenly. "I know I was at the point where I was really catching on and starting to become a good receiver. And then there were some things in my personal life, like my drug problems, that I needed to get in order and that didn't allow me to reach my full potential."

Still, though colored with regret, the boy from Lampasas looks back with humble gratitude on his pro days. "Looking at the overall picture, I have so much to be thankful for.

Photo courtesy of the *Lampasas Dispatch Record*

JONES was the No. 1 overall pick by the New York Jets in the 1980 NFL Draft

Even though I might not have reached my full potential in football at that level, I still have so much to be grateful for because of the experiences that I've had."

If Jones's life had been a movie, it would probably have ended here, with his retirement. Little did he know that his life script was in store for another, shocking scene. This time, it had nothing to do with his amazing athletic exploits.

It began on a spring day in 2005. Jones's expression takes on a tinge of distress as he relates the story:

> It was completely out of nowhere. My good friend Ham Jones and I were going fishing right down on the Colorado River by the airport. We were going down a trail by the water and there was a tree that had fallen across the trail. It was about three or four feet up off the ground and I stepped up on it, and then I slipped and came down on my heels. My legs were locked and it jammed my back because it couldn't absorb any of the shock. It hurt me so bad.
>
> I had to lay there for about thirty minutes because I could hardly breathe. We thought we were going to have to call an ambulance. We barely got out of there because it was a big, steep hill that we had to climb. I went to the doctor and they told me that I had a compression fracture in two places.

For the next five months, Jones waited to see if rest would cure his compound back fracture. During this time, the pain intensified to the point that it nearly paralyzed him:

> I ended up being on a cane for four or five months, but my condition kept getting worse. About three weeks after I hurt my back, my chest starting hurting real bad. It felt like an iron ball was burning right in my chest under the bone. It was about the size of a pool ball and it felt like it was on fire. I had to go to the emergency room on two different occasions, but they couldn't find out what was wrong

with me. This was getting worse and worse all the time. I was having trouble getting in and out of bed. I could barely lay down and I could barely get up. It just kept getting worse.

After about five months, it finally got so bad that [former Texas teammate] Donnie Little set it up so I could go see the team doctor. I explained to the doctor how I had hurt my back with the compression fracture and she said, "Johnny, something is going on with your bones. You shouldn't have gotten a compression fracture from that short of a fall. I want you to take these two tests."

As it turned out, the fracture was the least of his worries. Two days later, the tests confirmed his worst fears.

"I came back that day and by then I was barely getting around," Jones continues. "I was in pretty bad shape. I had started to lose my height. You could really tell I was hurting bad. When I came back from taking those two tests, the doctor said, 'I'm about 95 percent sure that you've got multiple-myeloma.'

"What the hell is that?" Jones asked.

"Bone cancer," she replied.

Immediately upon receiving his diagnosis, Jones checked into the hospital. He was in so much pain by then he couldn't have walked out of the building if he tried. Jones was left wondering whether he'd ever see anything again outside the four walls of his new home. He recalls,

I'd walked around for five or six months without knowing I had it. The reason I had the compression fracture was that the cancer had already weakened my bones. It had already started before I fell, but I had walked around for five months before anyone linked it to cancer. By then it had already hit me.

It was so bad that I almost didn't come out of the ICU. When I first went into intensive care, they didn't think I was going to make it, with all of the complications I was having. Things were starting to shut down, but they were able to stop it. My kidneys started to fail and everything was just going haywire. They finally got everything back on track and they turned it around.

At that time it was touch and go. Something would come up and then they would take care of it. I can't even sit here and tell you everything that went wrong. It was the kidneys one day and it would be something else at another time.

I almost died.

Almost.

Just when things seemed at their worst, Jones miraculously recovered. The cancer went into remission and remains so today.

"The type of cancer that I have, a little more than 50 percent of the people live a little longer than two-and-a-half years and 50 percent live a little less," Jones states bluntly. "For mine to be in remission right now, something had to happen that was really good."

JONES gets a round of applause during his induction ceremony into the Texas High School Hall of Fame

Photo courtesy of Cathy Kuehne

Even during his darkest days, Jones fought off feelings of hopelessness. "I have been so blessed throughout my life. I've always had so many loved ones and friends that loved me, and even in this situation there was so many people that cared about me that I never carried that feeling of despair. I never once sat up and worried about dying. I never thought about it. I never thought for a day that I wouldn't make it."

Although his life was no longer in imminent danger, the road to recovery was arduous:

> When I first got out of the hospital, I could barely walk. I was in a wheelchair when I got out, but I made myself walk into my house. I could barely walk and everyone was telling me that I had to move out of my house because I couldn't be going up and down the stairs. I remember that just to shower, I'd have to sit and rest for thirty minutes after I was done. That's how far I've come in the last two years. To be able to get showered and dressed on my own is like a feeling of accomplishment. After running in the Olympics, I've got to go back and feel good about just being able to get out of the shower.

With a second lease on life, Jones is determined not to take his days for granted. He's taken up new hobbies, such as photography, and he has learned how to derive satisfaction from the small things in life. "The little things should always mean something," Jones concludes. "When you really get so close to death like that, you appreciate everything so much more. The things that we do in life that really matter don't have to be the big, glamorous things, They don't have to be the Texas Relays. They don't have to be the state meet. They don't have to be the Olympics. I could go out here and put together one of my tower photos, and when I see that put a smile on someone's face, that gives me as much joy as catching a big touchdown, winning a big race, or anything else."

Whether he's cultivating his love of photography, enjoying Sunday dinner with his loved ones, or simply walking to and from his car without a cane, Lam now has another moniker to attach to his life story.

He's now Johnny Lam Jones—cancer survivor.

Chapter Five

JAMES BROWN AND THE 1996 BIG 12 CHAMPIONSHIP

IT AIN'T BRAGGIN' IF YOU DO IT

Twelve of the most memorable words ever spoken by a Longhorn player came from a very unlikely source.

Although James Brown is remembered as one of the most exciting players to appear on the Texas gridiron, he wasn't known as a "go-to" guy when the media needed a sound bite.

No, as the 1996 Longhorns prepared for the first-ever Big 12 Championship game against the defending national champion Cornhuskers, seniors Dan Neil, Tyson King, and Mike Adams were the favorites of reporters looking for a good fifteen-second quip. King was a good source for spicy quotes about upcoming opponents, while Adams provided some local color to each media session. Neil combined attributes of both these players, offering insightful comments without infuriating the other team, but adding in some of that good ol' boy charm that made for an entertaining interview.

Brown was different. As flamboyant as the star quarterback may have seemed to Texas fans throughout a career in which he rewrote numerous school passing records, he was every bit as quiet and low-key off the field as he was the center of the Longhorn universe on it.

So when he finally uttered the words that would ultimately define his football career, they seemed strangely out of character for the soft-spoken kid from the Golden Triangle.

As it turned out, Brown had already been thinking about Nebraska during Texas's previous game, a 51–15 pasting by the Longhorns of in-state rival Texas A&M. That victory clinched the Big 12 South title for UT.

"I was just looking back at some of that old film and I remember seeing a clip where I was on the sideline at the game and I was saying, 'Bring it on Nebraska. Come on, Nebraska,'" Brown says today. "I guess we were just focused."

As 21-point underdogs to the Big 12 North champion Huskers, Texas players found themselves in an unfamiliar role. One of the nation's top pro-

Photo courtesy of Dave Campbell's 40 Years of Texas Football

BROWN FIRST EARNED his reputation as a leader and big-game performer in 1994, when he led the Longhorns to a 17-10 victory in his first career start against Oklahoma

grams, the Longhorns had never been anyone's patsy. Even in their worst years, opponents knew that the guys under the horn-emblazoned helmets would always put up a good fight.

Yet coming into this game the unranked Longhorns were almost an afterthought to the national media—and not without reason.

These Huskers were ranked among the top five nationally in six of the top eight offensive and defensive statistical categories: third in scoring offense (44.1 points per game), fifth in rushing offense (296.4 yards per game), third in scoring defense (10.5 points per game), fourth in rushing defense (77.8 yards), fourth in total defense (232.9 yards per game) and fifth in passing efficiency (84.8 rating).

In fact, after winning back-to-back national championships in 1994 and 1995, the Huskers weren't just the Big 12's best heading into the conference's first season—they were the NCAA's reigning dynasty. The team didn't just beat people so much as they pounded them into submission.

The 1996 Longhorns were a different story. After losing four of their first seven games to the likes of No. 9 Notre Dame, No. 19 Virginia, unranked Oklahoma, and No. 8 Colorado, this Longhorn team deserved its underdog status, having bounced between "good" and "mediocre" for most of the season.

Nevertheless, neither Brown nor his teammates regarded the showdown with Nebraska as a lost cause.

"They're not unbeatable," Adams remarked after the big win over A&M. "They're a great team, they have a great head coach, a legacy and all that stuff, but they are human just like us."

Reporters, however, apparently disagreed. At the Longhorn media luncheon on the Monday before the game, nearly every Texas player was asked to comment on the team's underdog status. The media seemed to feel that the squad should not even bother showing up to take on the Husker juggernaut.

For Brown, a full hour of this line of questioning was tiring. When a Dallas reporter harped on the same theme, the quarterback decided to speak his mind. As he remembers:

[*Dallas Morning News* reporter] Chip Brown asked the question. It was at the end of the day. I was just tired of the same questions. Everyone kept asking how we felt about being 21-point underdogs and how it felt knowing that we were going into a game that we could potentially lose. That's not the type of team we had that year. We had a good team and we had a lot of good players. We had a lot of confidence. A lot of those guys are in the NFL. There was just a lot of confidence.

So Brown told the reporter what he really thought, with little inkling of the notoriety his simple remark would quickly achieve.

He said, "I don't know...I think we're going to win by three touchdowns."

Brown didn't regard his comment as big news, but his bravado immediately captured attention in Nebraska. In the Tuesday edition of the *Lincoln Journal-Star*, a five-column headline read: "Texas QB: We'll win big." The next day, Nebraska All-American defensive end Grant Wistrom appeared at the Huskers' own media event wearing a leather jacket and a big smile.

"Any time anybody says anything that is kind of a direct challenge, of course it motivates you a little bit," Wistrom said. "You probably think about that stuff until kickoff. After that, you just think about the game. Hopefully, I'll have a chance to sack him. If I don't, they might be beating us by three touchdowns. Who knows?"

Wistrom's fellow defender, Mike Minter, also seemed indifferent to Brown's statement. When asked to comment on Brown's prediction, Minter merely replied, "I guess he's very confident."

If Nebraska players weren't taking the media's bait, the same could not be said for Husker fans. Brown recalls,

I remember on either Tuesday or Wednesday, I got some flowers from Nebraska fans. They sent me some lilies. Aaron Babino was my roommate. Derrick Lewis was there. I didn't know that a lily was a funeral flower. I just gave it water and put it in the window. I wanted to thank those Nebraska people. I didn't know. It wasn't until a year later that I found out that was a funeral flower. Their attempt to rattle me didn't work because I was ignorant.

While the ire of Nebraska fans may have been lost on Brown, the anger of his head coach came through loud and clear. The volatile John Mackovic had kept the team on an emotional roller coaster all season. And the disconnect between him and his players seemed to grow in the lead-up to the Nebraska game. The players felt loose, riding a four-game win streak during which they averaged nearly forty points per game. But Mackovic was in a constant state of tension, and this grew into fury when he heard about Brown's comments. He ordered Brown to explain his actions to the entire team. Brown remembers,

> Mackovic was on a little tear. He was chewing people out and threatening to throw people off the team. He was getting after people for every little thing. Mike Adams had gotten in trouble. It was just every little thing and he would blow it up. We were just there to play football, that's what we were thinking.
>
> Every Monday before our first practice we would have a team meeting to go over our agenda for the week, and then we'd go out and have a little walk-thru. He mentioned what I said in the meeting, and I was like, "Yeah, I said it and that's how I feel." It wasn't a big deal. Everyone was like, "Yeah, yeah, yeah." Most of the players looked around at me and what not. That's about all it was and coming out onto the field I didn't think too much of it. I figured everyone would be like, "Well that's just J.B."
>
> But I remember Dan Neil specifically coming over and saying, "I'm glad you said that. That's the way I feel, too." Then Chris Carter came and told me the same thing. Even Priest [Holmes] said something to me. He just looked me in the eyes and was like, "Yeah, I feel you."

Texas players today claim the Nebraska game may have been won in that very meeting when Brown not only owned up to his comments, but ensured his teammates knew that he believed every word of it. It turned out to be a unifying moment for the players, who rallied around Brown's defiance.

"James said exactly what a lot of us had been thinking, but we just didn't say it," Neil says after ten years of reflection. "When Mackovic made him stand up in front of us and explain what he had said, we were all like, 'Alright! Let's go out and play.' That motivated all of us and we believed what he was saying just like he did. We *needed* him to say that."

Mackovic, however, was clearly unmoved. In a post-practice talk with reporters on Tuesday, he quickly grew impatient with all the questions about Brown's comments, which by then had made national news.

"I'm not going to talk about it. I won't answer any questions about it," Mackovic told the assembled reporters. After an uncomfortable short moment of silence, a local cameraman from KEYE-TV told Mackovic that he appreciated Brown's comments because he felt it showed confidence.

Flabbergasted, Mackovic stared down the questioner. If looks could kill, then Mackovic was swinging a samurai sword with every glance at the sports writers. Finally he exclaimed, "Didn't I just say I'm not going to talk about it?"

Reporters continued to implore Mackovic to comment on Brown's remarks, but the coach refused each entreaty. "People try to make too much out of it," he said dismissively.

The UT Sports Information Department put Brown off limits to the media. Meanwhile, his teammates not only continued to support him, but they themselves also began predicting a big win against the Cornhuskers.

The team had suddenly developed an edge that had been missing during the entire Mackovic era. Truth be told, the players were beginning to sound downright cocky, especially in light of the weakness of the Longhorn program for more than a decade.

Much of the pressure fell squarely on Brown's shoulders—and the quarterback thrived on it. Two decades after the fateful events of 1996, Brown explains that he has always performed best when he is riled up:

I love competition, man. Even today, [former Longhorn running back] Shon Mitchell and I play on the same flag football team and we've won two championships in a row. We're out there high-fiving. I just love competition. I can't play the game unless I'm really upset, unless I have a grudge or a reason to go out and play my hardest.

There was a time when we played SMU in Dallas and Coach Mackovic took us all out of the game because we knew we were going to beat SMU and we really weren't serious. But, it was different in big games. When we played Notre Dame that year I was very focused, even though we didn't win. The big games are the ones that I loved to play. Yeah, maybe I [needed it]. It gave me motivation. I need fuel.

I played better when I was on edge and when I was upset.

The Longhorn players may have been itching for battle, but the same could not be said of the fans. A poll conducted the night before the game showed that 82 percent of the Longhorn Nation believed the Huskers would win.

In fact, the 'Horns could not sell their full allotment of game tickets; they returned several thousand, which were then sold to the general public or to Nebraska fans. UT's challenge was now compounded by the fact that the Huskers would have an effective home-field advantage in St. Louis. One bowl official remarked, "I guess Texas still helps with TV ratings, but if they don't travel that's a big strike against them. Are they afraid of who they are playing—or just scared to travel?"

> **I can't play the game unless I'm really upset, unless I have a grudge or a reason to go out and play my hardest.**

By the end of the week, the Huskers had had enough Texan braggadocio. There was already some tension between the two programs stemming from UT demands for stronger academic requirements in the old Big Eight Conference. Now, after several days dominated by news of the Longhorns' predictions of victory, Nebraska unloaded a few verbal salvoes their own.

Only days after praising Brown and the entire Texas team, Grant Wistrom changed his tune. "Texas is trying to crimp our style," he alleged. "They need a little reminder of the pecking order."

On Friday, Nebraska linebacker Mike Minter declared his feelings on the rivalry: "There's more than just what goes on on the field at stake. [There are] philosophical differences. We have our territory to protect."

Even the Nebraska coaching staff joined the fray. "Speaking only for me, I'm sorry for ever getting into the Big 12," lamented Nebraska defensive coordinator Charlie McBride. "The Texas stuff is troubling, the undue influence. We lost in the boardroom; we'll see how it goes on the field."

With tension growing, Brown largely dropped out of public view. As he recalls,

> I was just really focused in the final days before the game. I wasn't in school much that week and I just remember being really focused for the game. I had no idea how big the game was, really. I just knew it was the biggest game we had played up until that point. I think that had been one of the biggest games Texas had played in the last few years. I just knew that I was going to be ready.

ROLL LEFT WAS THE CALL

A chorus of jeers greeted the Longhorns as they took the field at the Trans World Dome an hour before game time on December 7, 1996. Although a small sliver of Texas fans was on hand, it was Husker red that dominated the stands. And the Nebraska faithful didn't show up just to see a coronation. After a week of jawboning, they were there to see blood.

But it was the Longhorns who drew first blood that afternoon, as they took the opening kickoff and marched eighty yards on eleven plays, scoring on a 5-yard run by Holmes to take a 7–0 lead.

The opening gambit sent a message to the 63,109 in attendance that Texas was not going to roll over for the two-time defending champions.

BROWN'S ABILITY TO ESCAPE the pressure of the swarming Nebraska defense was one of the biggest reasons for Texas's offensive explosion in the Big 12 title showdown against the Huskers

Photo courtesy of the University of Texas

"I think we set the tone with that possession," Neil remarked after the game. "There were no big plays, just a methodical drive. It put some doubt in their minds."

The Huskers responded with a touchdown of their own late in the first quarter when DeAngelo Evans capped off Nebraska's own 12-play, 80-yard drive with a 2-yard scoring run that tied the game.

After the two teams traded field goals, the Longhorns landed the next big blow when the oft-injured Holmes exploded through the Nebraska defense for a 61-yard touchdown run that gave the Longhorns a 17–10 lead.

Holmes's run triggered a series of big plays for the Longhorns that lasted through the rest of the game. For every punch that the Huskers landed, the Longhorns seemed to answer with a counter-punch. Brown remembers how the Longhorns raised their game for the big-time match-up:

> Just looking back at the game, that's just the type of mindset that we had. I remember Grant Wistrom was chasing me and I jumped, ducked, and stopped. Usually in that situation I might have run out or bounds or thrown the ball away, but not in this game. I put my foot into the ground and got up the field and gained about eight yards. That was something I hadn't done for a while. The shit talking focused me, really and truly.

Both teams successfully moved the ball across the field in the first half, with the squads scoring on seven possessions combined. Having scored first, the Longhorns benefited from this pattern, as the Huskers stayed close but could never wrestle away the lead. Going into halftime, the Longhorns were on top, 20–17.

In the locker room, the players recalled the pep talk that Mackovic had given before the game. As he later told reporters, "I told the players that they were playing for more than themselves. I told them that they were playing for the spirit that lives in all of us."

The Longhorns may have been playing for spirit, but there was also a Big 12 championship at stake for both teams and a potential slot in the national title game on the line for Huskers.

Both squads came out ready for battle in the second half, but neither managed to score in the third quarter. In the fourth, Phil Dawson connected on a 47-yard field goal to put Texas up, 23–17, with 8:30 remaining in the third quarter.

After that, however, the Huskers began to rally. A combination of two drives totaling twenty-eight plays, 123 yards, and nearly twelve minutes of clock time gave the Huskers their first lead of the game, as Evans returned to the end zone with 2:11 remaining in the third quarter. Husker kicker Kris Brown connected on a 24-yard field goal with 10:11 left in the final quarter to extend Nebraska's lead to 27–23.

With the game beginning to slip away from the Longhorns, Brown and his teammates dug in their heels. It was at this moment that Brown would cement his legacy in Longhorn lore. As he remembers, despite the score being close the entire game, he'd been confident of victory almost from the beginning:

> I feel like I knew we were going to win the game early on. There was a play earlier in the game that occurred and I just knew it was our day. I was in my own end zone and on a third down play, [senior tight end] Pat Fitzgerald made a one-handed catch over people and kept his feet in to get the first down. I think that play showed the type of mindset that we were in.
>
> Our backs were to the end zone at the time and we were down in the area where we had scored our last touchdown. We were going that way and we were backed up to our own end zone. I had to make a move because it was almost a safety, and I threw a pass that a lot of people probably thought I shouldn't have thrown. It was over one guy's head, but I saw him stumbling and I knew that he couldn't jump. I threw it and Pat caught a good pass. That's when I knew.

DID YOU KNOW?

The university's scoreboard, dubbed "Godzillatron," was the largest high-definition screen in the world at its creation. It is still the largest high-definition screen in college sports, sizing up 84 percent larger than the video screen at the University of Nebraska.

Brown's field goal had given the Huskers a little breathing room, but it didn't last long. Just three plays later, Brown hooked up with sophomore wide receiver Wane McGarity on a 66-yard touchdown pass that put the Longhorns back on top, 30–27.

The Huskers had dominated the Longhorns for most of the quarter, but with one flip of the wrist, Brown recaptured the momentum for Texas.

After the Huskers failed to respond with points of their own, the Longhorn offense got the ball back on their own 7 with just over four minutes remaining in the game. The 'Horns moved the ball around twenty yards, but the drive stalled on the 29. Texas faced a fourth and one situation with just over two minutes.

If the Longhorns punted, they'd give the ball back to a Nebraska offense that had worn down the Texas defense in the second half. Mackovic, having more confidence in his offense than he did in his defense, decided to roll the dice and go for it.

"Roll Left" was the play the coach called in from the sideline. Brown recalls the moment clearly:

I remember that play well. We thought Mackovic went for it because he wasn't confident about the defense. He thought that at any time Nebraska was just going to bust us with a big run or just wear us down with that option. Our defense played well. They had some runs and they had some plays, but we stopped their option with guys who weren't NFL caliber linebackers, but who played the option well. Tyson King and Jonathan Hickerson had big games.

That play really is a simple play. I remember in the Notre Dame game, it was like the last play of the game and it was around fourth and five. We ran a play that we had never run before. It was a play that [Mackovic] had thrown in, maybe on a Wednesday. We went over it a couple of times. It was a play where Mike Adams would drag across. Mike Adams never really drove across on drag routes. He was always a deep threat that did comebacks and outs. That play confused us and we didn't have confidence in it. But Roll Left and Roll Right, we had been running that since I got here in 1993. That was a play that we all had confidence in.

Nebraska were thinking that if they stopped us, they win. If we make it, they lose. We had three running backs in the backfield. Pat Fitzgerald was back there with Ricky [Williams] and Priest [Holmes]. With those guys in the backfield and coming downhill, they had to respect the run. I just knew that. Priest had had a big game and I just wanted to sell my fake. With three people coming downhill they almost had to react. I remember my goal was to just give a good fake and when I'm at the top of my fake, back there where the tailback is, I have to get my head around to see what was coming because this was our last chance. I felt like a superstar in that game. I felt like I had to make plays. I was focused.

As Brown approached the line of scrimmage, the Huskers defense crowded the line in anticipation of a run play. As soon as the ball was snapped, Brown faked the handoff to Holmes, who had already gashed the Nebraska defense for more than 100 yards and two scores on the day. Holmes then faked one of his trademark moves—a high leap over the line that he often employed in short-yardage situations. The Huskers defense fell for the sleight—hook, line, and sinker.

"They call it an Oscar-winning role," Holmes later said. "I try to put my head down and make it so they can't see the ball. They have to think I have it."

At that moment, Brown rolled to his left and found himself matched up one-on-one with Nebraska linebacker Mike Minter, who was closing in on the quarterback like a missile. With the option to run or pass on the play, Brown's decision had to be quick.

In all likelihood, Brown only needed a yard to put the game away. But the 'Horns had not come to St. Louis to play a conservative game. In the confrontational spirit that Texas had displayed all week, Brown decided to go for the jugular.

"I had a crease to throw the ball, but I could have run the ball for a first down just as easily," Brown said in the aftermath.

Minter would recollect the play differently. "It was just me and him," he said. "He wasn't going to make the first down."

Just as it appeared that Minter might stop Brown short of the first down, the Longhorn quarterback pulled up and shocked Nebraska with a long throw to a wide-open Derrick Lewis.

With the Nebraska defense looking for a running play, the Longhorn tight end had slipped into the secondary. As Lewis pulled in the catch and rumbled down the field, the entire Husker defense gave chase, eventually dragging him down at the Nebraska 11-yard line.

The Longhorn sideline erupted in delirious pandemonium at the 61-yard bomb.

"Roll Left" had instantly become the play that would forever define the Longhorn careers of both Brown and Mackovic.

Still, the game was not yet over. According to Brown,

> **All right, we've got them right where we want them. They have run out of room. They can't throw a long pass. They've got to come right at us.**
>
> —UT Linebacker Johnny Treadwell, during a 1962 game against the Razorbacks, as Arkansas lined up on the Texas 3-yard line. Treadwell and Culpepper caused a fumble by Arkansas fullback Danny Brabham on the play. Texas recovered, drove eighty-five yards, and won 7–3.

I was focused. I was on my back down the field and was ready to run the next play. I was ready to huddle up the team, so everyone was running around and jumping, and I made this little gesture with my hands [to bring the players together]. But, I was already looking to Coach Mackovic for the next play we were going to run. I had to get us ready for the next play.

On the next play, Holmes capped off the drive with his third touchdown of the game—this one from eleven yards out—to give the Longhorns a 37-27 lead with only 1:53 remaining.

Nebraska was unable to recover from the shock of Texas's comeback. Any dreams of a miracle finish were dashed when the Huskers fumbled in the final minute of the game. Texas defensive lineman Cedric Woodard came up with the ball, sealing the most unlikely of victories for the Longhorns.

Nebraska might have reigned over the old Big Eight, but Texas established itself as the first king of the Big 12. At St. Louis, the 'Horns scored four touchdowns on a Nebraska defense whose starters had only surrendered five all season. Texas totaled 503 yards of offense, including 150 on the ground.

"That's why they make pencils with erasers," Mackovic quipped after the game.

For all the big plays that the Longhorns had made, after the game the only topic of discussion in either locker room was Texas's decision to go for it on fourth and one.

"When they snapped, I was amazed," admitted Huskers head Coach Tom Osborne. "When I saw the quarterback run, I was more amazed. When I saw him throw, I was really amazed."

Wistrom, so vocal in his disdain for the Longhorns earlier in the week, grudgingly gave credit where it was due. "If it doesn't work it's a really dumb call," he stated. "But Coach Mackovic is a genius."

SOUL OF THE GODFATHER

If Mackovic was a genius for calling the play, Brown was the wizard that pulled it off. The junior quarterback was sensational all afternoon, completing nineteen of twenty-eight passes for 353 yards and a touchdown. While he threw a pair of interceptions in the game, any miscues were quickly forgotten in light of the game's climactic finish.

"It was mainly James Brown," Wistrom replied when asked about the success of the Texas offense. "I thought he played very well today. A couple of times we thought we had him sacked for sure, but he just got out of it."

THE MYSTERIOUS ORIGINS OF "BEVO"

The football team was first called the Longhorns in 1904, but the first actual Longhorn mascot didn't appear before the student body until 1916, when 124 alums donated $1 each to purchase "the grandfather of all Texas steer" in the Texas Panhandle.

BEVO MADE HIS FIRST appearance on Thanksgiving Day against Texas A&M, 1916 (photo courtesy of Silver Spurs Alumni Association)

At half-time of a 7–7 game against Texas A&M on Thanksgiving Day, two West Texas cowboys dragged a "half-starved" steer onto the field, where it was formally presented to the Texas students by a group of Texas Exes. The Longhorns went on to score two touchdowns in the second half to beat the Aggies 22–7, which avenged a loss from the previous season.

The origin of the mascot's name, Bevo, is shrouded in mystery. It's clear, however, that the name was set by December 1916, when Texas Exes *Alcalde* magazine editor Ben Dyer stated of the school's new longhorn, "His name is Bevo. Long may he reign!"

The most popular theory of the name's origin centers on an old soft drink from the era, "Bevo," which was produced by the Anheuser-Busch brewery in St. Louis.

Texas alum Dan Zabcik has offered another theory on the origin of the Bevo name. Accoring to Zabcik, in the early part of the century, newspapers nationwide ran a cartoon by Gus Mager that usually featured monkeys as the main characters. In these cartoons, all the monkeys were named after their personality traits. The comic strip sparked a national fad, as people began nicknaming their friends by attaching the letter "O" to their names. The word "beeve" is a slang term used for steers that are destined to end up on someone's dinner plate. Thus, "Bevo."

Contrary to conventional wisdom among Aggies, the name Bevo has nothing to do with an event that occurred two years later, in 1917, when a group of Aggies broke into the South Austin stockyard where the steer was kept and branded "13–0" into its side, which was the score of the 1915 game won by A&M. According to legend, UT fans altered the brand to read "Bevo," and that's where the name came from.

A week after the Aggies' stunt, amid rumors that the Aggies planned to kidnap the animal, Bevo was moved to a ranch sixty miles west of the city. In 1919 the school decided to turn the animal into the main course of the 1920 football banquet. The Aggies that were actually invited to the event were served the side that had been branded, which still read "13–0."

In the victorious Texas locker room, while the entire squad wildly celebrated, Brown remembers that he sat alone:

> I don't think I really allowed myself to get out of the zone I was in until when we got back on the bus. When I came to the locker room, I just sat in front of my locker and I looked up and everyone was celebrating. I looked up and there was Derrick Lewis throwing water and everyone was celebrating. I was at my locker and still focused. I was really focused for that game. I wouldn't let myself or my teammates down, I guess in hindsight, because of the words that I said. I just remember how I felt at that exact moment. I was just so focused. I thought to myself, "We won, already. Get back to normal." That was something I had never felt before in my life, really and truly.

If the emotions were more intense than Brown had ever felt, the same could be said for the national attention that fell on him after the win in St. Louis. With hindsight, we see that Brown's legendary performance was hardly diminished by the Longhorns' 38–15 loss to Penn State in the Fiesta Bowl to end the season. Brown's defiant prediction of victory, followed up by the game of his life and the play of 100 lifetimes, had cemented his legacy. Reflecting on the game, Brown understands that it will long be remembered among the Longhorn Nation:

> Today I can look back and see that it was a big moment. I think it gave the fans more satisfaction than it actually gave me. At the time I was the most satisfied. I was ecstatic and I was feeling things that I had never felt before.
>
> It was a moment in UT history that a lot of people remember me for. I'm thankful that I was able to even be a part of that kind of history. It blows my mind. I never really knew what the Eyes of Texas were until I finished playing. The Eyes of Texas saw that play, they loved it and they all remember it.

While Brown went on to play professional football and win a championship while quarterbacking overseas, the NFL career that many expected for him never materialized. He's now back in Austin, living a quiet life as a property appraiser.

But his big moment in St. Louis still defines the way he approaches his life. As Brown explains,

That moment kind of keeps me on my toes. I have to stay a positive figure for the public because I do feel like I have a responsibility to keep myself out of trouble. I don't think young kids today care about what you've done in the past. They care about what you're doing now and that's my thing. I want these young kids to respect me. If I go somewhere and I'm around athletes, I want to be recognized as being just as good of an athlete as y'all. I'm a little older now, but I recognize what I've done in the past.

I'm a real estate appraiser and I go into a lot of people's homes. I'll give someone my business card and they'll get excited and ask if I'm *the* James Brown. I've been in people's houses and seen posters of me hanging up.

I don't mind it at all. I consider it a blessing to tell you the truth.

With his playing career behind him, Brown looks back at the events from that week in 1996 with a sense of satisfaction and accomplishment. If only for one moment in time, he was the emotional leader of a team that emerged as a champion.

On a squad that included future NFL stars like Ricky Williams, Priest Holmes, Bryant Westbrook, Dan Neil, and Casey Hampton, it was Brown that gave them their identity.

It was Brown that turned them into believers.

It was Brown that led them to greatness.

He was a fearless leader on the gridiron, but stepped out of the role when he was off the field. It wasn't until Brown emerged from his shell and publicly

Photo courtesy of the University of Texas

BROWN WILL FOREVER be remembered as the quarterback that led the Longhorns to the last Southwest Conference title and the first Big 12 championship challenged the notion of the Longhorns' inferiority that he suddenly came to embody the heart and soul of the program

Today, Brown looks back on those twelve words as something that expressed the feelings of the entire team:

> Maybe I did intend to say it. You can say that anyone could have said it, but everyone was at the media day. All of our players were there. Dan Neil, Chris Carter, Bryant Westbrook—all of the big-name players were there. That's something that Westbrook would definitely say, but nobody said it. Like everyone said, we were definitely a reflection of our coach. I just knew it needed to be said.

Brown sits up straight when the Die-Hard Fan asks him one last question: Would the Longhorns have won the game if not for his prediction?

A smile comes across his face. Brown knows he's being asked once again to engage in some controversial public speculation. But this time Brown doesn't take the bait.

"We'll never know," he replies.

Chapter Six

RICKY WILLIAMS
A PECULIAR KIND OF KING

Few players coming through any college football program have as colorful and controversial a story as does running back Ricky Williams. His Heisman-winning career at Texas is one of the most successful ever in college football, while his personal difficulties continue to fuel debate as to just what kind of man Williams is underneath the pads.

While his later career in the NFL would provoke controversy among the fans, there is no debating that Williams' four years on the Forty Acres provided some of the most exciting and successful moments ever witnessed on the gridiron. Williams—or simply Ricky, as he was known to Longhorn fans—enjoyed a storybook career at Texas, capped by his capture of the NCAA all-time rushing record. Fans flocked through the gates at Darrell K Royal–Texas Memorial Stadium to see the fullback phenom, whose fame spread across the country even before he reached the pros.

Despite being one of the most dissected players in Longhorn history, Williams perhaps remains one of the program's most misunderstood personalities. Known for his dreadlocks, piercings, tattoos, and ever-present smile, Williams was popular among fans for his good-natured, shy demeanor. But these traits, in fact, masked a profound social anxiety disorder and periodic bouts of depression. The extent to which these maladies brought on his later personal problems is still the source of much speculation today.

A product of Patrick Henry High School in San Diego, Williams was a celebrated prep athlete in Southern California who churned out 2,099 yards rushing and twenty-five touchdowns in his final season of high school ball.

When Williams signed with Texas in 1995, recruiting was much more low-key than it is today, when many recruits' every public comment is dutifully chronicled. Thus, despite his excellent high school record, Williams was virtually unknown to the Longhorn Nation until he first took the field in a burnt orange uniform for the 1995 season opener in Hawaii.

Williams immediately attracted widespread attention, rushing for ninety-five yards and two touchdowns in Hawaii. That first game set the tone for an outstanding freshman year in which Ricky, starting at fullback, rushed for a Texas freshman record 990 yards, averaged six yards per carry, and scored eight touchdowns. That year, Ricky put in some memorable performances against UT's toughest opponents, including a 113-yard rushing game against the Zach Thomas-led Texas Tech Red Raiders.

"I remember the game against Texas Tech. We were freshmen and Zach Thomas was the middle linebacker," says former Texas linebacker Dusty Renfro, who played four years with Williams. "He just destroyed Zach all day long. He was running over him, he stiff-armed him into the ground. That's when I really realized how physical Ricky could be—when I was watching him run the ball in that game against Zach Thomas. He owned Zach Thomas that day."

Less than a month after the Texas Tech game, Texas squared off with Texas A&M in College Station. The Longhorns were fighting to secure the final Southwest Conference Championship against a formidable Aggies team that came into the game with a 31-game home winning streak. But A&M simply couldn't contain Williams, who ran for 163 yards and two scores in Texas's first win in College Station in more than a decade.

Williams finished the season just ten yards shy of the ever-elusive 1,000-yard mark. But as noted by his former teammate, offensive lineman Dan Neil, Ricky never paid much attention to statistical records.

"Shon Mitchell had a thousand yards," Neil says. "We almost had two 1,000-yard backs. I came up to him [Williams] after the A&M game and said 'Man, why didn't you get a thousand yards?' He just kind of smiled and said, 'Ah, nobody told me. I didn't know.' It didn't bother him at all. That's Ricky in a nutshell."

Williams followed up his impressive freshman campaign with a sopho-more season that again saw him light up the stat books. He rushed for 100

WILLIAMS accepts the Doak Walker Award, given to the nation's top running back, from Walker himself following the 1997 season

Photo courtesy of Dave Campbell's 40 Years of Texas Football

yards seven times that year, totaling 1,272 yards, with twelve touchdowns on the ground.

Entering his junior season, Williams had gained national attention and was hyped as a likely Heisman Trophy candidate. Ricky lived up to the expectations, even though the 'Horns struggled through a disappointing 4–7 season. Williams battered and bruised defenses for a total of 1,893 rushing yards. He led the nation in rushing and scoring, a performance that earned him the Doak Walker Award, given to the best running back in the country.

Williams finished fifth in the Heisman voting. Many fans believed this was his last shot at the trophy, as Ricky was widely expected to declare for the NFL draft. After a difficult season, the Longhorns were entering a transition phase that would include the release of Mackovic and the rest of the coaching staff that had helped bring Williams to Austin. If Williams came back to Texas, he'd pass up a sure-fire top-five draft pick and a multi-million dollar contract. Meanwhile, there was no guarantee that the Longhorns would play any better in 1998 under their new coach, Mack Brown.

But Williams' career would be marked by his defiance of the conventional wisdom. On January 8, 1998, in front of a jam-packed media session in Bellmont Hall's Carpenter-Winkel Centennial Room, Williams shocked the crowd by declaring his intention to return to Texas for his senior season. Longhorn fans celebrated the news, which even provoked cheers among the reporters covering the announcement.

The decision was not spur-of-the-moment. After careful consideration, Williams decided that he didn't want to leave Texas with the frustrating 1997 season as his final memory. He told Brown that he would only return if the coach felt the Longhorns could field a winning team in 1998. Receiving that assurance, Williams only let the coaches know of his decision shortly before he officially announced it from the podium.

"There are certain things that money can't buy, like camaraderie and the team being together, and loyalty," Williams would later say about his decision. "Money can't buy those things."

A YEAR FOR THE AGES

Having secured another year of service from the nation's top college player, the Longhorns' transition period suddenly looked a lot less daunting. As former Texas wide receiver Wayne McGarity remembers,

> When Ricky decided he was coming back for his senior year, Mack kind of kidded and said we now have the top recruiting class in the country. And it was true. I'm not sure what the team would have been without Ricky. We had some pretty good players and great senior leadership. I know that we had some guys that were really trying to make a change and make some things happen because Mack Brown came in and set a different standard and a different tone of how football would be played at The University of Texas. But the fact that we had Ricky back there, granted, that was certainly going to help.

The 1998 season, however, did not get off to a promising start. After winning their opener against New Mexico State, the Longhorns dropped consecutive games to top-10 teams UCLA and Kansas State. The latter match-up was particularly demoralizing, as Texas barely put up a fight against the Wildcats, who pounded the 'Horns to the tune of 48–7. Williams gained just forty-three yards on twenty-five carries, provoking more speculation that he'd already lost his last chance at a Heisman. Other critics seemed ready to write off the team's chances before conference play had even begun.

And it was at that point that Ricky began leading the Longhorns to another storybook season.

After beating Rice, 59–21, in their next game, the Longhorns hosted Iowa State in week five. What was expected to be an easy win over the Cyclones turned into a game of high emotion for Williams.

Earlier in the week, Doak Walker, the legendary SMU running back, had passed away. Williams and Walker had met the previous year, after Ricky won the Doak Walker Award. The two quickly became close friends, and Williams hung a photograph of Walker in his locker. After Walker's death on September 27, Williams dedicated the remainder of the season to his late friend.

Williams took the field against Iowa State wearing a decal bearing No. 37—Walker's jersey number—on his helmet. He then ran all over the Cyclones, setting or tying six NCAA records over the course of the game. Williams found the end zone five times and posted a Texas record 350 yards rushing as the Longhorns creamed their opponents, 54–33.

The following week, in a game against Oklahoma, Williams switched his jersey from No. 34 to 37 in Walker's honor. Fittingly, the Cotton Bowl, site of the annual Texas-OU grudge match, is also known as "The House that Doak Built." Williams entered Doak's dwelling and proceeded to clean house, running for 139 yards and two scores in a cakewalk 34–3 Texas victory. After his first touchdown, Williams tapped his chest with both hands and then pointed to the sky in memory of Walker. Later, Williams repeated the tribute after a 78-yard TD run, although the play was called back on a holding penalty

After the game, Walker's children and their families joined the Longhorn team in the Texas locker room. Williams handed over his game jersey to the family.

"I met him and he made a big impact on my life. He was so humble," Williams said of Doak after the game. "He kept fighting back through good and bad. He lived the way I want to live my life. When I looked down at his number before the game, I started to get real emotional. It was an extremely special day."

The season hit another high note on Halloween, when Texas traveled to Nebraska to face a Cornhusker squad riding a 47-game home winning streak. After more than three hours of helmet rattling football, the Longhorns came out on top, 20–16, on a late touchdown pass from Major Applewhite to

McGarity. Williams rushed for 150 yards against Nebraska's famed "Black Shirt" defense, including some key runs on the game-winning drive to get the ball close to the goal line.

Ricky's tear continued over the next two games, setting up one of the most memorable moments in college football history during the Longhorns' regular-season finale against Texas A&M in Austin.

Texas had lost their previous game to Texas Tech, which meant that the Big 12 South title would not be on the line in the match-up against the Aggies. But the game drew a lot of attention for its implications to Williams, who needed just sixty-two yards to surpass Tony Dorsett as the NCAA career rushing leader. A national television audience and a then-record crowd of 83,687 fans, including Dorsett himself, provided an excited atmosphere even by Longhorn standards. The stands were like a powder keg ready to explode. And late in the first quarter, Williams lit the fuse.

With 1:13 remaining in the opening period, the jumbotron showed that Williams needed just eleven yards for the record. Setting up from the right hashmark on Texas's own 40-yard line, offensive coordinator Greg Davis sent in a play that would go down in Texas history—"L King Zin 53." Ricky stood seven yards behind the line of scrimmage, ready to strike.

Applewhite took the snap, turned left, and handed the ball to Williams four yards deep. Ricky darted left, heading for a hole between the left guard and tackle. Aggie linebacker Warrick Holdman slipped by the block of right tackle Jay Humphrey and tried to make the stop in the backfield, but Williams easily broke through, crossing the line of scrimmage through a hole formed by left tackle Leonard Davis and left guard Roger Roesler. Texas fullback Ricky Brown provided a key block on Aggie All-American linebacker Dat Nguyen, and Williams powered through an attempted tackle by A&M safety Rich Cody. Two steps later, he had the record—but Williams wasn't done.

Breaking into the secondary, Ricky angled left and sprinted downfield toward the left sideline. At the 15-yard line, approaching the boundary, Williams put on the breaks and cut back. McGarity threw a key block on safety Brandon Jennings, and Williams overpowered cornerback Jason Webster as he fell across the goal line.

The crowd erupted when Williams slipped through Cody's tackle. But that was nothing compared to the deafening roar it unleashed when Williams lunged into the end zone.

As always, Williams' close-knit family—his mother Sandy and sisters Cassie and Nisey—were in attendance. Reflecting on the play, Sandy cites the run as her favorite memory from Ricky's career. She particularly remembers two aspects of the play that later won the "Compaq College Football Play of the Year" award. First, she recalls that ABC sent a cameraman to her seat to shoot her reaction when Ricky broke the record. "I understand we all have our jobs to do, but can you imagine watching a football game with a camera right there in your face?" asks Sandy. "Honestly, part of my happiness of Ricky's record-breaking run was having that cameraman get the shot he needed and leaving."

More importantly, she remembers watching Ricky celebrate the moment with her daughters, who took to the field to congratulate their brother.

"It was a huge accomplishment, but more than that, it was a picture perfect moment watching all three of my children's faces as they embraced on the field," Sandy says today. "I was up in the stands and everyone around me was asking if I was going to go down. I said 'No, this is my kids' moment.' It was a great joy to watch Cassie and Nisey being rushed onto the field and then Ricky's look of surprise and delight when he saw them."

McGarity, who was split about ten yards wide to the right side of the formation at the time of the snap, also remembers the moment well:

> Obviously, I think everybody in the stadium knew that was a possibility at that time. I was on the other side of the field. The play wasn't even coming my way. I just remember the backside of the play. Once he cleared the line, I was going to get that safety. So I'm watching him run, and I knew he was going to break. I just made a bee-line to get

WILLIAMS finished his college career as the NCAA's all-time leading rusher, with 6,279 yards. In 1998, he ran for 2,124 yards to capture the UT single-season rushing record.

over there as fast as I could. There was nothing that was going to stop him from scoring, I guarantee that.

I remember thinking in my head as it's going on, "What a way to break this record." As it's happening, I'm telling myself that. I'm running as fast as I can to get over there. I probably ran the fastest forty yards I've ever run in my life. I happened to get in front of him right about the time he was making a move on the guy. I grabbed and pushed that guy into the end zone and right there in front of my face I got a chance to see probably the greatest record-breaking run ever.

You can call it holding if you want to, but that guy was not going to tackle Rick. I go back and look at that and I'm thinking "Wow, this is history here." I cried on the sideline. I cried because I was so happy for him. Everything that people said about him—that he was weird and all this crazy stuff—this guy just genuinely wanted to play football. He loved it. Every day at practice, he loved it. He would show guys what it would take to get there.

Added Texas linebacker Dusty Renfro, who played all four years at Texas with Williams, "We were all standing up on the benches, watching over everybody's head. It was exciting. Tony Dorsett was on the sideline with us and he was a childhood role model for a lot of us. It was just a neat atmosphere. We were playing A&M in a big game, a close game. It was just really exciting. That year in general was really exciting."

Williams finished the game with 259 yards rushing and a score. The ending was near-perfect, with Texas coming from behind to beat the No. 6-ranked Aggies on a last-second field goal. Williams recorded thirty-six yards in receptions in the game, which also gave him the NCAA career all-purpose yardage record previously held by Napolean McCallum.

After getting bypassed as a junior, Williams' extraordinary efforts in 1998 (2,124 yards rushing and twenty-five touchdowns) secured him an invitation to the Heisman Trophy ceremony. Williams was the runaway winner, securing the fourth-widest margin of victory ever. He joined Earl Campbell as the

Longhorns' only winners of college football's most prestigious individual award.

"There are only two Heisman Trophies at this school," says Neil. "Being one of them is a major accomplishment. People might question why he didn't leave early or why he came back. I think to me, it's really simple with Ricky. He was just a kid having fun. He was having a good time at Texas, so why was he going to go anywhere?"

Three weeks after accepting the Heisman, Williams strapped on the pads and a Texas uniform for the last time in his career. With its key victories over top-10 opponents Nebraska and Texas A&M, Texas made a move up the Big 12 standings and the national polls. The Longhorns accepted a slot to take on Mississippi State in the Cotton Bowl. At the time, Texas sat at No. 20 in the polls, with Mississippi State ranked at No. 25.

The 'Horns went on to thrash the Bulldogs, 38–11, giving Texas its first New Year's Day bowl win since the 1982 Cotton Bowl victory over Alabama. Williams rushed for 203 yards and two touchdowns, capping one of the most remarkable individual seasons in college football history.

"I'll never forget how he just demoralized Mississippi State in the Cotton Bowl," said Applewhite. "He was hitting them so hard and knocking guys out of the game that it didn't take them too long to not even want to try to tackle him anymore."

Texas finished the year ranked No. 15 in the Associated Press poll. Applewhite maintains that the team's achievements began and ended with Ricky Williams. "He was our team's success. As Ricky went, so did we. His presence had such an effect on what defenses could do to you. He limited them and therefore limited the coverages they could throw at us, which was a great benefit to me as a freshman quarterback," Applewhite declares.

Williams' choice to return for his final year set the table for what turned out to be a season that far exceeded most fans' expectations. After beginning the season at 1–2, the Longhorns had gone on to win eight of their next nine games.

In fact, Williams' decision changed the face of Texas football far beyond his senior year. The glaring spotlight that followed Ricky and the whole Texas

Photo courtesy of the University of Texas

WILLIAMS poses with his newly won
Heisman Trophy in December 1998

program over the course of his record-setting season lent UT a certain prestige that it had been lacking for some time. Williams' return, and the subsequent success that Texas enjoyed that year, opened avenues for Mack Brown to reel in some of the elite recruiting classes for which he and his group of assistants have become famous.

"He [Williams] was without a doubt the most integral part of our team's success and in many ways laid the foundation for Coach Brown and the Texas staff to reestablish themselves in the recruiting world," says Applewhite.

His sentiments were echoed by Renfro, the defense's fiery leader throughout most of his Longhorn career. "I think it helped propel Mack Brown and Texas tremendously," he says about Williams' senior-year return to Texas. "It was huge. It was a huge decision."

"NOT YOUR NORMAL NFL GUY"

With such a storybook career, and with so many eyes following his every move, one would think the world would have an amazing insight into Ricky's inner thoughts. But most fans and reporters never really cracked through his quiet outer shell to get to know the man under the pads.

Perceptions of Williams vary dramatically. Many fans, particularly those who followed his career at Texas, view him as a good-natured, soft-spoken guy with a compassionate heart. However, other observers—particularly those who have concentrated their attention on his NFL career—have a more negative impression of Ricky. This largely stems from a number of highly-publicized incidents involving Williams after he turned pro.

In order to obtain Williams with the fifth pick of the 1999 draft, the New Orleans Saints, led by head coach Mike Ditka, resorted to an unprecedented move, giving up their entire draft in 1999 as well as first- and third-round picks in 2000. As the only player in the whole New Orleans draft class, enormous pressure fell on Williams' shoulders; he was expected almost single-handedly to turn the team into contenders.

"In the draft, the Saints gave up everything to move up to get Ricky. Think about the pressure that put on him at that time," says McGarity, who played a short stint with Williams on the Saints team. "You go into your rookie year and *you* are the draft class. How difficult is that to handle?"

The Saints' opponents keyed in on Williams, who was a stand-out star on an otherwise unremarkable offense. Nevertheless, Williams performed well in his three years at New Orleans, averaging more than 1,000 yards per season despite missing ten games in his first two years due to injuries. He was the first Saints player to post back-to-back 1,000-yard seasons, and he would finish each of his first three years as one of the Saints' leading receivers.

"The one thing I'll say about Ricky and any other guy coming out of college, you do not get to pick which team drafts you. So much of it is where you go that determines your success," observes Neil, who regularly blocked for some of the NFL's most productive rushers while playing with the Broncos. "If you look at the guys that I played with in my career, they got drafted by a great team that loves to run the ball a certain way, so they were destined for success. Ricky, it didn't always fall into place for him with the team but he's always a ton of talent."

GAMEDAY HAUNTS

Best place to take a family of five before the game—**Bob Bullock Texas History Museum**—1800 N. Congress Avenue, (512) 936-8746

Best place to two-step away the night after a victory—**The Broken Spoke**—3201 South Lamar, (512) 442-6189

Best place to see co-eds in bathing suits 365 days per year—**Barton Springs Swimming Pool**—2101 Barton Springs Road (located in Zilker Park), (512) 476-9044

Best post-game radio talk—**ESPN 1530AM**

In 2002, as he prepared for his fourth year in the league, Williams was dealt to the Dolphins as part of a blockbuster trade in which Miami gave up two first-round draft picks. The move paid immediate dividends for Williams, who was pleased with his new teammates and felt relieved to get away from the unrealistic demands of the Saints' fan base.

"When I was playing football I crossed paths with him every so often," says Neil. "One thing I did notice, when I ran across him when he was in New Orleans, he just never looked happy. When I saw him in Miami, he seemed like a much happier guy and I could tell he was enjoying himself more at that point of his career."

The satisfaction Williams found in Miami was reflected in his on-the-field performance. He had an outstanding first year with the Dolphins, rushing for a league-high 1,853 yards and earning his first invite to the Pro-Bowl, where he was named the game's MVP. Williams followed that up with a strong second season in which he rushed for 1,372 yards.

And just when Ricky seemed on top of the world, everything unraveled.

In December 2003, he tested positive for marijuana. (It was his second failed test with Miami, although the first was unpublicized.) In response, the NFL handed him a four-game suspension in May. Two months later, with the Dolphins about to begin preseason training, rumors began spreading that Williams had failed a third drug test. Ricky then shocked the professional sports world by abruptly announcing his retirement.

It was not Williams' first brush with legal trouble. At UT in 1997, police had stopped Williams early one morning for running a stop sign on campus. When asked his name, he replied "Ricky Lynn Williams." His license, however, bore his birth name—Errick Lynn Williams—and the officer arrested Ricky for failing to identify himself. After being held overnight, the police dropped the charges and released Williams. Ricky chalked up the incident to a simple mistake and declined to pursue the matter any further.

In light of his positive drug tests, however, this story was recycled in the press as reporters suddenly began portraying Ricky as an out-of-control egomaniac. His dreadlocks and body jewelry, previously viewed as a colorful quirk of personality, suddenly cast a dark shadow over Williams' public image.

It was a stunning turn of events. In just three months, Williams' reputation had plummeted from that of an NFL hero to someone labeled as everything from a pothead to a quitter.

After his fall from grace, the introspective Williams struggled to find inner peace. He set off for Australia, where he spent time living in a tent, and he later returned to California to teach yoga and study Ayurveda, a form of holistic medicine.

"He did well playing football, but when he was done, he just said 'I'm done and I'm out of here,'" says Neil. "I admire him for that because there's a lot of pressure. A lot of people try to get him to keep going out there and keep playing and he just did what he wanted to do."

Williams' reclusiveness, his problems with marijuana, and his attraction to spiritualism, holistic medicine, and yoga have given rise to a public perception of him as an extremely eccentric, somewhat unstable person. But those who knew him best insist this image is inaccurate.

"I think he is misunderstood, definitely. Everyone says he doesn't care about playing football. That's a lie," McGarity states emphatically. "With all the things that were beginning to get written about him, I'd hate to play football too. Granted, some of those things are from his actions and I think he understands that. Ricky has an interesting spirit. I respect him because he never changed who he was. He never once tried to be somebody else. He just wanted to be Ricky. He's not your normal guy from around the NFL. He's not one of those cocky guys that drives around in Bentleys. I think that's the perception that people have when you get to the NFL—that you're supposed to be that way. But Ricky's not."

Williams returned to the NFL in 2005 after serving out his four-game suspension—only to be suspended again for the entire 2006 season and part of the 2007 season for testing positive for an undisclosed drug.

Once again the critics and national media pundits attacked Williams, with some portraying him as a brutish thug. And once again, his former

RICKY WILLIAMS rewrote the NCAA record book when he broke Tony Dorsett's career rushing record on this 60-yard touchdown run against Texas A&M

Photo courtesy of the University of Texas

↗ **ON FOURTH DOWN,** Vince Young scores the winning touchdown in Texas's 41-38 victory over USC that landed Texas its first outright national championship in over thirty years

» **YOUNG KISSES THE TROPHY** after beating USC

AFTER YEARS OF FRUSTRATION against the Sooners, the Cotton Bowl scoreboard told a different story in 2005

THE OKLAHOMA SECTION of the Cotton Bowl empties out while Texas fans celebrate the Long-horns' 28-10 victory over OU in 2006

LEGENDS: The 2005 Texas Longhorns

Photo courtesy of *Dave Campbell's Texas Football*

teammates came to his defense. Renfro takes particular exception to the perception of Williams as a dumb jock. Says Renfro,

> Ricky is a very, very intelligent person. I had an economics class with him in college and he would read everything he could get his hands on. He was just a fanatic. Ricky would read the textbook. He would be done with it in the first month or so of the class and get bored and then he wouldn't show up for a while. Not only would he read it, he would learn it. When he did come to class and the coaches would do spot checks on classes, he would show up and the professor would try to pick on him. He would just start rattling that stuff off. You could not put him on the spot because he knew it. It was amazing.
>
> A lot of people try to put him in that pro athlete category, say he's a good athlete but not very intelligent. But Ricky is exactly the opposite. He's a good athlete who is highly, highly intelligent.

Texas fans, having watched Williams for a full four years, have a more personal relationship with the Heisman winner than do the fan bases of his NFL teams. For the burnt orange faithful, talking about Williams is like talking about a close friend or relative. Insult Ricky around UT, and you just might have to fight your way through a heated crowd of his fans.

Perhaps the deep support for Williams among the Longhorn Nation can be attributed to the city of Austin's diverse population and tolerant nature, or maybe it's just that college football enthusiasts tend to get intensely attached to their star players. With Williams, it's probably a combination of both.

But above all else, it seems to be his quiet yet engaging personality that continues to win fans over. Nearly a decade after his career at Texas, Williams still proclaims his close attachment to Austin, and he regularly returns to the Capital City to visit friends and relatives. "I think the people that I hold closest to my heart are all in Austin," he commented recently while in Austin for a Gridiron Celebrity Golf Tournament.

"Really and truly, Ricky is a really positive guy," insists McGarity. "Having gotten a chance to know him over the course of the years, my impression of him has not changed."

This seems to be the consensus among his former teammates, although it was not always so. When he decided to return to the NFL in 2005, some of his teammates felt scorned by his abrupt retirement and voiced skepticism about bringing him back into the franchise. Those feeling, however, quickly dissipated after Williams addressed the team and candidly answered any lingering questions.

Today, Williams's relationships with his former Longhorn cohort remain strong, even if Ricky's shy nature and reclusiveness has caused him to lose touch with many of his former Texas teammates.

> **"I think the people that I hold closest to my heart are all in Austin."**

After serving out his suspension, Ricky briefly returned to the Dolphins in the 2007 season before an injury knocked him out for the rest of the year. When asked to speculate on Williams' future, McGarity and other former Texas teammates argue that nothing that Williams does should come as a surprise. He may play for several more years, or he could just as easily decide he's had enough and suddenly walk away. Neither scenario would come as a shock, and those who know him would accept either decision.

"Ricky's always kind of done his own thing," recalls Neil. "It didn't shock me where he ended up today—that he believes in meditation and that he's into some other alternative beliefs. Ricky was kind of a free spirit and I think he always will be. I enjoyed that about him. The one thing I have always admired about Ricky and I always will admire about Ricky is that he never played the game for the money."

Williams has stated that he has changed since his days at Austin. He's overcome much of his anxiety disorder and feels more comfortable among the public. It's been a surprising journey, but one in which he's finally found peace of mind.

Longhorn fans have stuck with him through thick and thin. And Ricky knows it.

"UT has the most awesome fans for any level of the game, collegiate or professional," declares Ricky's mother. "You can't have that kind of fan base and not have a great relationship with them. The whole school is like a big family that sticks together for the good times as well as the bad. A player who has ever worn burnt orange remains a part of that family for life. I know it means a lot to Ricky to know he always has a home in Austin and at UT."

Chapter Seven

THE PERFECT STORM:

THE 2002 RECRUITING CLASS

I f you're wondering when Mack Brown's Longhorns turned the corner as a program, look no further than February 6, 2002.

National Signing Day.

It was on that day that the program added the foundation that would eventually lead it back to national glory in the 2005 season, when the Longhorns won their first national championship since 1970.

At the time, head coach Mack Brown was already known as one of the most effective recruiters in the country. Having taken over a foundering program in 1998 with a team that had gone 4–7 the previous season, Brown began rebuilding the Longhorns, relying on aggressive recruiting tactics and an easygoing attitude toward the academic potential of his prospects. Although he didn't bring in any valedictorians, Brown recruited enough outstanding football talent in his first few years to turn Texas into a top 5 program.

Then came the 2002 class, when a number of factors came together to create a perfect storm of recruiting for UT. The class was so strong that its likes may never be seen again—at least not for many years.

By 2001, Texas's program was clearly on the upswing. Brown's recruiting efforts were reinforced by Tim Brewster, the team's tight end coach and a superb recruiter in his own right. There was an unprecedented degree of local talent in Texas that year, giving UT a leg up on prospects who wanted to stay close to home. And finally, as the year wore on, the growing likelihood that Vince Young would end up at Texas served as a magnet for the school to attract other promising players.

For recruits, the decision often came down to a choice between Texas and Oklahoma. In 2001 the Sooners, who recruited strongly in Texas, seemed to have the upper hand, having crushed the Longhorns 63–14 in their 2000 matchup. However, thanks to the circumstances described above, in the 2002 class the Longhorns reeled in almost every one of the star players they sought.

And what a haul it was. The class produced thirteen starters (of whom eleven would start against USC in the national championship game on January 4, 2006), ten All-Big 12 selections, five All-Americans, two major award winners, and nine NFL players. Of the twenty-seven prospects who signed letters of intent to play for the Longhorns in 2002, a record six were ranked as five-star prospects.

To put that last stat in perspective, after the 2002 class, it took Texas *five years* to attract that many five-stars.

The historic success of the 2002 class came with a price, however. Aside from attracting a number of top prospects who didn't pan out, Brown's intense focus on pure athletic ability meant that numerous players made the team who ended up flunking out of school or alienating their coaches. In fact, after this class, Brown instituted new recruiting standards that valued stronger academics and character. That's why we'll probably never see another class like that of 2002.

This chapter describes the construction of the 2002 recruiting class, which included the key players who went on to win the national championship for Texas. We'll discuss each of the twenty-seven prospects, beginning by recounting the buzz on each recruit as he was being feted by Texas. Then, we'll describe the recruit's decision to enroll in Texas, constructed from contemporary articles written by the Die-Hard Fan. Finally, we'll take a look at what became of the recruit once he donned the burnt orange.

JUSTIN BLALOCK—OFFENSIVE LINEMAN—PLANO EAST

The hype: As the nation's top interior lineman and one of six five-star prospects from the Lone Star State, Blalock was one of the most important targets in the entire 2002 class.

December 20, 2001: When Justin Blalock woke up this morning, he felt like celebrating his eighteenth birthday by giving himself a gift.

Blalock called the University of Texas coaching staff and let them know that he was committing.

"I guess it was an early present for my birthday," Blalock said.

According to Blalock, the commitment to Texas was a matter of when and not if.

> " Texas is like a home away from home. "

"I knew I wasn't going to go anywhere else," Blalock declared. "When I saw the unity of the team, it just seemed really genuine. Texas is like a home away from home."

Blalock chose the Longhorns over a handful of the nation's finest programs, including Oklahoma, Michigan, and Florida.

"It's a great school and a great program, but I had no idea how close the players were," Blalock said. "That really impressed me and helped me with my decision."

Blalock's commitment is the fifth major verbal pledge that Texas has received this week.

"It's really been incredible in recent days," Blalock said of the Longhorn's recruiting class.

So, what happened? Blalock was a four-year starter for the Longhorns who earned All-Big 12 honors in his final three seasons while picking up

JUSTIN BLALOCK, one of the top recruits of the 2002 class

Photo courtesy of US Army All-American Game

third-team All-American honors as a junior and consensus first-team All-America honors as a senior. As a senior, he became the first player in school history to start in fifty consecutive games. Blalock was eventually drafted in the second round of the 2007 NFL draft by the Atlanta Falcons and started fourteen games as a rookie.

LARRY DIBBLES—DEFENSIVE END—LANCASTER

The hype: One of the great battles for the Longhorns in this class was the recruitment of the four-star Dibbles, who was regarded as the nation's No. 6 strong-side defensive end. The Longhorns were forced to battle a number of national powers to land Dibbles' signature.

December 25, 2001: Although it wasn't something that he had planned to do, Larry Dibbles made a little history with his decision to commit to the University of Texas on Tuesday.

"I called Coach [Mack] Brown and told him that I was committing and he told me that in all his years of coaching, I was his first Christmas Day commitment," Dibbles said.

Considering that Dibbles is the best defensive end prospect in the state of Texas and one of the top overall players in the Lone Star State this year, it's appropriate that his commitment to the Longhorns stands out above the normal verbal pledge.

"I was with my family yesterday, and I just felt comfortable about the idea of going to Texas," Dibbles said. "It wasn't planned or anything. Everyone was asking where I was going to go and I just felt comfortable with Texas. It wasn't until yesterday that I really knew where I wanted to go."

Dibbles chose the Longhorns over a bevy of national powers, but his final decision came down to Texas and Oklahoma.

According to Dibbles, his official visit to Texas on December 14 helped to steer him toward the Forty Acres.

"I had a very good time on my visit," Dibbles said. "It was an extraordinary visit. Most of the guys that visited Texas that weekend that were uncommitted had been with me the week before, when I visited Oklahoma. It gave us a chance to have something to compare it to. It's always good to meet guys from around the state and country that are like you."

Considering that Texas has received a verbal pledge from five of the six recruits that entered the weekend uncommitted, it would appear that the visit was a smashing success.

"We really got along on the visit and had a good time together," Dibbles said. "The players at Texas are not a bad peer group. Nobody is arrogant. It seemed like a good trip for all of us."

As for his own decision, Dibbles mentioned that the Longhorn program offered him the right combination of things that he was looking for.

LARRY DIBBLES, one of the many recruits who chose Texas over Oklahoma

Photo courtesy of US Army All-American Game

"I knew that I wanted to go to a school that had great academics, could offer me playing time, and would be able to compete for a national championship," Dibbles said. "If I didn't think I could play with the very best, I shouldn't be playing football. The way I see it, the better my surroundings are and the harder I'm forced to work, the better I'm going to be."

Dibbles added that his commitment to Texas would relieve him of some of the stress that he's endured over recent weeks because of the hectic recruiting process.

"It's a pressure off my shoulders," Dibbles declared. "Whenever someone asked me today where I'm going, I was able to say that I had committed to UT today. You can't lose with them. There's always going to be some people that don't like them even if they bought them a new house. But I feel very good about my decision."

So, what happened? A two-year starter for the Longhorns at defensive tackle, Dibbles twice earned All-Big 12 honors. During his Longhorn career, Dibbles played in forty-one games and recorded 107 tackles, two-and-a-half sacks, fourteen tackles for loss, nineteen quarterback pressures, and three forced fumbles. His best season came as a junior in 2004, when he earned All-Big 12 honors after posting forty-nine tackles, five tackles for loss, one-and-a-half sacks, nine pressures, a fumble recovery, and a forced fumble.

CLINT HANEY—RUNNING BACK— SMITHSON VALLEY

The hype: In the early years of the Mack Brown era at Texas, the staff would often give out scholarships at their June summer camps. Haney was one of the "summer camp surprises" who gave stellar performances in the camp. Overall, Haney was considered a solid prospect, although he wasn't one of the top recruits.

June 11, 2001: The Texas Longhorns picked up their fifth verbal commitment for the 2002 class late last week when Smithson Valley, Texas running back Clint Haney gave the Longhorn coaching staff a verbal pledge to become a Longhorn.

"He's going to start out as a running back for them, but he can play just about anywhere," Smithson Valley coach Larry Hill said. "He can catch the ball real well out of the backfield or he could line up in the slot and play wide receiver, and even though he hasn't played there he could play on defense as well."

The six-foot, 190-pound Haney really opened the eyes of the Longhorn coaches at their first mini-camp when he displayed tremendous speed and quickness during the tests. "He had run a 4.27 at the Texas A&M camp and he ran in the 4.3's at Texas," Hill said. "He also did very well in their shuttle drills. He's just a terrific athlete."

July 30, 2002: Some of the top high school football players from the state of Texas will be playing in the Texas Coaches Association All-Star game in Houston on Tuesday night. One player that won't be able to play due to injury is future Longhorn athlete Clint Haney.

However, after seriously injuring his arm this summer, Haney is just happy that he's close to returning to 100 percent.

"I was on the lake with my cousin and girlfriend, and I got my arm caught in the handle while I was wakeboarding," Haney said. "I tore two muscles in my forearm. As soon as it happened it looked like I had a softball under my skin on my forearm."

As amazing as it sounds, Haney is relieved that the injuries he suffered weren't any worse.

> **"I talked to the Texas trainer and he told me I was lucky because it should have ripped my arm off."**

"I talked to the Texas trainer and he told me I was lucky because it should have ripped my arm off," Haney said. "He said that it could have been a lot worse."

As it stands, the arm is feeling much better and Haney claims that he'll be ready to practice at full strength when freshmen report next week.

"I'm ready to go," Haney declared. "I still have a little damage in my thumb, but I'm ready. It's not going to be a problem."

According to Haney, Texas fans can expect to see him do a little bit of everything early in his career.

"I talked with Coach [Greg] Davis a while back and I'm going to go both ways," Haney said. "I'll be playing free safety on defense and I'll play running back and the inside slot on offense. We'll see what happen."

Haney and the rest of the freshmen class will report to Austin next Monday and will participate in their first practice on Tuesday.

So, what happened? Haney never recovered from that summer's wakeboarding accident. He was forced to give up football without ever playing a down for the Longhorns.

ALBERT HARDY—FULLBACK—GALENA PARK

The hype: Hardy might be the best true fullback prospect that the Longhorns have signed under Brown. He was rated as the nation's No. 4 fullback prospect by Rivals.com and he was a consensus state top 25 player.

October 22, 2001: There are times when the life of a star football recruit is tough, and then there other times when being one of the elite is oh-so-sweet.

Just ask Albert Hardy, who was given the VIP treatment during an unofficial visit to Texas this weekend for the Longhorns game against Colorado.

"They gave me the prettiest Texas Angel at the game. She's a twin," Hardy asserted with a sly smile. "I had a great time. The game and everything else was real nice. I love the atmosphere there."

According to Hardy, the Longhorns are the team to beat as far as recruiting is concerned.

"Texas is still my number one school," he said. "I've pretty much narrowed it down to five schools. I think I'm taking Michigan off and my final five are Texas, LSU, Alabama, Florida, and Colorado."

As for his success on the field, Hardy has rushed for 1,186 yards and ten touchdowns through the first ten games of the season.

"We beat C.E. King 9–0 this weekend," Hardy pointed out. "I had about 140 yards. It took a while, but I finally got a big run late in the fourth quarter and got into the end zone."

December 16, 2001: Throughout the recruiting process, Albert Hardy has heard the warnings come from everyone, whether it was from his peers or college coaches from across the nation.

They told him not to go to Texas because he'd never see the field as long as Cedric Benson is there.

On Monday, Hardy committed to the Longhorns and had a message for those people.

"A lot of people told me not to come to UT because of Cedric Benson," Hardy claimed. "They didn't think I could do it. But I'm not the type of person who will back down from a challenge. I think I can go in and compete and earn playing time with him. We'll make a great combo."

Hardy had been leaning toward the Longhorns for some time, but it wasn't until his official visit to Austin this past weekend that he realized it was time to pull the trigger on his decision.

"I really love the place," Hardy said. "I can see myself being happy here for four years. I really liked the recruits that came in with me. We had a lot of fun."

When asked if there was a recruit with whom he hit it off the best, Hardy replied, "Oh, Larry Dibbles. That's a wild boy. He's a little crazy, but we had a lot of fun together."

So, what happened? Hobbled by injuries, Hardy was a little-used fullback in the 2003 and 2004 seasons before health concerns forced him to give up the game.

AARON HARRIS—LINEBACKER—NORTH MESQUITE

The hype: Harris was a four-star prospect who was ranked No. 53 overall nationally by Rivals.com. Lone Star Recruiting ranked him as the state's No. 8 prospect.

December 2, 2001: While many Texas fans would like to forget Colorado's victory over the Longhorns in the Big 12 Championship Game, the day wasn't a total loss.

With the 'Horns looking to shore up the linebacker position in this year's class, they were able to pick up one of the Lone Star State's finest early Saturday afternoon.

"At about noon yesterday I was sitting with my parents and we were talking about how the situation at Texas was right for me, and we agreed that it was best that I go ahead and commit. They have a great family atmosphere and the ability to win championships," Harris declared.

The six-foot, 230-pound Harris, who had offers from almost every major Division I program in the nation, was scheduled to visit Texas A&M, Oklahoma, and Florida in the coming weeks, but those plans have changed.

AARON HARRIS fulfilled his vow to make an impact at Texas

"I'm just going to visit Texas on December 14," Harris said. "I'm not going to take any other visits."

According to Harris, the opportunity to come in as a true freshman and potentially earn heavy playing time was a big factor in his decision.

"That was one of the main reasons I decided to commit," Harris revealed. "I want to go somewhere where I can make an impact."

So, what happened? A three-year starter for the Longhorns at middle linebacker, Harris earned third-team All-America honors by the Associated Press as a senior, while also being named a semi-finalist for the Butkus and Bednarik Awards. He played in fifty-one career games (comprising thirty-one starts) and recorded 282 career tackles, twenty-eight tackles for loss, nine-and-a-half sacks, seven forced fumbles, and two interceptions. His best season came in 2004, when he earned consensus All-Big 12 honors after posting 118 tackles and 10 tackles for loss.

TULLY JANSZEN—DEFENSIVE TACKLE—KELLER

The hype: Janszen was regarded as a very good—but not great—defensive tackle prospect coming out of high school. As this class was starting to pick up steam, Janszen was one of Texas's first head-to-head recruiting wins against Oklahoma that year.

August 2, 2001: A little less than a month ago, Tully Janszen took an unofficial visit to Texas and came away impressed with the family atmosphere that he experienced from the coaches, players, and everyone associated with the program.

Janszen gave a commitment to the Longhorn coaching staff today because of the chemistry he noticed on his visit.

"Everyone made me feel like I was a part of the team while I was there and made me feel like I was one of them," Janszen said. "I just felt very comfortable with the players that I spent time with."

According to Janszen, he came to a final decision between his top two schools (Texas and Oklahoma) a little more than a week ago, but waited a few days before acting on his desire.

"I guess I made up my mind about a week ago," Janszen said. "I talked with my mom and she said that I should wait a few days and if I still had the same feeling then I guess I know where I should go. Texas just felt like the right place."

So, what happened? Janszen struggled with injuries throughout the early portion of his career, but he eventually earned a niche as a deep-snapper. In fact, it was Janszen who snapped the ball cleanly on Dusty Mangum's game-winning field goal in the 2005 Rose Bowl.

MARQUIS JOHNSON—WIDE RECEIVER— CHAMPAIGN, ILLINOIS

The hype: One of the original ringleaders in this recruiting class, Johnson was a Parade All-American and had a close relationship with wide receiver coach Tim Brewster, a former player at Illinois. After this five-star prospect committed to Texas, he made a point to involve himself personally in the recruitment of several Longhorn targets, including Vince Young.

October 2, 2001: If you didn't know that Champaign (IL) Centennial wide receiver Marquise Johnson had a great time on his official visit to Texas this past weekend, it only takes about five seconds on the phone with him to confirm it.

"I'm just chilling and enjoying life as a Longhorn," Johnson replied when asked how he was doing.

According to Johnson, it only took one weekend in Austin to know that his future was cloaked in burnt orange.

"They want me to be in their family and I want to be in their family," Johnson said. "The fans are great and now I've got something to prove. It's time to go to work."

One of things that impressed Johnson was the relationship that the receivers had with one another.

"When I got there, I met Roy [Williams] and Sloan [Thomas], and we hung out in their room and watched the Oklahoma game," Johnson said. "We just clicked right away. That's the thing about Texas. I never felt uncomfortable the

Photo courtesy of US Army All-American Game

MARQUIS JOHNSON, a five-star prospect who never quite panned out

whole time I was there. They all wanted me to come there and become a part of the team."

Johnson, who is regarded by many as the best player in the Midwest and is rated by Rivals100 as the No. 3 receiver in the nation, is the fifteenth commitment for the Longhorns.

"I think I've set myself up long-term," Johnson said. "Texas is family and that's for life."

So, what happened? Shortly after signing day Johnson was involved in a car accident that nearly took his life. While recovering from the accident and a knee injury he'd previously suffered in a basketball game, Johnson had some qualification issues because the NCAA arbitrarily redflagged his passing SAT score. After failing to qualify for the fall, the staff decided to pass on Johnson. He spent a year at a junior college and then signed with Texas Tech, where he failed to make much of an impact in their program.

MARCO MARTIN—DEFENSIVE TACKLE—MESQUITE

The hype: Martin was a five-star talent who dropped in the rankings at the end of his senior season due to a serious knee injury stemming from an illegal chop that he suffered in the state playoffs. While in high school, the 300-pound Martin often played running back and had a couple 80-yard runs to his credit. He was considered a top prospect before the injury.

December 17, 2001: There's no question that this weekend will go down as one of the most bittersweet moments in the life of Mesquite, Texas defensive tackle Marco Martin.

While his team was celebrating its first state title on the Alamo Stadium field in San Antonio, Martin was on the sideline wearing a leg brace because of an ugly chop block that knocked him out of the game in the opening minutes of the contest.

"It was pretty upsetting, and I told the team at halftime that they had to go out and win the game," Martin said as he fought back tears. "We had come too far to let anything keep us from our dream."

Martin's teammates took his words to heart and overcame a 13–0 halftime deficit with two second half touchdown that allowed the Skeeters to escape with a 14–13 win.

Still, Martin can't help but think about the play during which he was injured.

"On an earlier play, he pulled me down to the ground by my jersey," Martin said. "When I got up, he asked for help and I didn't help him up. I guess that made him mad. The guard was trying to hold me up and he just dove at my knee. I really wish there was something I could do about it."

December 20, 2001: The last few days have not been easy for Marco Martin.

With an MRI scheduled for Thursday for his injured right knee, it's been hard for Martin not to feel somewhat down about his recent injury. One person that was able to comfort the six-foot-four, 300-pound Martin was Texas head coach Mack Brown.

"It was Coach Brown that called me and really comforted me," Martin said. "He told me some stuff that made me feel really wanted. He said that they wanted me at Texas before I was injured and that they wanted me just as much after the injury. He let me know that they really wanted me at Texas and that made me feel good."

It also made him realize that Texas was the place where he wanted to spend the next four to five years of his life.

"I had known for a while that Texas was a school I had really liked," Martin said. "Plus it's close to home and my mom can watch my games without having to go to the trouble of flying."

Martin, who chose the Longhorns over a legion of other suitors including Texas A&M, Tennessee, Florida State, and Florida, said that the chance to play with some of the other great recruits that Texas is signing in the 2002 recruiting class was another reason for his decision.

"That's what I want to do—play with other great players," Martin said.

So, what happened? Martin never fully recovered from his knee injury, which prevented him from reprising the star role he'd played on the gridiron in high school. Although he stayed in the program and tried to make a complete comeback, Martin was never a major contributor to the Longhorns' success.

EDORIAN MCCULLOUGH— CORNERBACK—NORTH GARLAND

The hype: McCullough was one of six five-star players in the class. An elite-level sprinter, he may be the fastest player that Mack Brown has ever recruited.

January 21, 2001: According to Garland (Texas) North Garland cornerback Edorian McCullough, his college decision ended up not being much of a decision at all.

It was a no-brainer. A slam-dunk.

"I've committed to Texas," McCullough said. "I knew before I visited there this weekend that that's where I was going. It's where I've always wanted to go."

The five-foot-eleven, 190-pound McCullough visited the Longhorns this past weekend and said that any reservations he might have had were thrown out the window.

"They knocked my socks off," declared McCullough, who was hosted by Texas safety Nathan Vasher. "But I knew I was going there. The players and I got along great."

THE RECRUITS, JANUARY 2002

Top row (left to right): Justin Blalock; Larry Dibbles; Albert Hardy; Bottom row (left to right): Aaron Harris; Larry Dibbles (left) with Marquis Johnson

Earlier this morning McCullough had reported that he wanted to wait until later this week before he announced a decision. But endless phone calls from reporters changed his timetable.

"I just wanted to get it over with," McCullough said.

McCullough's commitment gives the Longhorns the state's top defensive back prospect and the No. 3 cornerback in the nation according to Rivals100.

So, what happened? McCullough played with the Longhorns as a true freshman in 2002, but ended up leaving the school due to academic problems. He transferred to the City College of San Francisco and signed to play for Oregon State in February 2005, but never actually played for the Beavers. He later signed a rookie free agent contract with the Jacksonville Jaguars, but he didn't make the team.

MATTHEW MELTON—SAFETY—TYLER JOHN TYLER

The hype: Melton wasn't a national prospect, but he was one of the state's top defensive back prospects and had offers from most of the schools that recruit the state of Texas.

October 17, 2001: For the last few weeks, defensive back Matthew Melton has been toying with the idea of committing to the University of Texas.

On Wednesday, he made it official

"It was down to Texas and Texas A&M and I just felt more comfortable at Texas," Melton said. "I sat down with my parents and talked it over and decided to make my commitment.

According to Melton, the decision to become a Longhorn was one that excited the Texas coaching staff.

"Coach [Brown] told me that he was putting my scholarship in a drawer and that he wanted me to visit on December 13, 14, and 15 with the rest of the guys who have committed," Melton said. "I think they like me because of my versatility and my aggressiveness. I'm a guy that can come in during blitz packages and cover the slot as well as any cornerback. I'm also a very aggressive player against the run."

Melton added that he largely knew he was going to be a Longhorn once he made the decision that he wanted to stay in Texas.

"I feel like an enormous weight has been taken off of me," he stated. "I wanted to tell everyone, but we're having some problems with individualism on our team and we need to address that. The coach asked me if I wanted to tell the newspaper, but I told him not to call. I think he was happy about that."

So, what happened? A career back-up with the Longhorns, Melton played in more than forty games at UT but remained, for the most part, a role player.

DUSTIN MIKSCH—WIDE RECEIVER— ROUND ROCK WESTWOOD

The hype: Miksch was another player who earned his scholarship at the June summer camp that year. He was the only two-star prospect in the entire class.

June 14, 2001: Wide receiver Dustin Miksch has had orange blood flowing through his body for his entire life.

For years Miksch has attended Longhorn games as a fan with his family and dreamed about suiting up in burnt orange and running onto the field in front of the Longhorn faithful.

On Thursday morning, Miksch's dream came a lot closer to reality when he gave a verbal commitment to the UT coaches.

"I called the Texas coaches at 11:15 this morning and I talked with Coach [Greg] Davis," Miksch said. "They couldn't really talk about recruiting at the camp, so I just wanted to see what they thought about me. They offered me a scholarship and I went ahead and committed."

The six-foot, 167-pound Miksch is one of the best wide receivers in the state and was easily one of the top players on hand at the Longhorns' second camp session this week.

"I ran a 4.35 and won the fastest man competition," said Miksch, who also won the fastest man competition at the Texas A&M camp last week. "I felt like I did real well. I caught the ball really well

Miksch, whose father Ronnie lettered as a wide receiver for the Longhorns from 1977–78, explained that playing for Texas is something he's thought about his entire life.

"My dad played for Texas back when they were No. 2 and lost to Notre Dame in the Cotton Bowl," Miksch said. "I've always gone to the games and I would get chills when the players would run out onto the field. I've always been a Longhorn fan."

So, what happened? Frequently fighting injuries, Miksch was never quite able to get his college career off the ground. He was placed far down the depth chart, although he earned a letter in 2006.

MARCUS MYERS—LINEBACKER—
PFLUGERVILLE CONNALLY

The hype: Myers was one of the few local products in the class, and he earned his scholarship at the team's summer camp in June. A versatile prospect, the staff envisioned Myers as being able to play on either side of the ball.

June 27, 2001: The Texas Longhorns have a certain criteria that they look for when they recruit linebackers.

They like them big, physical, and most of all, they like them faster than a speeding train.

Enter Pflugerville (Texas) Connally linebacker Marcus Myers.

The six-foot-three, 215-pound Myers was one of the Longhorns' camp standouts this summer and became their ninth commitment for the 2002 recruiting class when he accepted a scholarship offer on an unofficial visit to the school this afternoon.

"I had been leaning towards them for a while," Myers said. "So, when they offered this afternoon I went ahead and accepted it."

Myers chose the Longhorns over Texas A&M, Texas Tech, Oklahoma, Oklahoma State, and Northwestern. The Aggies, Cowboys, and Red Raiders have all offered.

"I went to both the Texas and A&M camps this summer and I felt like I did real well," Myers revealed. "I had a lot of fun at both camps, but I kind of felt like Texas probably wanted me the most. The UT coaches were real nice to me and they met my mom and my dad at the camp."

The Connally standout really landed on the 'Horns' radar screen when he was timed in the 4.5's at the UT camp, where he showed tremendous all-around athleticism. According to Myers, the biggest reason for his commitment was that it gives those close to him a chance to watch him in person.

"This allows my dad, my family, and my friends the chance to watch me play close to home," Myers said. "The coaches told me that they had been watching me closely and that I was what they needed in a linebacker for their 4-3 defense. They liked my speed and hustle and they said I was the type of player that could get it done on the field and in the classroom."

So, what happened? Myers started out at linebacker for the Longhorns, but after several seasons as a back-up he moved to fullback on offense. He was a total team player who earned a national championship ring in 2005.

BRIAN PICKRYL—DEFENSIVE END— JENKS, OKLAHOMA

The hype: The nation's No. 2-ranked defensive end prospect, Pickryl possessed elite-level pass rush skills and was a dominant player at one of the best high school programs in the state. There was some concern at UT, however, about his history of shoulder injuries. The fact that he was a five-star prospect from the Sooner State made him a personal favorite to many.

December 3, 2001: Christmas might not be for another twenty-two days, but the Texas Longhorns received one of their biggest presents of the recruiting year on Monday.

Jenks, Oklahoma defensive end Bryan Pickryl, who is the top player in the state of Oklahoma this year, has given an oral pledge to play for the Longhorns.

"I've made my decision and it pretty much came down to what I thought was best for me," Pickryl said. "They stood out to me because they have exactly what I'm looking for. They have a great engineering program and they have great tradition in football."

According to Pickryl, the fact that he has family in the Austin area made the decision even easier.

"Having two uncles and a grandparent close by me will really help," he added.

Still, Pickryl made it clear that there were many reasons for his decision.

"Texas was just that appealing," Pickryl claimed. "I've talked with Coach Brown and Coach McCrary a number of times and they are the kind of people I want to dedicate the next four years to. I'm very secure in my decision."

Pickryl, who visited Texas back in October, also visited Missouri and was scheduled to visit Michigan and Oklahoma, but those trips have been canceled.

"The coaches were very enthusiastic and they are ready for me to get down there," Pickryl said. "I'll be reporting on January 13."

So, what happened? Pickryl showed up and made an immediate impact at Texas, joining the starting line-up early in his Longhorn career. However, his shoulder problems continued to plague him after his arrival at Texas, eventually forcing him to walk away from football despite all his talent.

CHASE PITTMAN—DEFENSIVE END— SHREVEPORT, LOUISIANA

The hype: Pittman's bother Cole was a member of Mack Brown's No.1-ranked recruiting class in 1999. A projected starter in 2001, Cole died in a car accident in the months leading up to Chase's recruitment. A defensive lineman and big-time prospect in his own right, Chase's matriculation at his late brother's school was widely hailed as a defining moment for the Longhorn Nation.

September 6, 2001: Emotions will be at an all-time high this weekend in Austin as the University of Texas dedicates its game this Saturday against North Carolina to the late Cole Pittman, a junior defensive tackle from Shreveport, Louisiana who was killed in a one-vehicle accident this February.

The entire Pittman family including his brother Chase, who will be making his official visit to Texas, will be on hand for a special ceremony to be held before the game.

"It's amazing that a whole city can remember a kid and I'm his brother," Chase Pittman declared. "That's just amazing."

While the entire state of Texas plans to honor a lost son on Saturday, it's something that Chase attempts to do on a daily basis.

"It's hard to go an hour or even twenty minutes without thinking about him," Pittman said. "I think about him all the time. Last week I wore his number in our first game. I remember looking in the mirror before the game and seeing his number and it was hard. I ended up getting cramps later in the game, and I think it's because I lost so much fluid from my eyes."

Still, Pittman finished the game as Evangel's leading tackler with eight tackles, two sacks, and two tackles for loss.

"The field was in really bad shape," Pittman said. "It's hard being 260 pounds and trying to tackle a guy who is 190 pounds and moving in every direction when the field is in such a mess."

As far as the recruiting process goes, Pittman said that it's come down to Texas and LSU.

"I went to LSU on an official visit this past weekend and it was great. I love LSU," Pittman said. "I'm going to go to Texas this weekend and then come home and rest. I'll talk with my dad about it and then make a decision."

September 16, 2001: Chase Pittman said he has decided to "play for the best team in America."

That team is the Texas Longhorns.

Pittman, who is ranked as the No. 10 defensive tackle by Rivals100 and is a four-star selection, confirmed what had been widely rumored for more than a week by announcing his decision earlier this morning in front of a packed congregation at ECA.

> **"I'm just so proud that I'm going to get the opportunity to play at Texas and help carry on what my brother started."**

He said he has decided to play football at Texas, where he'll carry on the legacy built by his brother Cole, who died tragically in a car accident earlier this year.

"I think Coach Brown is the best coach in America," Pittman said. "I already am convinced that Texas is the best team and school around. I'm just so proud that I'm going to get the opportunity to play at Texas and help carry on what my brother started."

Pittman picked Texas over LSU and Oklahoma. He visited Texas last weekend for the North Carolina game. Before the game, Texas honored Cole's memory in a pre-game ceremony.

"It's always felt like family," Pittman said. "Even before what happened with Cole. But now it's my home away from home."

So, what happened? Pittman appeared to be developing into a solid player for the Longhorns, but the memory of Cole in Austin was too much for him. He eventually transferred back home to play for LSU, where he emerged as a starter at defensive end. Pittman was drafted in the seventh round of the 2007 NFL draft by the Cleveland Browns.

BRIAN ROBISON—LINEBACKER—SPLENDORA

The hype: There was very little hype over the linebacker Robison, even if he was one of the state's top athletes. Overall, Robinson was probably one of the three least heralded prospects in the class.

July 10, 2001: There was a brief moment yesterday afternoon when Brian Robison must have felt a little uneasy.

Robison was in the middle of an unofficial visit to the University of Texas, along with his mother and grandmother, and had just informed Texas assistant coach Darryl Drake that he wanted to commit to the Longhorns when a moment of silence took place.

"I had just told Coach that I was committing and he just stared at us for a few seconds and finally he just got this real big smile on his face," Robison said. He told me that he was so happy, but that he was literally speechless that I was committing because he hadn't been expecting it at all. He told us he was real happy and came over and gave all of us hugs."

After making his commitment official, Robison spent some time getting to know some of his future teammates.

"I met Chris Simms, Mike Williams, and some of the new recruits that play defensive back," Robison said. "They were all real nice and treated me well."

According to Robison, there were only a few questions that he wanted to ask before he announced his desire to become the Longhorns' eleventh verbal commitment.

★★★

TOWER TRADITIONS

There is no greater feeling among Longhorn fans than to look up at the University Tower and see it light up in burnt orange after a victory in any sport. When it was first constructed in the 1930s, the tower was the only building in the city of Austin that competed with the dome of the State Capitol on the Austin skyline. The tower was lit up for the first time by a flood of orange lights in 1937. Today, specific lighting configurations are used to commemorate different kinds of occasions:

TOWER ENTIRELY WHITE
Standard Tower Lighting

TOWER WITH WHITE TOP AND ORANGE SHAFT
Academic and Staff Achievements
>> Faculty academic achievements (Academic Convocation)
>> Student academic achievements (Honors Day)
>> Staff achievements (Staff Recognition Day)
>> Academic team achievements with #1 displayed
>> Other events at the president's discretion

TOWER WITH ORANGE TOP AND WHITE SHAFT
Athletic Achievements
>> Football regular season victories, except Texas A&M
>> Non-Bowl Championship Series (BCS) victories
>> Other events at the president's discretion

TOWER ENTIRELY ORANGE
Significant Athletic Victories
>> Football victories
>> Texas A&M

>> Big 12 South
>> Big 12 Championship Game
>> Big 12 Regular Season Team Championship
>> Big 12 Tournament Championships
>> Student organization sports club national championships

Campus-wide Accolades
>> UT's Birthday—September 15
>> Commencement
>> Texas Independence Day—March 2
>> Other campus-wide events at the president's discretion

TOWER ENTIRELY ORANGE WITH #1 DISPLAYED
Athletic Championships
>> Football Bowl Championship Series (BCS) 1 vs. 2 win
>> NCAA championships for all other sports

DARKENED TOWER WITH WHITE CAP AND OBSERVATION DECK
Solemn Occasions
>> UT Remembers (annual memorial service)
>> Tower Garden Dedication
>> Significant solemn occasions, e.g. Texas A&M Bonfire Tragedy
>> Other occasions at the president's discretion

TOWER TOP SPLIT ORANGE AND WHITE WITH ORANGE SHAFT
Symbolic Campus Events
>> Gone to Texas—welcoming new students to campus
>> Other events at the president's discretion

"I asked them about me playing linebacker and whether or not they would move me," Robison said. "They told me that I was being recruited as a linebacker and that I was on their board as a linebacker. The only way they would move me is if I asked to be moved or if I got up to like 275 pounds and lost some of my speed and quickness."

So, what happened? After emerging as a starting linebacker as a redshirt freshman, Robison eventually moved to defensive end, where he earned at least honorable mention All-Big 12 honors for three straight seasons. A starter on the 2005 national championship team, Robison was a fourth round pick of the Minnesota Vikings, with whom he started five games as a rookie in 2007.

AARON ROSS—CORNERBACK—TYLER JOHN TYLER

The hype: After arriving in Austin as a member of the 2001 recruiting class in August, defensive back Ross was sent home after several practices because of NCAA Clearinghouse issues. It may have been an unprecedented situation; after Ross was accepted at Texas, the NCAA found that several of his high school credits from San Antonio did not transfer when he switched schools to Tyler. The star recruit was then forced to go back to high school. Having discharged this obligation, he returned to Texas as part of the 2002 recruiting class.

August 24, 2001: The Texas Longhorns will be without one of their top freshman for the entire 2001 season.

Longhorn head coach Mack Brown announced on Friday that freshman cornerback Aaron Ross will miss the season as he clears up some NCAA Clearinghouse issues.

"I have some (NCAA) Clearinghouse issues I need to get resolved in order to rejoin the team," said Ross, a six-foot-one, 180-pound defensive back. "I'm going to get those issues worked out so I can return to Texas in January."

Ross has been one of the top newcomers to the Longhorn team this fall and had figured to play as a true freshman.

December 16, 2001: You'll have to forgive Aaron Ross if he wasn't blown away by his official visit to Texas this weekend.

The truth is, Ross has been there and done that.

The six-foot-one, 180-pound Ross signed with Texas in February, but was forced to sit out the fall semester because of an NCAA Clearinghouse issue that centered on his transcript from San Antonio Fox Tech, the school that he attended before moving to Tyler.

"Basically, I was just trying to show Matthew Melton a good time this weekend," Ross said. "I'm just glad all this is over and I can get back. It was a pretty messed up situation."

Despite his bad fortune, Ross thinks he might be better off in the long run.

"It was probably better because I'll probably play all four years now," Ross said. "Jammer will be gone and there's a chance to play."

Ross is expected to battle with fellow true freshmen Cedric Griffin and Michael Huff for the vacated cornerback spot in the spring.

So, what happened? The former four-star prospect was forced to sit out another year before eventually arriving in 2003, where he made an immediate impact as a true freshman. As the school's No. 3 corner, Ross played a huge role in Texas's national championship season in 2006. A full-time starter for the first time in 20006, Ross earned consensus first-team All-America honors and was awarded the Jim Thorpe Award as the nation's top defensive back. After one of the biggest roller coaster rides that any Longhorn football player has ever ridden, Ross was a first round selection of the New York Giants in 2007. He earned a Super Bowl ring as a rookie.

LYLE SENDLEIN—DEFENSIVE TACKLE— SCOTTSDALE, ARIZONA

The hype: Sendlein followed his brother, Austin, to Texas as one of the top prospects in the state of Arizona. Although he was listed as a defensive tackle, the Longhorns had big plans for the underrated Sendlein.

June 3, 2001: The Texas Longhorns have picked up their fourth verbal commitment for the 2002 recruiting class.

According to his mother, Scottsdale (Arizona) Chaparral defensive tackle Lyle Sendlein committed to the Longhorns on Saturday.

"There's a new rule that says they can't offer anyone during the camp," Carrie Sendlein said. "They offered him yesterday and he's very excited that he's going to be a Longhorn."

The six-foot-four, 270-pound Sendlein, who is the son of former Texas star Robin Sendlein and brother of current UT linebacker Austin Sendlein, is regarded as one of the top players in the state of Arizona. He had offers from a host of national powerhouses.

"Robin is actually down in Austin right now and is celebrating with them," Mrs. Sendlein said.

So, what happened? Sendlein moved to the offensive line as soon as he arrived in Austin, later emerging as the best center Mack Brown ever had in his decade-long tenure in Austin. After starting in his final two seasons and earning All-Big 12 honors in both years, Sendlein was a rookie free agent pick-up of the Arizona Cardinals, with whom he made two starts in his first year in 2007.

GARNET SMITH—LINEBACKER— ARLINGTON LAMAR

The hype: Many considered Smith to be the top pure linebacker prospect in the Lone Star State in 2002. The four-star Smith was rated one of the nation's top ten outside linebackers, but he was probably better known for flip-flopping between Texas and Oklahoma for several months during the recruiting process.

October 30, 2001: Like sands through the hourglass....

In what has become one of the craziest recruiting stories in recent years, Arlington (Texas) Lamar linebacker Garnet Smith returned from his official visit to Tennessee this weekend as an uncommitted player.

There's no question that the past two months have been wild ones for Smith, and now there's reason to believe that the ride has only just begun.

Let's review.

On September 10, Smith made a commitment to Oklahoma, citing the Sooners defense and his relationship with Sooner assistant coach Brent Venables as the major reasons for his decision.

Two days later, Smith changed his mind and committed to Texas, claiming that his heart was in Austin and that his family wanted him to become a Longhorn.

For the past few weeks, Smith has openly talked about taking other official visits before he makes a final decision. His trip to Knoxville this weekend was the first of five scheduled visits.

"The visit went great," Smith said. "Being inside the stadium and seeing everything up close was great. It was a whole lot different that the other places I've seen. There's 108,000 people there for a 6:30 p.m. game. When I got there at 9:00 a.m., people were already tailgating. Just having a chance to do the Vol Walk with the players and watching their fans was great."

Smith said he had such a good time that he almost committed.

However, Tennessee coach Phil Fulmore told Smith to take his time and make his other visits before making yet another commitment.

"Yeah, he told me that I didn't need to be committed," Smith said. "He was real honest with me and I liked that."

When asked if that meant he was no longer a Texas commitment, Smith said yes.

"Based on my visit, you can say that," Smith said. "I still like Texas, but I'm leaning to Tennessee. I'm just being honest."

Smith added that he has scheduled official visits with Alabama, LSU, Oklahoma, and Florida in the coming weeks.

The omission of Texas on his official visit list is glaring.

"I'm not sure right now if I'm going to visit," Smith said. "I'm not sure how I feel about them."

> **"** It's only going to get better at Texas. We're going to compete for national championships every year. **"**

When asked if it was fair to say that the Longhorns were slipping on his list, Smith replied, "I would say they are definitely slipping. I'm just being honest about that."

December 16, 2001: There have been times this year when the status Garnet Smith seemed unclear.

But on Sunday night, Smith made it very clear that he's burnt orange through and through after his official visit to Austin this weekend.

"As far as I'm concerned, being down there at UT is the closest thing to heaven on Earth," Smith said. "This weekend was just incredible. The players all got along like we had known each other our whole lives. The players that are going to be in this class with me—guys like Aaron Harris and Matthew Melton are great players and great guys. This is going to be a great class."

According to Smith, the seventeen recruits that were on hand in Austin relished every second of the weekend.

"During the whole weekend we were always doing something together," Smith said. "Even when we were at the hotel, we were playing games. I don't think we ever slept. If we don't get every recruit that was there this weekend, I'll be shocked."

As for the possibility of taking other visits, Smith quickly nipped that in the bud.

"I'm finished with visits," Smith declared. "I didn't have the best season this year, and I wanted to prove that I'm the best linebacker in America. I'm going to a program that is going to allow me to prove that. It's only going to get better at Texas. We're going to compete for national championships every year."

So, what happened? After all the twists and turns of his recruitment, Smith ended up being a flash in the pan for the Longhorns. Although he emerged as a starter early in his career, injuries limited his progress, and he eventually decided to transfer.

KASEY STUDDARD—OFFENSIVE LINEMAN— LITTLETON, COLORADO

The hype: As the son of former Longhorn lineman Dave Studdard, Kasey was regarded as the best prospect in the state of Colorado and was recruited from coast-to-coast. A two-way star in high school, the four-star prospect was seen as someone that could excel on either side of the ball in college.

January 12, 2001: "I've made a decision and I have committed to play for Texas," Kasey Studdard has announced. "It came down to family and me following my heart. This was a really a tough decision for me. It's the hardest thing I've ever done.

The six-foot-two, 275-pound Studdard chose the Longhorns over Colorado, Miami, Tennessee, and a host of other major powers.

In reality, his recruitment ended up as a two-school battle between the Longhorns and Buffaloes.

"I hate having to tell them no, but my heart is at Texas," Studdard said. "I just feel like that's the best place for me."

Studdard added that last week's appearance in the U.S. Army All-Star Game in San Antonio helped push him over to the Longhorns. Counting Studdard, the Longhorns were represented by eight commitments in the game.

GAMEDAY HAUNTS

Best place to find a hot bowl of chili outside the stadium—**Texas Chili Parlor**—1409 Lavaca Street, (512) 472-2828

Best place for a man to get a shave or haircut before the game—**El Rey**—311 W 5th St # 100, (512) 472-5858

Best place to get away from football altogether—**Shady Grove**—1624 Barton Springs Rd., (512) 474-9991

"It was cool getting to hang with those guys," Studdard said. "Plus, I played real well and I proved to myself that I can play with anyone."

So, what happened? After moving to the offensive line on a full-time basis as a redshirt freshman, Studdard became a three-year starter for the Longhorns, emerging as a first-team All-Big 12 selection during his senior season in 2006. A sixth-round draft pick of the Houston Texans in 2007, Studdard played in three games in his first season.

DAVID THOMAS—TIGHT END—FRENSHIP

The hype: As the top tight end prospect in the state of Texas, Thomas was viewed as a must-have after posting outstanding numbers as a receiver at Frenship during his junior and senior seasons.

June 24, 2001: For the last few weeks, Wolfforth (Texas) Frenship tight end David Thomas has struggled to make a decision between his top three schools—Texas, Texas Tech, and Oklahoma.

When it was all said and done, Thomas just followed his heart.

"Everything was pretty even," Thomas said. "I have supported the Longhorns my whole life and when it was time to make a decision, I just couldn't say no to Texas."

The six-foot-three, 210-pound Thomas indicated that he had been leaning to Texas for a while and decided today to go ahead and make the call to the Texas coaching staff.

"I had probably known for the last week that I was going to commit to Texas," Thomas revealed. "I called them today and talked with Coach Brown and Coach Brewster. They seemed excited."

As far as his future position is concerned, Thomas said that the difference in systems ended up not playing a huge role in his decision.

"There were a few differences, but it doesn't matter whether I'm playing receiver or H-back or even a little tight end," Thomas said.

Thomas, who is the Longhorns' eighth verbal commitment, is considered by just about everyone to be the top "H-back" prospect in the state of Texas.

As a junior, he earned all-state honors after posting fifty-five receptions, 1,103 yards, and fourteen touchdowns.

So, what happened? Thomas eventually became the best tight end in the history of the Longhorn program, establishing records for receptions, receiving yards, and touchdowns at the position. Thomas was Vince Young's favorite target during the 2005 national championship run and became a third round draft pick of the New England Patriots.

ROBERT TIMMONS—WIDE RECEIVER— FLOWER MOUND MARCUS

Timmons had few peers when it came to pure talent. A sure-fire five-star prospect if not for his off-field issues, Timmons had been in trouble for much of his youth and was actually homeless at one point during high school. There probably wasn't a player in this class that was expected to contribute as much as a true freshman as the immensely skilled Timmons.

> **"If you look at the film you'll see me make linebackers collide in mid-air and people dive and miss. Just look at the film."**

May 11, 2001: Robert Timmons has heard all the comparisons, which make him smile just a little.

"I recruited Peter Warrick in high school and I never thought I would say it, but this kid is another Peter Warrick," one college coach said recently after visiting Flower Mound Marcus High School. "He has the same moves after the catch that Peter has."

"He is as good as Roy Williams minus three inches," Flower Mound Marcus coach Randy Mayes said. "I never thought I would coach another player like Roy, but I have been blessed again."

The comparisons to other receivers go on and on.

But who does Timmons himself think his game most mirrors?

"Style-wise, it's Peter Warrick all the way," Timmons remarked with a laugh. "If you look at the film you'll see me make linebackers collide in mid-air and people dive and miss. Just look at the film."

His on-field ability has assured that just about every big-time college program in the nation has walked through the doors at Marcus this year to take a look at the gifted receiver.

"I love Florida State to the fullest," said Timmons, whose only offer at the moment is from Texas A&M. "I really like Tennessee, too. I'm also looking at Kansas State and Georgia Tech. Those stand out to me right now."

February 4, 2002: It's been a long road at times for Robert Timmons.

However, after spending this weekend in Austin for his official visit, the talented receiver now knows that the path he is traveling runs straight through the University of Texas campus.

The six-foot-two, 200-pound Timmons committed to the Texas coaching staff after receiving an offer from Texas head coach Mack Brown on Sunday night.

Although Timmons was unavailable for comment, Marcus head coach Randy Mayes was able to confirm that his star pupil was walking around town with a burnt orange smile.

"This is good for Robert and it's good for Flower Mound Marcus," Mayes said. "Robert has had some difficult times, but this is a good situation for him."

Timmons is considered by most to be the Lone Star State's top wide receiver and is regarded as one of the top overall talents in the state.

So, what happened? Timmons played as a true freshman in 2002 and appeared to be a budding star for the Longhorns. However, after arguing with the coaching staff about his perceived lack of playing time, Timmons abruptly quit the team before the start of the 2003 season. He never resurfaced as a player anywhere else.

NEALE TWEEDIE—OFFENSIVE LINEMAN—ALLEN

The hype: This lineman from Allen was one of the first top national prospects to commit to the Longhorns. A two-way star in high school, Tweedie was projected as a franchise offensive left tackle prospect.

July 5, 2001: According to Allen, Texas offensive lineman Neale Tweedie, he knew from the first day that he visited the University of Texas that he would likely commit to the Longhorns when he was ready to make a decision.

The six-foot-four, 265-pound Tweedie set off some fireworks in the Texas football offices on July 4 with news of his verbal commitment to the Longhorns.

"Really, when I visited there early on in the recruiting process, I knew that Texas was where I wanted to go," Tweedie said. "Once I met the coaches and some of the players I felt the chemistry that they have, the bond between coaches and players. The only thing that kept me from committing then was that I had not seen any other schools up close."

After taking unofficial visits to Texas A&M and Notre Dame, Tweedie was ready to make a decision.

"I just figured I can't go wrong," Tweedie said. "They have always been a winning program and it just felt like the place for me. It really didn't take me long to make a decision."

Now that his decision has been made, Tweedie is turning his attention to his senior season.

"I'm just taking this one year at a time and right now I'm thinking about my senior year in high school," Tweedie stated. "When it comes time to go to college, it will come. But, with the new offense we have at Allen I'm really going to spend the rest of this summer working on getting stronger. I need to work on getting stronger in my upper body."

So, what happened? Tweedie never managed to add the weight needed to be a full-time offensive lineman. He eventually became a solid role player for the Longhorns at tight end, but was never a starter in Austin.

BRETT VALDEZ—OFFENSIVE LINEMAN— BROWNWOOD

The hype: The very first commitment in the 2002 recruiting class, Valdez was probably the least heralded of the linemen recruits that year.

THE RECRUITS, JANUARY 2002

Left to right: Kasey Studdard; Rodrique Wright; Vince Young; Seven future Longhorns

July 24, 2001: When Brownwood (Texas) offensive lineman Brett Valdez was trying to decide whether or not to accept an early scholarship offer from the University of Texas, he received some advice from an unlikely source.

An Aggie.

In fact, the advice came from an A&M football player of all people.

"Jared [Morris] is my best friend," Valdez declared. "When he was a senior and I was a freshman, we just started hanging out and have been best friends since then. He never pressured me to go to A&M, although he wanted me to go there and he said A&M was going to offer. He just told me that I needed to go where I felt I needed to be."

According to Valdez, only one place was right for him.

"I actually liked Florida State and might have committed if they had offered me early on," Valdez said. "But when I walking around the Texas campus, I knew Florida State was not the school for me. I know that I could spend five years at Texas and be happy."

Thus, despite the fact that Texas signed the best offensive line class in the country this past February, Valdez agreed to become the first Longhorn commitment of the 2002 recruiting class.

"I love competition, and if I didn't have good competition then I wouldn't be in a situation that will push me to become the best," Valdez said. "After my sophomore year I went up against most of those guys at the Texas summer camp. It helped me, knowing that I had worked against Jonathan Scott, Will Allen, Roman Reeves, and Mike Garcia. I went up against every one of them, and I know what's ahead of me."

Another reason Valdez found Texas so attractive was the relationship he has developed with the Longhorn coaching staff.

"I wouldn't want to play for any other coach than Mack Brown," Valdez said. "I think me and Coach Brown had a good connection from the start. He's someone that I want to win for. When they offered me in March, he told me that they wouldn't likely offer another guy on the line until June."

So, what happened? Although he was very popular among his teammates, Valdez never made a big impact on the two-deep as an offensive lineman. He finished out his entire football career in Austin.

MICHAEL WILLIAMS—LINEBACKER—LINDALE

The hype: This small town prospect seemingly emerged out of thin air during the fall of 2001 to become one of the most highly recruited players in Texas. He sparked a particularly ferocious recruiting battle between Texas and Oklahoma.

January 6, 2002: After months of deliberation, it appears that the Texas Longhorns have finally won the recruiting battle for Lindale, Texas linebacker Michael Williams.

"I committed to Texas today," Williams said. "I'm a Longhorn."

The star linebacker committed to Texas after his mother and grandmother visited the Forty Acres this weekend to take a closer look at the Longhorn program.

"My mom went down there this weekend and that's kind of what I've been waiting for," Williams said. "She wanted to see the school for herself and I wanted her approval."

The six-foot-four, 225-pound Williams, who is one of the Lone Star State's top defensive players, has been trying to choose between Texas and Oklahoma for several months. He said the recent talk of Oklahoma coach Bob Stoops leaving for Florida didn't help the Sooners cause, although he admitted that he had been leaning toward the Longhorns for a while now.

"I don't want to go somewhere where there's not any stability," Williams said. "I know that Mack Brown's not going anywhere."

So, what happened? Williams went through a roller coaster career with the Longhorns before transferring to Texas College in 2005, where he earned All-Conference honors. He played linebacker in nine games for the Longhorns as a true freshman before being moved to defensive end. As a sophomore in 2003, Williams posted six sacks and fifteen pressures in a back-up role. He missed the 2004 season with the Longhorns due to academics.

RODRIQUE WRIGHT—DEFENSIVE TACKLE— ALIEF HASTINGS

The hype: At one point in the recruiting process Wright was ranked as the state's top prospect, a title he earned until Vince Young took it from him with a sensational senior season. Wright was a five-star prospect and one of the nation's top two defensive tackles.

December 17, 2001: Heading into this weekend's visit to Texas, Alief (Texas) Hastings defensive tackle Rodrique Wright knew he favored the Longhorns over the other schools he was considering, but the idea of a commitment seemed a little far-fetched.

My, how things can change over the course of a weekend.

"The visit was fun and I could tell that they really wanted me," Wright said. "I wanted to stay close to home, play in a winning program, and get a good degree. If you put all of those together, it made sense for me to commit."

The six-foot-five, 330-pound Wright said that the chemistry among the players was one of the most impressive parts of his visit.

"I probably liked just hanging out with the guys the most," Wright said. "My host was Kalen Thornton, and we hung out with Cory Redding almost the whole time. There was a group of us that were not committed that really hung out with each other. Larry Dibbles, Travis Leitko, and Justin Blalock all talked a lot this weekend, and I wouldn't be surprised if we all ended up there. We really started to bond while we were there."

According to Wright, he's looking forward to the opportunity of getting back together with his new crew of friends.

"In two weeks we'll be together again for the All-Star Game in San Antonio," Wright said. "I was talking to Dibbles, Leitko, Aaron Harris, and a few others, and we're all going to be playing in the game together. We'll probably bind even more while we're there."

While Wright didn't expect to leave town yesterday committed, a conversation with Texas head coach Mack Brown helped change his mind.

"I was the last person to meet with Coach Brown," Wright said. "I really thought I would take a couple more trips because I had those visit dates set. But, after I spoke with Coach Brown, I met alone with my parents, separate from the coaches, and we just figured it would be a waste of time to visit those other schools if I already knew where I wanted to go. That's when I decided to commit."

So, what happened? A three-time consensus All-Big 12 selection, Wright earned consensus All-America honors as a senior and was a finalist for the Lombardi Award. Wright started in forty-five career games and compiled 227 tackles, seventeen-and-a-half sacks, forty-two tackles for loss, sixty-seven quarterback pressures, and six forced fumbles. He also earned Big 12 Defensive Freshman of the Year honors in 2002. Wright was selected in the seventh round of the 2005 NFL draft by the Miami Dolphins.

SELVIN YOUNG—RUNNING BACK—JERSEY VILLAGE

The hype: Young was the state's top running back prospect, rated the nation's No. 5 player at his position by Rivals.com.

December 19, 2001—The Texas Longhorns are on a roll.

Hours after picking up a commitment from one of the nation's top defensive tackle prospects in Mesquite, Texas star Marco Martin, the Longhorns scored yet another major commitment when Jersey Village, Texas running back Selvin Young announced his decision to become a Longhorn.

"I thought about it a lot," Young said. "I prayed about it a lot at night, and I know it's the right choice. I'm real excited about it."

The six-foot, 195-pound Young selected the Longhorns over Oklahoma and Colorado, among others.

"I've liked them since my sophomore year," Young said. "I've just always wanted to go there and now I'm a Longhorn.

Young was one of seventeen prospects who attended the Longhorns' biggest recruiting weekend of the year this past weekend in Austin. The relationships built there turned out to be a major factor in Young's decision.

"I bonded down there with those guys last weekend," Young said. "That's really what did it. I'm not really a people person, but your football team has to be a family and that's what they have down there. Everyone believes in one another and that's how you win."

So, what happened? Young was one of the true feel-good stories from this class. Despite battling a number of injuries and having some academic problems at Texas, Young eventually emerged as a starter on the 2005 national championship team. After his career at Texas concluded, he made the Denver Broncos roster as an undrafted free agent and started eight games as a rookie in 2007.

VINCE YOUNG—QUARTERBACK— HOUSTON MADISON

The hype: During his senior season Young emerged as the nation's top overall prospect, enticing tens of thousands to his games each week to see his next miracle play. He was the most high-profile recruit in the history of the city of Houston, and probably the most highly-recruited player ever signed by

VINCE YOUNG, who changed the face of Texas football

the Texas program. His arrival signaled a new era in Texas football.

August 21, 2001: With just two weeks to go until his first game of the season, Houston (Texas) Madison quarterback Vincent Young is in the process of fine tuning his game for the season opener.

"We had a scrimmage this weekend against Houston Washington," Young said. "Things went alright. I ran for a score and was eight of eleven throwing the ball. I thought we did okay."

Young open his season with a home game on September 7 against Aldine.

As far as recruiting goes, Young continues to maintain that there's not much to report.

"It's the same six schools," Young said. "Miami, Florida State, Texas, LSU, Kansas State, and Southern Miss."

When told that it had been reported on several occasions that Texas was no longer under consideration, Young seem surprised.

"They have always been on my list," Young said.

Young was then asked if he felt like the Longhorns were still serious contenders for his signature in February.

"Yeah, they have a fair shot," Young said. "Really, I'm just wide open and don't have a favorite right now. The schools are all the same."

January 13, 2002: It's all about the love.

Whether it was from the Texas players, coaches, or fans, Vincent Young received a lot of love on his official visit to Austin this weekend.

"There's a lot of love down there at Texas, and that's what I was looking for before I visited," Young said. "They made my mom smile and that's all I needed to see. I committed to them this afternoon."

In landing the six-foot-five, 190-pound Young, the Longhorns picked up the nation's top overall prospect and a player that could possibly add dimensions to the Longhorn's offense that have never been seen in Austin.

"Coach Brown came into a meeting with the quarterbacks on Saturday and told me right away that he didn't want me as a wide receiver or a defensive back," Young said. "He wanted me as a quarterback. That's exactly what I wanted to hear."

According to Young, the visit was a great chance for him to learn more about the program, but it also turned out to be an introduction to Longhorn fans.

During halftime of Saturday's Texas-Baylor basketball game, Young received a standing ovation from the Erwin Center crowd when he walked courtside on his way out of the arena.

"I was a little embarrassed, but I loved it," Young said. "Coach Brown told me that any time I want to give the fans some love to just show the 'Hook 'em' and that's what I did."

Young added that the chemistry between the players and coaches was another factor in his decision.

"The chemistry was just great," Young said. "I got along with all the players. B. J. [Johnson] was my host and I hung out mostly with the receivers."

So, what happened? Developing into arguably the best player in the history of the Texas program, Young changed the entire culture of the Longhorn program. As a junior in 2005, he led the 'Horns to their first national championship since 1970 and finished second in the Heisman Trophy balloting. He won numerous other major awards, set a host of Longhorn records, and ended his career at Texas with a surreal 30–2 record as a starter. He was the No. 3 overall pick of the 2006 NFL draft by the Tennessee Titans, and he quickly emerged as one of professional football's most dynamic young talents.

Chapter Eight

BACK IN PASADENA
THE 2005 LONGHORNS

O n a sultry summer night in the heart of Austin, Texas, the booming sounds coming from a snow white new model Cadillac Escalade drowned out the sounds of intense, heavy breathing.

Under the bright lights that surrounded the practices fields at the University of Texas, nearby cars sped by along the adjacent I-35 overpass, creating a white noise effect behind the shaking baselines that poured from the makeshift practice sound system.

It was a strange sight—vehicles full of Longhorn players moved through the parking lot and straight onto the field. There, some players were already warming up for the night's workout, while others relaxed to the music blasting from one of the player's cars.

An incoming freshman approached senior cornerback Cedric Griffin, who was standing in line waiting for his next warm-up rep. As Griffin stared intently ahead at the action in front of him, nothing could break his concentration from the anticipation of his next battle.

After several failed opportunities to grab Griffin's attention, the precocious freshman stepped aside, realizing the hopelessness of any attempts to engage in friendly banter with his new teammate.

Moments later Griffin was standing inches across from sophomore wide receiver Limas Sweed, who had earlier caught a quick slant against him.

Seconds before Griffin was set to resume sparring with Sweed, a voice boomed across the field that could be heard over both the music of Mike Jones and a loud honk from a semi-truck traveling on the upper deck of the highway.

"Hey Ced, are you ready? I don't think you're ready," Vince Young, the team's leader, shouted in his immediate direction.

For just a moment, Griffin's concentration was broken as he glanced at Young and flashed a slight hint of a smile. However, in the time it might have taken to decipher whether or not Griffin had given way to Young's taunt, the action began with the suddenness of the gates opening at a horse track.

As both players engaged in a game of cat and mouse, Sweed made a move toward the outside boundary. Turning his shoulders back toward Young, Sweed saw the ball was already in mid-flight. Just as Sweed lifted his hands to receive the pass, Griffin surged in front of him and knocked the ball violently to the ground.

"I came here to work," Griffin commented seriously to nobody in particular.

Within seconds, Griffin was mobbed by fellow defensive backs who wanted to revel in his deft defense of Young's aerial assault. After a series of high-fives, Griffin skied into the air and collided in celebration with one last teammate.

It was Young.

Suddenly, as a different Mike Jones song began broadcasting across the field, Young was back among offensive teammates, trying to lure junior offensive lineman Kasey Studdard into helping him turn the practice field into a well-lit dance floor.

As a team, this group of Longhorns had arrived with the intent of accomplishing two things—they were going to work *and* party.

OUT WITH THE OLD SCHOOL, IN WITH THE NEW

Nearly eight months after its Rose Bowl victory over Michigan, which represented not only the school's first BCS win but also the most important victory in Mack Brown's coaching career, this team had settled into a comfort zone. For most of the decade the program had been consumed with beating Oklahoma, but this group had been liberated of that particular obsession.

If previous Longhorn teams had been distracted by the glaring media spotlight that comes with playing college football in Austin, this group seemed not to mind the attention. The tense, white-knuckled approach that had prevailed among the team for years was suddenly replaced by a carefree, loose, and easy style.

The preseason expectations of the Longhorns were so high that they bordered on unrealistic. The only way this team was going to exceed them all was for the players to bond tightly, turning the team into a single, inseparable unit. The process began with these summer workouts, whose atmosphere often resembled that of a summer cookout. Former Texas quarterback Matt Nordgren, a senior then, recalls the scene:

> The difference was in those seven-on-seven's that year. Everybody was there, I'm not kidding you. The offensive and defensive lines were out there doing pass rush and pass sets. Every night, everybody made every workout. It was like a party. Every night we were out there. Everyone's friends were out there. The music was playing. It was such a fun deal. Everybody fell in love with playing football with those guys.
>
> It got to the point where nobody wanted to miss anything because the coaches couldn't make us accountable. Nobody could make us accountable except for ourselves. What you didn't want to

do was not be there when everyone else was there. It wasn't just once, either. Every single time, guys were out there just battling. Nobody wanted to drop a ball or bust an assignment because every person on the team was out there busting their butt.

After dropping only one game in 2004—a 12–0 loss against Oklahoma in the Cotton Bowl—Texas was an overwhelming favorite in 2005 to win the Big 12, even if the Longhorns had yet to accomplish the feat under Mack Brown's direction.

The burnt orange faithful had grown accustomed to "close, but no cigar" kind of seasons, but everything seemed to change following Young's five-touchdown performance against Michigan.

On that first day of January 2005, no sooner had Dusty Mangum's field goal squeaked through the uprights to give Texas an exhilarating win than Young was already establishing the team's goal for the next year: return to the Rose Bowl.

Pasadena was the site of the 2005 Rose Bowl, and was also slated to host the national championship game the following season.

"*We'll be baaaack*," Young intoned during the victory celebrations.

That vow echoed throughout Austin for eight months leading up to the start of the 2005 season.

With a majority of the previous year's starters returning for another season, including Young and a bevy of future high NFL draft picks, the Longhorns expected a big season. There were also high hopes for younger players such as running back Ramonce Taylor and wide receiver Limas Sweed, who were expected to upgrade the team's playmaking ability.

"I remember back in the beginning when we were in six o'clock workouts and nobody was showing up late and nobody missed workouts," says David Thomas, then an All-Big 12 tight end on the team. "There was a lot of self-policing among us to make sure that everyone was showing up on time and everyone was doing their work. I think when we beat Michigan and won our first BCS game that kind of got us going and it gave us a taste of the big stage.

Knowing that we had been there and that the national championship was being played there the next year, that experience motivated us a lot."

"I think what was different is that there were a lot of returning guys," adds Nordgren. "We had only lost a few guys from the previous year. I think it was Derrick Johnson and Cedric Benson, and that was about it. For the most part the core of the team was intact. Even more important was the fact that we had an established offensive line, which anyone who knows anything about football will tell you is the most important thing. We were really confident that we could run the football and throw. We knew that we would have the time to do whatever we needed to do. Quite frankly, that might have been one of the greatest offensive lines in the history of the game."

If the immense amount of talent wasn't enough to signify that this Longhorn squad was about to transcend every team that had graced the Forty Acres since Richard Nixon was in office, then the confidence displayed by their head coach should have.

> **"Quite frankly, that might have been one of the greatest offensive lines in the history of the game."**

For years Mack Brown had walked the Longhorn sidelines with a persona that reflected that of his team. Although a great coach in his own right, Brown's resume lacked a championship pedigree, which made him a perfect ambassador for a program that many across the country felt was a historic underachiever.

Over the course of the seven previous seasons in Austin, the constant smile that Brown once wore gradually gave way to a tight-lipped sense of urgency. While a lot of top coaches are motivated largely by individual glory, Brown primarily wanted a championship to reward the starving Longhorn faithful for their decades of patience.

Traditionally, Brown had kept tight control over the reigns of the club. But a funny thing happened in the very early stages of the 2005 season.

Brown let go.

"In years past you could sense how serious he was before games," recalls Texas wide receiver Brian Carter, then a fifth-year senior. "I'm not saying that

LONGHORN COACH Mack Brown, who in 2005 eased up on his control of the squad

he wasn't serious that season, but he just seemed much looser and I think that really radiated throughout all of us."

Indeed, no sooner had the Longhorns resumed workouts together in August than Brown proved his willingness to allow Young and Co. all the freedom they needed.

"We've even played some music to start practice because they said they needed to have a little beat started before practice starts, and it's fun if they want to do that," Brown commented after one of the first practices. He then explained the reason for his cool demeanor leading up to the season opener against Louisiana-Lafayette on September 3: with sixteen returning starters and NFL talent dripping from the two-deep, he was confident in his team.

And of course, he had a special talent leading the squad.

"It's fun to have a mature guy that's not [just] surviving at quarterback," Brown said of Young. "He's getting better every play and Vince makes them compete and get after it. He is like the coach on the field."

This was Young's team, and Brown wasn't about to micromanage the personality right out of his players. Not with this group. The old school method of trying to mold a team's collective character to fit his own vision had repeatedly failed. Yes, he still preferred conservative game plans and disliked the thought of living on the edge with young players. But Brown understood that with a player like Young leading the team, he could afford to let the players have some more say in how the squad was run.

The leadership on this team was different than any he had coached previously. Perhaps the single biggest contribution Brown made that season was his acceptance that this team didn't need to be pushed or prodded in the usual ways. As soon as the decisions about the two-deep were finalized in August, Brown backed off in a way that would have made Bear Bryant cringe. Nordgren recalls the change:

> It's funny because not one time in the season during practice did we hit with pads. We never wore pads. The last month of the season we probably didn't even wear shoulder pads. We were in shells maybe the first week of practice and maybe some the second week, but for the most part we never hit. We never tackled, we never ran before practice, we never ran after practice, and we never ran during practice. We just ran our plays and we were feeling good. Every play was run at the same speed as it would be run in a game because nobody was tired. When we got to the game, because nobody was hurt or tired, we could go out and run 100 plays at absolute full speed for the entire game, and we never got tired.

Nordgren smiles at the thought that this approach flies in the face of every old coaching rule in the book.

"Even on Wednesday practices we'd spend half of the day in the bubble," Nordgren says with a laugh. "We'd be inside and in the air conditioning getting ready to play, with unlimited amounts of water, Gatorade, and gum. It was like a country club. A lot of coaches would say, 'That isn't the way we want to operate. We want to run sprints after practice. We want to put pads on so that we can hit.' But you know what? When we got to game days, nobody was hurt and everybody had fresh legs."

Carter concurs:

> Coach Brown did a good job that year of taking it easy on us. We would rarely practice during the season in full pads. There were times when we would just be in our shorts during practice. The main thing is that we were fresh. Our practices weren't that intense, but when we did work we worked hard. I think our overall workout ethic, as well as our talent, really was the key ingredient.

As the preseason came to a close amidst high expectations, Longhorn fans looked forward to putting the team's new training regime to the test.

LET THE GAMES BEGIN

Any doubts Brown may have had about the team's laid-back style quickly disappeared in the first few weeks of the season.

In what can only be described as a light tune-up for a showdown with Ohio State slated for the following week, the Longhorns blasted Louisiana Lafayette, 60–3, in Austin to open the 2005 season.

"I felt like it was a perfect opener for us," Brown said after the game. "We were ready to play. I thought our guys were in great shape. We played everyone that was eligible....Our players were a lot better than Louisiana-Lafayette's."

There could be no denying that, as Young completed thirteen of fifteen passes for 173 yards, while accounting for four touchdowns in helping Texas build a 39–3 lead at the half.

With Young and the rest of the starters on the sideline midway through the third quarter, the only real significance of the second half was the showcasing of Texas freshman running back Jamaal Charles.

A native of Port Arthur, Texas, the highly recruited Charles represented the program's best chance at replacing the productivity of Doak Walker Award winner Cedric Benson, who had been a top-five pick in the NFL draft that spring. Although he had never played in a college game before the 2005 season opener, Charles possessed the kind of speed that could change the complexion of a game in the blink of an eye.

While the initial game was a walk-through for most players, it was a baptism by fire for Charles, who was expected to play a prominent role in the looming match-up with the Buckeyes.

For years, Brown had seemed to subscribe to Joe Paterno's classic theory that every freshman in your line-up meant a loss on your schedule. Heck, this was the same Mack Brown who refused to start Cedric Benson back in 2001 until after the team lost to Oklahoma.

Yet at the start of the 2005 season, Brown swore to the media that Charles would be a factor from day one. And indeed he was, rushing for 135 yards with a touchdown in his Longhorn debut.

Fellow freshman Henry Melton added sixty-five yards and two touchdowns on just six carries.

"They're freshmen, but they're unusual freshmen," Texas offensive coordinator Greg Davis noted after the game. "I think they will continue to get better."

FRESHMAN RUNNING BACK Jamaal Charles was expected to make an immediate impact for the Longhorns in his first season

Having easily dispatched the Ragin' Cajuns, the Longhorns turned their attention to the game that was already highly anticipated throughout the nation.

INTO THE LION'S DEN: UT VS. OHIO STATE

To suggest that by 2005 the Oklahoma Sooners had become a concern for everyone that sported burnt orange would be an understatement for the ages. One of the great sidebars to the run for the national championship in 2005 is the way the Longhorn program was able to turn the page on its fixation with the Sooners without first defeating its arch-rival.

Whether it was the memory of the win over Michigan or the focus on the early season match-up with the Buckeyes, there was unusually little talk about the Sooners in the off-season. In the wake of five consecutive losses to Bob Stoops's juggernaut, it almost seems absurd to argue that the Longhorn Nation had simply gotten over several of the most embarrassing losses in school history.

63–14. 65–13. Those weren't scores from previous games as much as they were four-letter words in Austin that might lead to a child's mouth getting washed out with soap.

Yet strangely, in the summer of 2005, 'Horn fans overlooked OU and concentrated on Jim Tressell's boys at Ohio State. In an era where cross-regional match-ups between national powerhouses had gone the way of the giant otter, the contest between the No. 2 Longhorns and No. 4 Buckeyes served as a national championship elimination game. The Longhorns could conceivably still get to Pasadena if they lost to the Buckeyes, but Texas's destiny would lie outside of its own control.

"Thank goodness both of these teams are rated in the top 10, so if something is going to happen to one of the two, it is not going to put you out of the mix for the rest of the year," Brown said during the week of the game. "You will still be within reason and have very difficult conference schedules that can still get you back up there. Until we see a playoff system of some type, I do not think we will see any more games like this."

The 'Horns were facing a formidable Ohio State team that would produce twenty NFL draft picks over the following three years. Texas was also battling history, as no team had ever beaten the Buckeyes at the Ohio State stadium at night. The game would be broadcast nationwide, giving the entire college football world a chance to see what these Longhorns were made of. The Texas players seemed to revel in the challenge.

"We like playing on the road," junior offensive tackle Justin Blalock declared prior to the game. "I'm not sure why. Last year it was our personality and going into other stadiums and being spit on and yelled at was motivation. We just soaked it up and said, 'Bring it on.' It's just an attitude thing. We just want to use it to push us in the game."

Looking back, Carter agrees that the players thrived on the enmity of opposing fans:

> One of the things that I can just remember very vividly is just the excitement of being on the road. Honestly, I liked playing on the road better than at home because when you're on the road it's just the players and the coaches. It's a hostile environment and everyone has to come together. There was just something about running out in that big stadium and having everyone boo you. There's something about running into a stadium and having 80,000 people yelling at you.

As it turned out, an Ohio State-record 105,565 people showed up to jeer the 'Horns in the big showdown. Thomas recalls the intimidating scene:

> One of the things I'll always remember is when the captains walked out through the door and saw the crowd situation, and what it was going to look like playing in the Horseshoe. Just the four of us all

THIRD-YEAR SOPHOMORE
Billy Pittman is off to the races in the first quarter of Texas's game against Ohio State

Photo courtesy of *Dave Campbell's Texas Football*

walking out together and seeing how big the crowd was, that has always stayed in my mind.

If the Longhorns were being led into the lion's den on a still Columbus night, their opening drives sent the message that they wouldn't go down without a fight.

After traveling nearly the length of the field and kicking a field goal on their first possession, the Longhorns struck gold on their second drive when Young capped a 12-play, 84-yard march with a five-yard touchdown pass to Billy Pittman.

The first quarter was all Texas. Before halftime, however, the Buckeyes scored sixteen unanswered points on three field goals and a touchdown. The Longhorns' 10–0 lead turned into a 16–10 deficit, as the Ohio State defense settled in and began defending Young's scrambling, while the Buckeye offense started to click behind the play of second-string quarterback Troy Smith. The future Heisman Trophy winner had started for the Buckeyes in 2004, but a two-game suspension issued before that season's Alamo Bowl game had kept Smith off the field for Ohio State's 2005 season opener. Senior Justin Zwich had started that game as well as the Longhorns match-up, but Smith started getting the majority of the snaps as the game moved into the second quarter.

With only thirty-one seconds remaining in the half, Texas took over at their own 46-yard line. That was enough time for Charles to take a screen pass from Young, break several tackles, and pick up thirty-six yards to put the 'Horns in scoring position.

Two plays later, senior David Pino connected on a 37-yard field goal to cut the lead to 16–13 as time expired in the half.

The two teams played serve and volley at the beginning of the third quarter, as Ohio State kicker Josh Huston kicked his fourth field goal of the game, while Pino added his third to make it 19–16, Buckeyes.

Another Ohio State field goal later increased their lead to 22–16. Then, with a little over five minutes remaining in the game, a pivotal moment occurred.

With the Buckeyes facing a third and goal from the Texas 5-yard line, Zwick returned to the field and seemed to connect with senior tight end Ryan Hamby for a touchdown that would have given the Buckeyes a two-possession lead. However, Hamby struggled to hold onto the ball. As he tried to ensnare the pass, Cedric Griffin came across the back of the end zone and nearly decapitated the Buckeye tight end, who dropped the ball harmlessly on the turf.

Young now had a chance to make the Buckeyes pay for their mistake. Trailing 22–16, he entered the Longhorn huddle with 5:00 remaining in the game. The Longhorns were sixty-seven yards from paydirt.

After allowing Young to break for a series of big runs early in the game, the Ohio State defense, led by future first round picks A.J. Hawk and Bobby Carpenter, had done a terrific job of forcing him to rely on the passing game.

The strategy had worked for more than half the game, but with the clock winding down, Young flipped the switch and once again established his dominance. Carter remembers the moment:

> When we ran on the field, it was like we already knew that we were about to go score. When Vince got in the huddle, man, he's got this confidence that everyone feeds on. I just remember running onto the field thinking, "We're about to go score right now." Everyone was just real calm and confident. There were no worries.
>
> I remember being in the huddle and you could just feel the crowd and the tension and the stress. The crowd was overbearing. Maybe that was just me, because I was a little older, but the overall feel was that, "Hey, this is what we do. There's three minutes to go, we're down by a touchdown—we need to go score." We just started moving the ball. We knew that they were vulnerable. We just knew that we had to execute.

After twice converting third down situations into a new set of downs, Young was looking at a second and nine situation from the Ohio State 24-yard line with less than three minutes remaining.

Facing a similar situation against Michigan in the Rose Bowl, Young had used his legs to carry the day. Yet on this spectacular fall night, watched by a good part of the college football world, Young showed everyone just how adept he'd become at the passing game.

With absolute perfect protection from his front line, Young dropped a pass at the corner of the end zone into the hands of a back-peddling Sweed. And just like that, the Longhorns tied the game.

Vince Young had struck again.

After Pino added an extra point to give the 'Horns a 23–22 lead, the Texas defense stepped up and ensured that Young's late-game heroics wouldn't be wasted. They forced a Zwick fumble and later sacked him in the end zone for a safety to secure a 25–22 Texas victory.

"I was the first one to get to him in the end zone," says Thomas, describing Sweed's climactic touchdown. "That was such a big play for him. That was probably the biggest play he had made at that point in his career. The fact that we won, I was so proud of him for stepping up on such a big stage."

The moment was memorable for Nordgren as well:

> I'll never forget Vince throwing that pass in the back of the end zone to Sweed. I was a little bit on the edge of my seat. It was so loud. I called the plays into Vince, and Greg [Davis] would call the plays down to me through the headphones. You couldn't even hear the play call through the headphones. That's how loud it was. Vince is just one of these guys that really doesn't care about the defense. He'll throw the ball anywhere. He reads the entire field. He just decided that he was going to throw it up. There really was no reason for it because Limas was double-covered and the route wasn't as long as it's supposed to be, but he just threw it up to his guy and said we'll see what the hell happens.

Although the late-game magic was nothing new for Young, it served as a great confidence boost for the emerging Sweed. The former Brenham star had been a dynamic prospect when he arrived at Texas in 2003, but his development had been a bit slower than some had hoped. Yet with the spotlight shining on him, Sweed made a catch that fundamentally changed how he was viewed around the nation.

"That was probably the biggest play he had made at that point in his career."

"I think that was probably the defining point in Limas' career," Nordgren says. "I think before that, he was probably a little tentative with his play, but he wasn't yet in the national spotlight. What that did was not only give us confidence in Limas, but it gave Limas confidence in himself. At that point in the season, that allowed us to have a big-play receiver. That play launched him and launched us."

Of course, the Longhorns had no illusions that the wild win would mollify their detractors. "I don't think you ever silence critics anymore," Brown told reporters after the game. "Critics are critics because they're called critics, and that's what they're paid for. We have to go back and beat Rice next week and there will be critics in the morning."

Nevertheless, the nation was forced to take notice that the 'Horns had shocked the Buckeyes in their own house. Nordgren maintains that winning that game was "the craziest thing we had ever done." Above all, he credits one man for the victory:

I think honestly it goes back to Vince Young and the way that he was able to turn this into a player's team. At any point when there might have been a reason for nervousness or if hesitation might came, if it was a big play or a big drive or a big game, everyone just rallied around him. Everyone would just look at Vince and he would have the calmest look on his face. It was like he was back to being fifteen years old and playing football in his backyard back in Houston.

According to Thomas, the victory gave the Longhorns confidence looking ahead to their upcoming games:

We knew that we were going to set ourselves up pretty good if we won that game. We knew going into that game that they were probably going to be one of the best teams in the country and if we could beat them then we could probably play with anybody. We approached that game like it was a one-game season and it was the most important game of the year. That was probably one of the most difficult environments I have ever played in. It's such a big stadium and we were playing at night. With all of those people and with the way that stadium is built, it's really loud. Just being in such a hostile environment really prepared us for everything that awaited us for the rest of the season.

With the Buckeyes out of the way, the No. 2 Longhorns were off and running toward the Rose Bowl.

EXORCISING THE GHOST: UT VS. OKLAHOMA

In the following two weeks, the Longhorns pummeled Rice 51–10 and then opened up their Big 12 schedule by crushing Missouri 51–20 on the road.

As the Longhorns put points on the scoreboard at a dizzying rate, the defense began to settle in under new defensive coordinator Gene Chizik.

Up next for the Longhorns was the one team that had served as Brown's kryptonite for the last five years—the Oklahoma Sooners. Although the Sooners entered the game with two losses, this was still a match-up that haunted the Longhorns. The week of the game, Coach Brown told the media that his lack of success against OU made him "feel like I've let our team down and the school in this game."

The players, however, didn't seem weighed down by recent history. As Nordgren remembers,

> We were just a bunch of kids having fun. We might as well have been playing the games on Wednesdays. We were just having so much fun that it didn't matter who we were playing or where were playing. Coach Davis would always say before games when he wanted to fire us up, "You can go mark it off in the parking lot. You can go draw up the boundaries in the parking lot and we'll go play right now." That's how we were at that time. It didn't matter that we were playing Oklahoma.

In the final days before the game, Young flashed some frustration over all the hype about the 'Horns-Sooners rivalry.

"I'm just ready to play," he told the media that week. "I'm ready to get out there and make some noise, just to answer all of the people that are thinking that Texas might go out there and be uptight with it. I'm just looking forward to getting ready to play the game. I just want to get out there and get this game over with because everyone gets crazy about the OU-Texas game."

On the opening drive of the game, the Longhorns served notice that their long offensive drought against Stoops's defenders was a thing of the past. After being shut out by Oklahoma the previous season, the Longhorns traveled eighty-two yards on their opening possession to take a 7–0 lead on Young's 15-yard touchdown pass to Ramonce Taylor.

As Carter recalls, the quick score proved that the Longhorns were no longer facing the unbeatable Sooner juggernaut of previous years:

> You could pretty much tell as soon as the game started that this was a different Oklahoma team than in years past. They just didn't have the firepower. Their line wasn't that strong. Adrian Peterson was hurt as well. They had a freshman quarterback. Honestly, they were just like another team. The fact that it was Oklahoma made it even sweeter, but I honestly think we were so focused that we weren't caught up with what had happened last year or in any other year. We were focused on the next team we were playing and we just wanted to go out and execute.

If Taylor's touchdown sent a message, then a series of big plays from the Longhorn offense later in the first half served as knockout punches.

First, Charles spun free of a potential tackler at the end of the first quarter and raced eighty yards to give the Longhorns a 14–6 lead.

After a 37-yard field goal from Pino extended the Texas lead to 17–6, the 'Horns delivered a devastating blow in the final seconds of the second quarter. With less than thirty seconds remaining in the half and the Longhorns facing a first and fifteen from their own 36-yard line, basic strategy called for Texas to take a knee and carry their 11-point lead into the locker room.

SENIOR DEFENSIVE TACKLE Rod Wright had a big game against Oklahoma, including a 67-yard touchdown run

However, Texas offensive coordinator Greg Davis had different plans. He wanted to go for OU's jugular right then and there.

"That might have been his most unbelievable play-calling that I've ever seen," Nordgren claims. "Everything that he called was open. Literally, we ran fifteen plays in that game that we had never run before in his entire career. Every time he called a play, he knew it was going to work."

As the clock ticked down, Young slowly rolled to his left and threw deep to a wide open Pittman along the Texas sideline. When Young first released the ball, it appeared as if he might have overthrown his intended receiver. But as the ball hung up in the air, the speedy sophomore receiver ran underneath it and hauled it in.

Before Pittman even reached the end zone, his right hand flashed the "Hook 'em" sign to the Texas fans who were already celebrating in the stands.

"That was a great example right there of just how great [Davis's] play-calling was," Nordgren says. "Literally, that play we ran before the half, we'd never run before, ever. We saved it for that game and he saved it for the right, exact time."

That play, giving Texas a 24–6 lead, effectively ended the game even before halftime. In the final thirty minutes, the deflated Sooners only served as stress relief for the Longhorns, who relished dishing out a little bit of the pain that Oklahoma had been inflicting on them for years.

As the Texas offense continued to put points on the scoreboard, the defense pounded Sooner quarterback Rhett Bomar into the ground. After hitting Bomar time and again, Texas defensive end Brian Robison emphatically punctuated the butt-kicking with a bone-jarring shot to Bomar's body that forced a fumble. It was scooped up by senior defensive tackle Rod Wright and returned sixty-seven yards for a touchdown.

For Thomas, the 45–12 victory over the Sooners was a standout moment in the season. "We had never walked off the field from the Cotton Bowl still undefeated, so it was a huge burden off our shoulders," he declares. "The seniors that year were really proud that we had broken that streak. I remember singing 'The Eyes of Texas' to all our fans and feeling how full of excitement the Texas side was, and then running into the tunnel where the Oklahoma fans were and seeing how empty it was. That was a proud moment for me."

As Nordgren recalls, the win over Oklahoma got some Longhorns thinking about the likelihood of ending the season with a Bowl Championship Series game. "It was awesome and I think that getting that monkey off our back helped us throughout the rest of the year," Nordgren says. "It was the same every year. It was either going to be us or Oklahoma that played in a BCS game every year, so it was almost like whoever won that game was going to have an excellent shot at winning out the rest of the year, and to be ahead of the other one, which would put us in a BCS game."

Carter, however, took things one game at a time:

> Everybody had [OU] in the back of their minds, but honestly, we were more into thinking about the games from a week-to-week basis. If you really look at how we played, we only had like two close games all year. We were so focused on our next opponent and we were so excited about having a chance to go out on the field and make plays—that's all we were really focused on. Oklahoma wasn't really on our minds. We weren't thinking that we had to come into the season and beat Oklahoma or that we even had to win a national championship. That's not what we were thinking about. I'm thinking about catching a touchdown. What are you thinking about? I'm probably going to intercept a pass. I'm going to get a sack. It was just a lot of fun and everyone was trying to make plays. If everyone takes care of their job like that, we're going to win.

"I remember singing 'The Eyes of Texas' to all our fans and feeling how full of excitement the Texas side was.... That was a proud moment for me."

Having cleared the OU hurdle, the Longhorns really hit their stride over the next several weeks.

First, Texas faced No. 24 Colorado in the first of two consecutive home games against ranked opponents. Young barely broke a sweat in completing twenty-five of twenty-nine passes for 336 yards and two touchdowns, while adding another three touchdowns on the ground in a 42–17 win over the Buffalos.

The next week the Longhorns faced No. 10 Texas Tech, which entered the game with a perfect 6–0 record. It may have been another highly-anticipated match-up of two top ten teams, but for the Longhorns, it was simply the next game on the schedule.

Although Young performed at what he called a "C+" level, Texas jumped out to a 31–10 halftime lead and completely destroyed the Red Raiders by the end of the third quarter.

The 52–17 win over Tech gave the Longhorns an unblemished 7–0 record for the season and a fourteen-game winning streak going back to 2004. The offense was averaging fifty points per game and the defense was creating turnovers and big plays.

However, if this team thought the rest of the season would be an easy road to the championship, a night in Stillwater, Oklahoma would quickly change its tune.

SHOWDOWN AT STILLWATER: UT VS. OKLAHOMA STATE

The odds looked good for the Longhorns coming into the match-up against OSU. They were on a roll, set to face off against a wounded Cowboy squad. Riding a horrendous four-game losing streak, which included a 34–0 slaughter at the hands of Colorado at home, a 62–23 drubbing by Texas A&M, and a 37–10 pounding by Iowa State the previous week, the Cowboys were hobbled by their weak quarterback.

Sidelined by an injury, starting quarterback Bobby Reid had been replaced by Al Pena. The backup had performed terribly in the previous two weeks, throwing eight interceptions, fumbling numerous snaps, and getting sacked four times.

In order to avoid overconfidence, the Longhorns assumed that Reid would recover in time to start the game.

SENIOR TIGHT END
David Thomas had a standout game in Stillwater, including this 20-yard touchdown reception in the first quarter

Photo courtesy of *Dave Campbell's Texas Football*

"The biggest difference in where Oklahoma State is right now is that they didn't have Bobby Reid the last two weeks and we think they'll have him back, and he's a guy that's a lot like Vince. He can make a lot of plays with his feet and arm," Mack Brown pronounced on the Monday before the game.

So when Pena jogged onto the field for the first series of the game, it seemed that OSU wouldn't stand much of a chance against the surging Longhorns. Little did Texas realize that they had walked into an ambush led by none other than Pena himself, who happened to hail from Leander, Texas, only a stone's throw away from the UT campus.

After stalling on a three-and-out on the first OSU possession, Pena caught fire on the next drive, connecting with D'Juan Woods for a 49-yard touchdown pass to give the Cowboys an early 7–0 lead.

The Longhorns quickly responded with an 11-play, 62-yard drive capped by Young's 20-yard touchdown pass to David Thomas. The PAT was blocked, however, preserving a one point lead for the Cowboys.

That drive turned out to be Texas's highlight for the entire first half.

As soon as the Cowboys regained possession, they unleashed their running attack, punctuated by the speed of freshman Mike Hamilton and senior Greg Gold. Eight runs, seventy-six yards, and a Julius Crosslin touchdown later, the Cowboys had extended their lead to 14–6.

On Texas's next offensive play, Young was intercepted by OSU defensive back Daniel McLemore at the Texas 38-yard line. The return set the Cowboys up with a first and ten at the UT 17. Seconds later, Pena ran into the end zone.

Down 21–6 in the first quarter, the wheels seemed to be falling off Texas's Rose Bowl Express.

Although the Texas defense settled down and began effectively countering OSU's assault, the Longhorn offense was stuck in second gear. After scratching their way to a field goal to make it 21–9, Young gave up his second turnover of the evening, a fumble at the Texas 29-yard line.

Riding the energy coursing through the OSU stadium, Pena dropped back and threw across the middle to Luke Frazier, who watched the ball get deflected right into the hands of his teammate, Woods. With this surprising gift in tow, Woods sprinted into the end zone to give the Cowboys a 28–9 lead.

The shocking turn of events was inexplicable. Pena, who came into the game looking like the second-string back-up that he was, suddenly could do no wrong. He was having the game of a lifetime, while the superstar Longhorn quarterback had more turnovers than touchdowns.

Young and Co. got another field goal before the half, putting them in the locker room down by sixteen points. While most teams in that position would probably spend halftime on the receiving end of a tongue-lashing from the coaching staff, the Longhorns decided to move to a different beat.

Literally.

Nordgren recalls the scene:

> I'm telling you right now that it was the craziest thing. Vince wanted it to be a player's team. I've never seen coaches do such little coaching. At halftime we had our little meeting and we did our little deal,

but before the game started again we did something else. We had this little Bose music system that Michael Huff brought with him on every road trip. We had different people's iPods and we took that little speaker and set it right in the middle of the room and we turned it up as loud as possible. People were dancing, everybody was rapping, and everyone was having a good time. Literally, that's what we did in every game, so in that particular game we turned on the Bose, and we were all dancing, singing, and having a good time.

Vince turned it down and said, "Hey, I want you guys to know that the first half is on me. I'm going to go out in the second half and take over. You watch and see. You guys have to be there with me." All of the guys were hyped up and we believed him.

Young had vowed personally to change the dynamics of the game. After the second half got underway, he accomplished that in exactly fifty-two seconds.

Facing a third down and ten from his own 20, Young dropped back to pass, then rolled to his right. With defender Donavon Woods bearing down on him, Young showed a pump fake that sent the Cowboy leaping into the air.

As Woods watched helplessly in mid-air, Young sprinted past him down the sideline. Eighty yards later, the quarterback was in the end zone for a dramatic score that changed the momentum of the game on a dime.

According to Nordgren, the play was simply a matter of Young keeping his word:

> He called it. He said he was going to come out and take it in for a touchdown on the first drive. He said that. It was like Babe Ruth pointing into the left field stands and calling his shot. He said, "I'm taking the game over right now. Are you guys in?" Of course, we were in.

Number ten had seized the game, and there wasn't a thing the Cowboys could do about it. From that point on, Young was unstoppable. By game's end, he had rushed for 267 yards, passed for 239 more, and accounted for four touchdowns. The Longhorns put thirty-five points on the board in the second half while completely shutting down the OSU offense, leading to a spectacular 47–28 come-from-behind victory.

"The play that changed everything was when Vince pump-faked that guy and ran for a touchdown," Carter remembers. "That changed everything. Pretty much after that, it was all downhill for them. Football is all about momentum. You could feel the momentum shift and when it started going in our direction they could never recover. They got knocked off their feet and they couldn't get back up."

"That set the tone for the second half," Thomas concurs. "We knew when we scored that quick that we could get the lead and then not give it up. That year when our team was behind, we never panicked. There was always calmness on the team and we never got down on ourselves when we got behind. That game and the national championship game were similar because we never panicked. We just stayed steady and we knew that we could come back."

The comeback was so swift and so stunning that the Texas players couldn't help but admit their awe of their own quarterback.

"The guy's a character," senior tight end Neale Tweedie said after the game. "He's so confident and he just knows he's going to make something happen. It's just a matter of time."

"Everything Vince does is great for our team," UT junior safety Michael Griffin added. "He turned this game around. Vince does things that I think not too many people can do."

Before the season was through, Young would have more than a few chances to prove it.

THE ALL-TEXAS GRUDGE MATCH: UT VS. TEXAS A&M

The Longhorns only seemed to get better as the season wore on. After the victory over OSU, Texas made swift work of its next two opponents, Baylor and Kansas, trouncing the pair by a combined score of 128–14.

With a 10–0 record and a No. 2 ranking that they had held throughout the entire season, the 'Horns looked to their last two games of the regular season—a match-up with arch-rival Texas A&M, and a Big 12 Championship game against Colorado at Reliant Stadium in Houston.

Heading into the game against the Aggies in College Station, the Longhorns had dominated the series for the previous ten years and won the last five match-ups. The Aggies had a 5–5 record in Dennis Franchione's third season coaching the team, and few, if anyone, expected the team to put up much of a fight against Texas, which was now two wins away from punching its ticket to Pasadena for a second straight season.

Like Oklahoma State back in October, the Aggies were having some trouble at the quarterback position, with some observers predicting that an injury would keep Reggie McNeal out of the game. This would leave only redshirt freshman Stephen McGee to take snaps.

With so many people writing off the Aggies, a lot of attention turned from the game itself to Vince Young, who was in a dead heat with USC running back Reggie Bush for the Heisman Trophy.

The previous week Bush had made national headlines with a 513-yard, two-touchdown performance against Fresno State that had seemingly put him ahead of Young in the Heisman balloting with only a few weeks left in the season. For Young to have any chance at overtaking Bush, he'd need his own breakout game against the Aggies.

"If you pick the most valuable player in the country, it has to be Vince," Brown said that week. "We wouldn't be sitting here today without Vince. I do remember with Ricky [Williams] that he won the Heisman, lost the Heisman, won the Heisman, lost the Heisman, and won the Heisman. How do you know? If you go on the season, Reggie had a phenomenal game and they talked about him struggling and not having as good of a year. Last week he

DID YOU KNOW?

Legendary record producer David Geffen of "Geffen Records" dropped out of the University of Texas. He went on to become one of then most powerful men in the music business, with an estimated net worth of $6 billion.

was out of it and this week he won it. I think what will happen with voters is at the end, they'll sit down and take a deep breath and do what they think is best for the year."

Even Young did his best to deflect attention from the Heisman race.

"What I do is prepare myself each week....I just play the game of football," Young replied when asked about Bush's performance four days before the A&M game. "At the end of the game when we see our stats, I'm not out there trying to make plays because someone else made great plays, like we're competing. He's just out there making plays. He's not trying to make plays because I was or am the front-runner for the Heisman. He's out there making plays for his teammates. It's the same thing with me as well."

With Young and Co. having everything to play for, many fans felt the Aggies would be served well if they could just keep from getting embarrassed.

As it turned out, there's a reason why they still play the games.

In the week leading up to the game, rumors spread that the Longhorn faithful had been scooping up large quantities of tickets from A&M fans. On game day—the morning after Thanksgiving—these reports rang true, as there was a much larger burnt orange tint than usual to the giant crowd of 86, 617.

And the assembled 'Horns fans began celebrating early, showering the crowd with long-stemmed red roses midway through the first quarter as Texas jumped out to an early 14–0 lead. The Aggies looked doomed as McGee indeed filled in for McNeal.

A beat-down of historic proportions seemed imminent, along the lines of the walloping Texas had dished out to Baylor, Kansas, Colorado, and other teams. The 2005 Longhorns had proved ruthless in running up the score and simply breaking the will of their opponents. In scoring 652 points that season while allowing just 213, Texas was so dominating that most of their games were effectively decided by halftime.

Yet with a two-touchdown lead against the Aggies and all the momentum in the world, the Longhorns suddenly began to fall apart.

The Texas defense became disoriented by a new option offense designed for McGee. Texas coaches would later confirm that they had not prepared at all for the possibility that the Aggies would run the option with McGee. Expecting an injured McNeal to play in his final home game, the coaches didn't foresee any running threat emanating from the A&M quarterback position.

To make matters worse, Young just couldn't get things clicking all day. Whether he was distracted by the Heisman talk or not, he just didn't perform up to the standard he had set all season.

Thus, before the end of the first quarter, the game's complexion changed dramatically.

After McGee led the Aggies down the field for a field goal that cut the lead to 14–3, Young was intercepted by safety Melvin Bullitt just before the end of the quarter. Facing a first and ten from the Texas 35-yard line, Franchione called on a little trickery that sent the Longhorns reeling. The Aggies lured an aggressive Texas defense into playing the run as freshman running back Jorvorskie Lane darted toward the right hash-mark with the ball. He then pulled up and unleashed a shock pass to Jason Carter in the end zone.

Aggie fans at Kyle Field suddenly came alive as the Longhorns showed some rare signs of weakness. Meanwhile, the Aggies continued to pound away with their new running game.

After a stalled Texas drive, A&M's seldom-used running back, Brandon Leone, capped off an 85-yard drive with a 16-yard scoring run. In a matter of minutes, the Longhorns had given up fifteen unanswered points. The Aggies had missed the PAT on one of their touchdowns and blew an attempted two-point conversion on the other, but they still had captured the lead, 18–14.

It wasn't until close to halftime that Texas managed to get its offense moving again. With 3:35 remaining in the second quarter, Young hit former walk-on Ahmard Hall with a 14-yard touchdown pass. That was enough to put the Longhorns back on top, 21–15, going into halftime.

The Longhorns received the kickoff to start the third quarter. But any hope that they would quickly put away the Aggies dissipated on the third play of the quarter, when A&M defensive end Jason Jack recovered a Young fumble at the

Texas 15-yard line. Two players later, McGee was in the end zone on an 11-yard touchdown run, once again putting the Aggies in the lead, 22–21.

Texas kept the seesaw battle alive a few minutes later. With his team facing a fourth and one from the A&M 44-yard line, Brown called for a fake punt. Linebacker Rashad Bobino, a former redshirt freshman, pulled it off beautifully, rushing for six yards for a first down with an additional fifteen yards tacked onto the end of the play due to a facemask penalty.

The play was another momentum-changer. A reenergized Young quickly led the Longhorns down the field, setting up an 8-yard touchdown run by Ramonce Taylor to put the Longhorns back on top, 28–22.

Four plays later, Texas safety Michael Griffin blocked a punt by Justin Brantley. Cedric Griffin scooped it up and returned eleven yards to extend Texas's lead to 34–22.

Texas had regained its biggest lead since the first quarter, but the Aggies refused to go quietly. Another McGee touchdown run capped off an eight-play, 65-yard drive to cut the lead to 34–29 going into the final quarter. It was only the second time in the entire season that the Longhorn lead was five points or less at that point in the game, the first instance having occurred back in the second game of the season in Columbus.

With the spotlight focused squarely on Young, the quarterback aimed finally to put the game out of reach. He never really did it, but he led two drives that got close enough for David Pino to kick field goals. The Texas defense, however, stepped up when it counted and shut out the Aggies for the quarter.

It was a win for Texas, but it wasn't pretty. What was expected to be a blowout turned into a nail-biting 40–29 slugging match. The defense allowed 277 yards rushing and struggled through most of the game with sudden-change defense. Twice they gave up touchdowns within seconds of a Texas turnover.

The picture was not much brighter on offense. Young seemed to transform from Superman back into Clark Kent for the game, completing thirteen of twenty-four passes for 162 yards and a touchdown. He was sacked

» JUNIOR SAFETY Michael Griffin starred in the outstanding 2005 Texas secondary

Photos courtesy of *Dave Campbell's 2006 Texas Football*

» VINCE YOUNG holds the championship trophy in Houston's Reliant Stadium moments after leading the Longhorns to their first Big 12 title since 1996

three times, fumbled twice, and threw an interception. On the ground he was limited to just nineteen yards on eleven carries.

In other words, goodbye Heisman.

Nevertheless, the win gave the Longhorns their first 11–0 record since 1983. Now, only a rematch against Colorado stood in their path to California.

If the A&M game cured the team of any signs of overconfidence, the results of the Colorado match-up risked reimplanting them. In what can only be described as a brutal annihilation, the Longhorns demolished Colorado, 70–3, in Houston. If anything, the final score understated the extent of the bloodbath; the Buffs were lucky that the Longhorns didn't hit them with triple digits.

Thomas remembers the lopsided match-up:

> I don't think anyone ever expected to win that game 70–3. We just started rolling and we really put it to them. That was one of the few games where I don't think I even played a series in the second half. I just stood on the sidelines the entire second half because we were up so big.
>
> I got a chance to sit back and really soak it up. Looking up into Reliant Stadium, it was full of burnt orange, which was pretty neat. I got a chance to enjoy the moment and enjoy winning the Big 12 Championship. Everyone had their roses on the sideline. Getting to carry that trophy around Reliant Stadium was pretty special for me.

Young was coldly efficient in his first performance following his sub-par outing against A&M, completing fourteen of seventeen passes against the Buffs for 193 yards and three touchdowns, while adding another fifty-seven yards and a touchdown on the ground. In all, Texas scored ten touchdowns in the first three quarters and none in the fourth.

Ironically, Nordgren recalls the blowout as an example of Coach Brown's reluctance to run up the score on weaker teams:

In that Colorado game, we could have scored 100 points on them easily. We could have set all kinds of records. Trust me, I know. I'm the quarterback that went out there and played the whole second half. Literally, there were times that year when we would be down on someone's 10-yard line with five minutes to go and he [Brown] would run three fullback dives knowing that we're not going to score, and then he'll just kick the field goal.

That's just the type of guy Mack Brown is. He didn't ever want anyone to think we were rubbing it in their face. He would rather not have all of the accolades and have everyone think we're a good group of guys. I think that was kind of good for us to peel back a little bit. There were guys that wanted us to go and score more points, but that's not what we were about. USC did that, but that wasn't us.

As the Longhorns concluded the regular season with the first Big 12 championship of Brown's tenure, a spot awaited them in the BCS title game to play No. 1-ranked and defending national champion USC.

Just as Young had predicted, the Longhorns would be back in Pasadena.

A GAME FOR THE AGES: UT VS. USC

Despite their outstanding season, the Longhorns quickly learned that most of the national media expected them to play a bit role in the grand story of USC's coronation. In fact, fans and reporters alike frequently debated that season whether the 2005 Trojans were the greatest team in NCAA history.

Hype aside, USC had an outstanding squad. After winning a piece of the national championship in 2003, the Trojans had whipped Oklahoma the previous season in the BCS title game. They were entering the match-up against Texas with a thirty-four-game winning streak, far overshadowing Texas's own nineteen-game win streak. The Trojans were quarterbacked by 2004 Heisman winner Matt Leinart and had the projected 2005 Heisman winner, Reggie Bush.

Young quickly grew impatient with the hyperbole surrounding USC. Shortly after the Texas-USC match-up was announced, he was asked by a reporter if the Longhorns felt intimidated by the Trojans. Young took the opportunity to throw down the gauntlet:

Intimidated for what? They are the same team as we are. I don't know why people think they are going to scare us, for one thing. We as a team have been doing the same thing. We've been to the granddaddy of them all. We've been in the big games as well. We've got a nineteen [game] winning streak going on. All of that [being] scared stuff, no, we're not going to be scared. We're going to be pumped and excited to go out and play. All of that nervousness, that's not a part of the University of Texas.

He wasn't finished.

They haven't seen a team like us, no. They haven't seen the different guys on our team that's gangsta. [Laughs] We've got some guys that are going to talk some trash. We're not just going to let you talk in our face....Guys on our team, when you say something wrong to them, we're going to say something back, and we're going to talk trash the whole game. That's just us.

As Nordgren recalls, Young's teammates watched him pick a fight with USC—and loved him for it:

It wasn't necessarily us being gangsta like you would hear in a rap song. If you're in a dark alley and someone is about to try and steal your wallet and beat you up, I'm going to tell you right now that you want to have Vince Young in that alley with you because that's the type of guy he is. All of us rallied behind that [comment]. When it comes down to getting down and dirty, these are the guys you want to have in a dark alley fighting for you. That's what he meant. It wasn't about being a gangster. It was about having the mentality that we'll fight for anything that we believe in.

"We were hot," Carter remembers. "We were real hot. We were like the underdog and you know we didn't like that. It made us want to fight. I don't think I've ever seen a game with so much hype, at least not one I've ever played in."

Young stirred the media pot some more later that week when he traveled to New York for the Heisman Trophy ceremonies. Although Bush had been projected as a runaway winner, Young was not only confident that he'd claim the trophy himself, but he let it be known that he *wanted* it in a bad way. He told reporters,

> The Heisman is always on my mind. It's getting closer and closer. You kind of wake up now thinking that you're already in New York. It's getting closer and closer. All I can do now is keep praying about it.
>
> I think my chances are real high. If [the voters] have been watching the games and how I'm a leader for my teammates—I hope they will see that the numbers I put up were basically in the first half [of the season]. In the second half, I've basically been on the bench. I hope they look at that. If I played a full game, I'd have some more stats, but coach Brown doesn't like to blow out people, so he'll put all of our starters on the bench. If they basically look at that and how I love my teammates, how we play together and how big of a leader I am to those guys, I'm pretty sure I should win it.

When the announcement came in that weekend that Bush indeed was the runaway winner, Young took it as a major snub by the national media. Nordgren recalls the moment:

> Oh yeah, I was in New York with him at the Heisman. When he didn't win, he felt like the A&M game was a determining factor. He

TEXAS FIGHT

"The Eyes of Texas" is always followed by the song "Texas Fight," UT's official fight song. Many people don't know that a more well-known version of the song is called "Taps," and its first strain is a sped-up version of the hymn played at military funerals. "Texas Fight" was written by Colonel Walter S. Hunnicutt in collaboration with James E. King, then director of the Marlin High School Band.

Its official lyrics are as follows:

Texas Fight, Texas Fight,
And it's goodbye to A&M.
Texas Fight, Texas Fight,
And we'll put over one more win.
Texas Fight, Texas Fight,
For it's Texas that we love best.
Hail, Hail, The gang's all here,
And it's goodbye to all the rest!
(YELL)
Yea Orange! Yea White!
Yea Longhorns! Fight! Fight! Fight!
Texas Fight! Texas Fight,
Yea Texas Fight!
Texas Fight! Texas Fight,
Yea Texas Fight!

Note: The line, "Hail, Hail, the gang's all here" is usually replaced with "Give 'em hell, Give 'em hell, Go 'Horns Go!"

felt like that was the game where he lost the Heisman. I think he'll be the first to tell you that he deserved it, and I think that was a huge factor for him.

That guy doesn't lose at anything. If you're sitting on the couch and someone pulls out some dominos, he'll fight you before he'll lose. You can call the sky blue and he can call it green, and you're not going to win that argument. He's a very emotional guy and that fired him up. He even told me that. He said, "I deserved it. I'm a better player." It pissed him off real bad and that's the last thing you want to do with that guy.

Feeling overlooked and unappreciated, Young and his teammates used the media hyping of USC as motivation for the big game.

"I know USC kind of had us underestimated," Carter says. "I think all the talk about them being the greatest team ever really motivated us. I think they thought that even though we had Vince at quarterback, that was all we had."

According to Nordgren, in the end the Longhorns themselves began hyping USC for their own purposes:

We wanted to build them up to be so big. We wanted it to be David versus Goliath for two reasons. For one, if we lost the game it wouldn't look as bad because we were supposed to lose. It doesn't look as bad if you lose a game that nobody thought you could win. But, if we win, it only makes us ten times better than anyone thought we were going into the game. We wanted to build them up to be the best team ever.

Even in the final moments before the game, Carter remembers the Trojans refusing to show the Longhorns much respect. "I just know that in pre-game, when you go out there and catch passes and things like that, they were just real cocky, all of them," he says. "I guess they were thinking they were just going to run over us."

After a dazzling pre-game show that concluded with a flyover by three stealth fighters, the Longhorns and Trojans began the game that many today call the greatest ever.

The Trojans took control in the first quarter when they parlayed Aaron Ross's fumbled punt into a LenDale White touchdown run to give them a 7–0 lead.

❝They just wanted to razzle dazzle and put on a show. We just wanted to win.❞

Heading into the second quarter, the Trojans had a chance to deliver an early knockout blow when Bush reeled in a 37-yard reception. However, at the Texas 18-yard line, he blew an inexplicable attempt at a backward lateral. The ball was recovered by Longhorn senior safety Michael Huff, recipient of the Jim Thorpe Award as the nation's top defensive back.

"I think Reggie throwing the ball back and kind of being Hollywood, I think that was kind of a symbol of what they were and what we were," Nordgren explains. "They just wanted to razzle dazzle and put on a show. We just wanted to win."

Young led the Longhorns to their first points of the afternoon on their next offensive series, as Pino connected on a 46-yard field goal to cut the lead to 7–3.

The first quarter had been a low-key affair, but the high-octane offensive shootout that everyone had anticipated was about to begin.

After another Trojan turnover, the Longhorns traversed the length of the field and took the lead on Selvin Young's 12-yard scoring run on a late option from Young. Television replays showed that Young's knee was down, but the Longhorns kicked the point after before officials could review the play. Although they missed the rushed PAT, the Longhorns had taken the lead, 9–7.

Nordgren recalls the controversial play:

> As soon as that happened, I knew he had his knee on the ground. As soon as Selvin got in the end zone, I ran and got all of the guys on the special teams and we got on the field. We had a couple of guys that weren't even on the field goal unit because we just wanted to hurry up and kick the extra point. We ran out there and got the damn thing off before they could challenge it. We kicked that thing so fast you wouldn't have even have thought there was a break in the action from the touchdown.

The Longhorns grabbed the momentum moments later, when Ramonce Taylor capped off a 4-play, 51-yard drive with a 30-yard touchdown run.

Down 16–7, the Trojans suddenly seemed to be reeling. However, USC bounced back in the final minute of the half with an offensive series that ended with a 43-yard field goal by Mario Danelo. At halftime, the score stood at 16–10, Longhorns.

The Trojans came out of the locker rooms ready for battle in the third quarter. After a three-and-out by the Texas offense, the Trojans retook the lead at the 10:36 mark when White found the end zone from three yards out, putting USC up 17–16.

No sooner had the Trojans taken the lead from the Longhorns than Young stepped right back into the spotlight, leading the Longhorns on a 7-play, 80-yard drive that took all of 2:02 off the clock. Young crossed the goal line on a 14-yard scoring run to give Texas a 23–17 lead.

Like a machine, the Trojans marched right back down the field behind the precise throwing of Leinart, who completed six of seven passes on the drive. White punched the ball into the end zone with a 12-yard touchdown run. The Trojans were back on top, 24–23.

The match-up had turned into a game of "anything you can do, I can do better" between Young and the entire USC offense. It seemed that the game's winner would be determined by whichever team happened to have the ball last.

"As soon as the game started I think they understood that we were a legit squad," Carter reflects. "They had a lot of talent over there and that was a game where the momentum just went back and forth. You have to commend them because we went out and grabbed the momentum and they came right back and grabbed it back. In the second half, we were going back and forth."

As the game entered the fourth quarter, Young had the Longhorns on the move again, but Pino missed a 31-yard field goal wide right that would have regained the lead for the Longhorns. Presented with a golden opportunity, the Trojans attempted to put the game out of reach on the next two offensive possessions.

First, Bush showcased his Heisman-winning skill with an electrifying 26-yard touchdown run that concluded with him leaping into the end zone from the five-yard line. That put USC up, 31–23.

After Pino cut into the lead with a 34-yard field goal on the next Texas possession, the Trojans finally found the separation they were aiming for all night, as Leinart moved the Trojans down the field in a matter of seconds and appeared to seal the game with a 22-yard touchdown pass to Dwayne Jarrett.

With 6:42 remaining, the Longhorns trailed 38–26. In order to clinch the school's first national championship since 1970, they'd have to score a pair of touchdowns while shutting down a USC offense that had carved up Texas defenders for four touchdowns in the second half.

It was time for Young to dip into his bag of magic tricks.

The Longhorn quarterback led his offense down the field on an eight-play scoring drive that covered sixty-nine yards in only 2:39. Young completed passes to David Thomas, Limas Sweed, and Quan Cosby before finally running into the end zone from seventeen yards out to cut USC's lead to 38–33 with 4:03 remaining in the game.

Now it was time for the Texas defense to step up. Already worn out by the video game-like production of the USC offense, the Longhorn defense had to shake off its weariness and find a way to get the Trojans off the field without scoring another point. In fact, with the Longhorns down to two timeouts and USC taking over at their own 34-yard line, all the Trojans needed was a pair of first downs to put away their third consecutive championship.

The USC drive got halfway to victory on its second play, when Leinart moved the chains with a pass to Jarrett that put the ball at their own 47-yard line. After White gained three yards and Leinart missed his fullback Brandon Hancock in the flat on second down, the Trojans decided to have White run the ball again on third and seven from midfield.

Hancock crashed down two yards short of the first, leaving the Trojans facing a tough decision. If they punted on fourth and two, they'd give the ball back to Young with a little more than two minutes left in the game. With Young already well-known for his late-game heroics, that wasn't an attractive option.

> **"It's coming. It's right around the corner. Keep your eyes open because the state of Texas and the Longhorns are on the warpath and we're making our way to a national championship."**
> —Cory Redding, upon signing with the Longhorns in 1999

The other move would be for the Trojans to go for it on fourth down. If they make it, they win. Of course, if they fall short, they turn the ball over to Young even closer to their own end zone.

With more confidence in his offense than his defense at that point, USC head coach Pete Carroll decided to go for the first down.

"I was never on the sideline thinking that we were going to lose, but on that one key play when they went for it, it pretty much entered my mind that this might be the game," remembers Carter. "I said a prayer and asked that we be able to stop them. I never thought that we were going to lose, but I did know at that point that we needed to make a play. I knew that much."

Amazingly, as the Trojans took the field for the biggest play of their season, their 2005 Heisman winner remained on the sideline. White was having a better night than Bush was, and after rushing for 123 yards and three touchdowns, Carroll decided to ride White's hot hand. Averaging six yards per carry that night, White only needed two on the play to effectively put the game away.

The Longhorns, however, were anticipating that the Trojans would go to White. As he lined up behind in the backfield, the entire Longhorns defense began inching closer to the line of scrimmage. When the ball was snapped and handed off to White, all eleven Longhorn defenders were already looking for the red-hot running back.

Charging toward the line of scrimmage like a locomotive, White was met by a host of Longhorn defenders who stopped him on contact. On his twentieth carry of the night, White had finally been shut down.

As the officials sorted through the mess of bodies scattered across the line of scrimmage, the Texas defenders celebrated deliriously.

It was Texas's ball. Or more specifically, it was Vince Young's ball.

"As soon as they didn't get the first down, we knew it was over," Nordgren argues. "Coach Davis said it on the phone. The whole team knew it and Vince knew it. That guy goes onto the field as stoic as ever. He looked like he might have been in the library studying for a test. He just does not care and everyone else out there is nervous as shit. It's the biggest game and the biggest drive in college football history."

GAMEDAY HAUNTS

Best place to go have a drink and feel like you are in a Sinatra movie—**The Belmont**—305 W. Sixth, (512) 457-0300

Best place to watch the rest of the day's action on a big-screen TV—**Third Base**—1717 West 6th Street, Building 2, Suite 210R, (512) 512.476.BASE

Best place to find a homemade chicken-fried steak—**Threadgill's Old No. I**—6416 N. Lamar, (512) 451-5440

The clock showed 2:09 remaining in the game and the Longhorns needed to travel fifty-six yards to take the lead.

After losing two yards on the first two plays of the series, the offense picked up a much-needed first down when Young connected with Quan Cosby for a gain of seven, with five more yards added on due to a facemask penalty. On third and twelve, the Longhorns had picked up exactly twelve yards.

"When the offense went onto the field I wasn't in the game, and I was pissed off," Carter remembers. "They had Nate [Jones], Quan, and Sweed. I was on the sideline thinking that this is my senior year, the game-winning drive, I'm not nervous at all. Man, I need to be in that game."

Seconds later, Carter got his wish.

"I was just like, 'Ooooh!' Carter says. "Man, I was so excited. I was ready for whatever. This is what you live for. When I got onto the field I just remembered thinking that this was big."

With the initial first down conversion out of the way, the Longhorn offense methodically moved down the field. After a completion to Carter picked up nine yards, Young rushed for another seven to get a first down and move the offense to the USC 37-yard line.

On the next play, Young hooked up with Carter once again for a 17-yard gain. With less than a minute remaining, the Longhorns were a measly thirteen yards away from making history.

After Young misfired on a throw to Sweed, he picked up five yards rushing on second down to set up a third and five from the 8. With thirty seconds remaining, the Longhorns called a timeout.

The plan for the next play was to have Young win it with his arm. However, Young once again missed Sweed in the end zone when his pass sailed through a crowded area in the middle of the field.

Nordgren remembers the play like it was yesterday:

> There was a low snap and it caused the timing to be off. That was the only mistake we made the entire drive. He [Young] took three steps on the drop instead of one and ended up not having the ball in his hands

Photo courtesy of *Dave Campbell's Texas Football*

LONGHORNS DEFENDERS celebrate after stopping White on fourth down

properly. He basically let the play come too close to the safety because the slant had beat the corner. We missed it because it was so close to the safety that it got to where Limas and the safety had collided, and when the ball came he didn't even have a chance to catch it.

"I had a curl and I pushed my dude off," Carter says. "I was thinking that I've got to win and he threw it to Sweed. I was wide open in the end zone and I would have caught it."

So the season came down to one final play. Facing a fourth and five on the USC 8-yard line, Young and Co. went back to the huddle with twenty-six seconds remaining.

As Greg Davis sent in the play, Nordgren was the first to hear the call:

> The very next play we called the same play. All the quarterbacks know that when coach Davis calls the same play back-to-back, he does it for a reason. There's no way for Greg to be able to communicate why he called the same play over again, but if he calls the same exact play from the same exact set, there's a good reason.

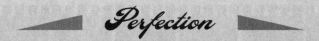

Perfection

THE 2005 LONGHORNS

DATE	OPPONENT	RESULT
September 3, 2005	Louisiana-Lafayette	W 60–3
September 10, 2005	at Ohio State	W 25–22
September 17, 2005	Rice	W 51–10
October 1, 2005	at Missouri	W 51–20
October 8, 2005	vs. Oklahoma	W 45–12
October 15, 2005	Colorado	W 42–17
October 22, 2005	Texas Tech	W 52–17
October 29, 2005	at Oklahoma State	W 47–28
November 5, 2005	at Baylor	W 62–0
November 12, 2005	Kansas	W 66–14
November 25, 2005	at Texas A&M	W 40–29
December 3, 2005	vs. Colorado	W 70–3
January 4, 2006	vs. USC	W 41–38

As Young walked up to the line of scrimmage, the USC defense immediately recognized that the Longhorns were in the same offensive set as the previous play. Trojan defenders guessed that Young would come right back to Sweed on the slant. Nordgren continues:

> We ran the same play, and Vince took the one step and he was going to throw it, right? Like he should have before? But he saw that they knew it was the same play. So what did the defense do when they saw that it was the same exact play? The cornerback, the safety, and a linebacker all ran straight to Limas—all three of them. That left nobody else over to the other side of the field, and when Vince took that one step, he caught everyone running directly for the slant, and he just took it and ran.

Right around the time that Young decided to pull the ball down and run, Carter was hoping that the quarterback hadn't decided to throw to him.

"The defensive back just grabbed me," Carter recalls. "I remember thinking, 'Man, if I turn around and this ball is coming, Lord help me because this dude is grabbing me and I'm not really open.'"

As it turned out, Carter wasn't open—but Young wasn't looking for him.

With Young starting to drift to his right and the Trojans playing the pass, a path opened up for the quarterback toward the end zone. In the blink of an eye, he was in there. With a successful two-point conversion, the Longhorns had seized a 41–38 lead.

Thomas remembers watching Young's climactic run:

> I just ran a diagonal over to the left sideline and I saw him tuck it down and run. There was nobody there for me to block because the play was going the other way, so I became a spectator and started watching. When he got to the 5-yard line, I just squatted down and jumped as high into the air as I could because I was so excited, knowing that he was in. I just ran over there and started celebrating with

all of the guys. That was just freaking unbelievable the way he played in that game.

"I turned around and I saw Vince running, I saw him run into the end zone, and I must have jumped twenty feet into the air," Carter recalls. "That's when you miss sports. Moments just like that. That was just an unbelievable memory and everyone was just so excited. It was crazy."

Although the Longhorns had taken a 41–38 lead, the game wasn't over yet. Up by a mere three points with nineteen seconds left on the clock, the 'Horns still had to weather one final storm from the potent USC offense.

The Trojans took over at their own 31, putting them around thirty-five yards away from field goal position. On the first play, Reggie Bush sent Longhorn fans into cardiac arrest by taking a short pass from Leinart and deftly converting it into a 27-yard gain.

With just seconds on the clock, USC opted for one more pass play to bring them within field goal position. The Texas defense tightened up, knowing they couldn't afford another mistake. Leinart took the snap—and misfired on a throw to Jarrett! What's more, the play cost the Trojans just a few more seconds than they had anticipated. After the blown pass, the clock read 0:00.

Pandemonium erupted from the Longhorn Nation—among the thousands of Texas fans at the stadium, as well as the millions across America screaming at their television sets. At long last the Longhorns were college football's national champions.

When the dust had settled, Young had given a performance for the ages, completing thirty of forty passes for 267 yards, while adding 200 yards and three touchdowns on the ground. For the second consecutive season, he earned MVP honors in the Rose Bowl.

Perhaps he hadn't won the Heisman, but on the greatest stage in the history of college football, in a match-up of two of the greatest teams ever, Young had risen to the occasion and won.

With the crystal national championship trophy in his hands, Young returned to the same stage that he had stood on a year ago when he made his boisterous prediction that the Longhorns would return to the Rose Bowl for a second straight season.

There were no predictions this time, just a few moments of pure glee.

"It's so beautiful," Young said after he received the MVP trophy. "Don't you think that's beautiful? It's coming home all the way to Austin, Texas, baby!"

Yes, the Longhorns had come back to Pasadena. And they were leaving as champions.

MACK BROWN (left) basks in Texas's Rose Bowl victory with Vince Young (center) and safety Michael Huff (right)

Photo courtesy of *Dave Campbell's Texas Football*

Chapter Nine

"ARE YOU A BELIEVER YET?"
THE VINCE YOUNG STORIES

The author of this book—the Die-Hard Fan—remembers pandemonium erupting in the Longhorn section of the Rose Bowl following Vince Young's fourth-down touchdown run in the waning seconds of the 2006 BCS National Championship game. The play had secured a thrilling 41–38 victory over USC.

From the moment Young crossed the goal line to put the Longhorns ahead with only nineteen seconds remaining in one of the greatest contests in college football history, the raw emotion in the stadium was overwhelming.

As I stood in a sea of burnt orange that night, there was jubilation and triumph among the Longhorn Nation. At every turn, complete strangers embraced each other as if they shared a winning lottery ticket. Family members kissed and hugged. Some sobbed with joy.

The only words I remember hearing in the chaotic first fifteen minutes after the play's conclusion came in the form of a five-word question.

"Are you a believer, yet?"

Standing close to me was a single USC fan. He showed no tears or contortions of rage, but his face was frozen in shock. More catatonic than anything else, the guy just stared blankly at the field.

Just ten minutes prior to Young's final touchdown, this fan had been taunting the Longhorn faithful, figuring his Trojans' twelve-point lead with a shade over six minutes left was as secure as Fort Knox. Standing next to this individual was his wife, who was decked out in a burnt orange No. 10 jersey.

"You are going to regret this," she told him. "Vince will not let us down. He does not lose. You just wait and see, you'll believe when it's all over."

And sure enough, just a few moments later, she was kissing strangers and doling out countless hugs to her entire row. Eventually, she turned her attention to her shell-shocked husband. She had warned him not to count out Young and Co., and now she was going to remind her hubby of that fact.

Shamelessly, the Die-Hard Fan eavesdropped on the couple's private moment. Having endured the guy's obnoxious boasting just moments before, I was expecting a big payoff for his victorious wife. Heck, if she had left him and walked away with Matthew McConaughey right then and there, it would have struck me as poetic justice.

But the woman opted for the high road. She leaned over to him, planted a kiss on his cheek, and asked a simple question.

"Are you a believer, yet?"

He didn't blink. Or smile. Or cry. He just stared off into space with a look of despair and disbelief.

Whether he was ready to admit it or not, our villain had been forced to become a believer. This singular moment will be burnt into his memory. For the rest of his life, this will be his Vince Young story

It's not uncommon for people to react strongly to Young's on-the-field performance. After all, he left a legacy at Texas that will be tough for any future Longhorn to match, compiling a staggering number of records and winning a plethora of awards. He rushed for 3,127 yards (No. 1 all-time among Longhorn quarterbacks) and thirty-seven touchdowns in just thirty-seven games, while completing 444 of 718 passes for 6,040 yards. He departed the program as Texas's all-time leader in total offense.

Young's stand-out season, of course, came in 2005, when he posted 4,086 yards of total offense, far surpassing Major Applewhite's previous single-season Longhorn record of 3,211 yards. Young's 3,036 yards passing ranked as the third-best mark in school history, while his twenty-six touchdown passes tied a school record. In addition to his excellence as a passer (he ranked third nationally in passing efficiency), Young thrived in the running game, rushing for 1,050 yards and twelve touchdowns. That year, he became the first player in college football history to pass for more than 3,000 yards and rush for more than 1,000 in the same season.

Oh, and he led the team to its first national championship in thirty-five years.

Following his Herculean 2005 season, Young was named the Big 12 Offensive Player of the Year and the Big 12 Championship MVP. He also won the Davey O'Brien Award (given to the nation's top quarterback), the Maxwell Award (given to the nation's top player), and he finished second to Reggie Bush for the Heisman.

After finishing his career at Texas with a stunning 30–2 record as a starter—the best ratio in school history—Young was selected with the third overall pick in the first round of the 2006 NFL draft by the Tennessee Titans.

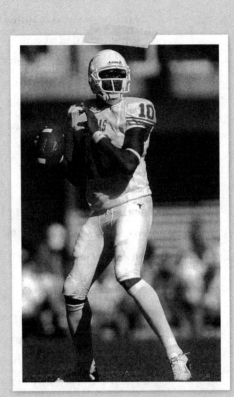

Photo courtesy of *Dave Campbell's 2004 Texas Football*

DOUBLE THREAT: At Texas, Young's precision passing complemented his incredible speed.

In his first season, Young took the league by storm, winning Rookie of the Year honors and leading his team to the brink of the playoffs. He is commonly regarded as one of the top players in the game today.

A superstar of Young's caliber tends to bring out strong emotions in people, such as the despondent USC fan sitting near me at the 2006 Rose Bowl, as well as his ecstatic wife. In fact, anyone who knows Young personally, or has simply rooted for or against him from afar, has his own Vince Young story. Having followed Young's career since his sophomore season at Houston Madison, you better believe I have my own share of stories about the man whose teammates called him simply, "VY."

The 2006 victory over USC will always be one of my favorites. But the one that really stands out took place less than three months before Young signed his letter of intent to play for the Longhorns in February 2002.

It was on a Saturday afternoon at a high school playoff game in the Houston Astrodome that I learned never to doubt Young's leadership and ability. In a match-up between two of the best teams in the Houston area, Young led the Madison Marlins against the Fort Bend Hightower Hurricanes.

By the time I saw the six-foot-five, 190-pound Young that day, he had already emerged as the nation's number one quarterback prospect. In one memorable game that year, he led his team to an amazing 61–58 win over state power North Shore, amassing more than 400 yards of offense in the process.

A lot of stories were circulating about Young's star power back then—one had Houston Rockets guard Steve Francis coming over to introduce himself to Young at a restaurant.

And his legend was about to grow a little bit more on this day at the Astrodome.

To better understand Young's accomplishments in that game, it helps to know something about his opponent. Hightower was an excellent team, especially on defense. They hadn't given up more than a handful of yards or points to any team all season. Young was taking on this powerhouse

THE EYES OF TEXAS

The official Alma Mater of the University of Texas was written in 1903 by John Sinclair in response to a request that a song be written for a cowboy minstrel show. Sinclair used an old saying from UT president Colonel Prather, who often told audiences to remember that "the eyes of Texas are upon you." Sinclair fitted the expression to the melody of "I've Been Working on the Railroad," and the tune is now played at the beginning and end of all official UT functions. The original manuscript hangs in the Alumni Center.

> The Eyes of Texas are upon you,
> All the live long day.
> The Eyes of Texas are upon you,
> You cannot get away.
> Do not think you can escape them
> At night or early in the morn—
> The Eyes of Texas are upon you
> 'Till Gabriel blows his horn

squad in what was most certainly a state championship contender elimination match.

As I secured my seat on the 30-yard line, electricity was in the air. Men and women, old and young, were speculating about what tricks Young would pull out of his hat. Those who had already seen him play that year were retelling their stories to a bevy of curious listeners.

And these were the *Hightower* fans! I had gotten comfortable in the Hightower section of the stadium, and there wasn't a shred of clothing in sight bearing Madison's baby blue. Yet those surrounding us, although rooting for the Hurricanes, had clearly come to see Young.

The talk was all about Young, and as the game started, it didn't take novices long to figure out why. Among the 30,000 on hand that night, those who were not yet believers soon would be.

On Madison's first drive of the game, Young marched his team seventy yards down the field in the blink of an eye. At the end of the drive, as Madison ran the option play to the right side of the field, the crowd got its first look at what was in store for the tremendous Hightower defense. Young pitched the ball to star running back Courtney Lewis just as the quarterback was about to get pummeled by numerous Hightower defenders. With much of the Hightower defense obsessed with Young, Lewis was able to turn the corner and race his way twenty-eight yards down the sideline to give Madison a 7–0 lead.

Hightower quickly responded with a touchdown of its own, but this had the unfortunate consequence of handing the ball back over to Young. As it turned out, the opening drive was a precursor of things to come.

As he jogged back on the field, we could feel the electricity in the air as the entire crowd stood up in anticipation. On this drive, Young would display the arm that would eventually lead the NCAA in passing in 2005. From fifteen yards behind the line of scrimmage, he threw a laser downfield that traveled nearly sixty yards in the air before landing in the hands of Joey Dancy for a 46-yard gain. That set up another Madison touchdown, giving Young's team a 14–7 lead.

The buzz in the stands turned into a roar. The score may have been close, but it seemed like everyone believed the game itself was a mere formality, and the only reason for watching was to see Vince Young do his thing.

Madison lit up the scoreboard later in the first quarter when Young rolled slightly to his right and unleashed a perfect pass that dropped beautifully over the outside shoulder and into the hands of Dancy in the right corner of the end zone.

The 40-yard throw—50, if you include the end zone—displayed a perfect mix of arm strength and touch. That he was able to launch a pass that long with seemingly minimal effort was one thing, but his placement of the ball, which he dropped in a spot where only the receiver could make the play, really grabbed the crowd's attention.

The Astrodome began going crazy. Even Hightower fans were high-fiving, laughing, and shouting in amazement. I remember staring in disbelief at the sight of fans cheering so emphatically for an opposing player whose success ultimately signaled the end of their team's season.

And Young was still just warming up.

Later, with Madison leading 23–7 and facing a first and 20 from its own 49-yard line, Young dropped back and then took off up the middle on a quarterback draw. Once he passed the line of scrimmage, Young split two Hightower defenders and turned the jets on, leaving everyone in his path as he raced untouched into the end zone.

Young was like a Ferrari on the Autobahn, while the rest of the players on the field were just trying to park their mom's Volvo in the family garage.

The spectacle sent the crowd into hysteria. Teenagers ran up and down the aisles and stairs. Grown men jumped up and down. And I just stood there dumbfounded.

As if that weren't enough, Young set up another first-half touchdown with a beautiful 40-yard throw reminiscent of his first scoring toss. Once again, it landed just over the outside shoulder of his receiver, who pulled it in just before running out of bounds.

The final eye-popping play of the day occurred in the third quarter, when Young scored yet again on a long touchdown run. This time several Hightower defenders had the angle on him, but Young again kicked it into high gear and left them all in his dust as he raced into the end zone.

Young went on to lead Madison to a 56–22 dismantling of Hightower. The quarterback finished the game with 403 yards of total offense and five touchdowns. He passed for 286 yards and three scores, while rushing for 117 yards and two more touchdowns.

As I departed the Astrodome, I had my cell phone glued to my ear, telling all who would listen about this Vince Young phenom whom I'd just seen in person for the first time.

In the years since, I've probably told this story at least 1,000 times. It's *my* Vince Young story. And this convinced me that the best way to tell the story of the greatest player in Longhorn history is to let those who know him best tell their own Vince Young stories.

In this final chapter, those who played with Young or watched him from the sidelines provide their own favorite memory of the young man that brought the Longhorn program back to national glory.

FORMER LONGHORN QUARTERBACK AND TEAMMATE MATT NORDGREN

In one of the games, we were playing at home, and it was a tight ball game in the third quarter. We were pinned back on like the 5-yard line and about ninety-five yards away from the end zone, and we needed to go down and have a nice drive. Really, we were just looking to change field position. We wanted to get the ball down on our side of the field.

There was a TV timeout and I just remember it being the biggest game of the year. During the timeout, when we got out on the field, Vince was in the huddle trying to get everyone fired up. He was so fired up, and he hadn't had that great of a game. He had the whole entire offense in front of him and he told them, "I want you to turn around right now." The whole offense turned around and the defense was just kind of standing there waiting for the end of the timeout. He walked around to the front of our huddle and yelled at the whole defense. His point was to get all of the guys to look over at him. He had the whole defense looking at him and nobody on offense knew what he was doing. Everyone was just staring at each other.

Vince started yelling and screaming at the defense that they didn't have anything on us, that they couldn't stop us and we were about to go ninety-five yards. He turned around and started slapping all of our linemen in the heads and getting everyone fired up. The next thing you know there are eleven guys out there on our offense and they are all yelling and screaming at the defense. They were yelling at the defense that they were going to mess them up. It was crazy. It was just one of those deals where he was on a whole different level than anyone else and he literally had everyone on our offense turn around and stare down the defense and basically tell them that we're about to kick their ass. We went down there and scored on a 95-yard drive. I've never seen that happen before.

FORMER LONGHORN HEAD COACH FRED AKERS

Like everybody else, when I first saw him on the practice field when he was a freshman, I couldn't believe how fast this big guy could move, and do it with almost no effort, or so it seemed. It was just a thing of beauty to watch. When he would start running and moving, he was always able to be just out of the reach of the pursuer. He was always able to throw the football just where it could be caught. I thought to myself, "My goodness, what an athlete!" That was my first impression of him and I never changed it.

> **66 There are only two players that I have seen that I could honestly say that they could dominate a game. The first one was Earl Campbell, and then there's Vince Young. 99**

I'll tell you, from the time that I was a player (I played against Texas in college at the University of Arkansas), from the time I was watching, and for the nineteen years that I was coaching, I believe there are only two players that I have seen that I could honestly say that they could dominate a game. The first one was Earl Campbell, and then there's Vince Young.

FORMER TEXAS RUNNING BACK AND TEAMMATE MARCUS MYERS

I'll never forget one summer when we were having seven-on-seven workouts. We'd occasionally scrimmage Texas State, and every time they would come out they would take a lot of trash. I don't know why, but they did it every time. This one time they must have brought their entire school up there because there were a lot of people there. For some reason this one guy was really talking a lot of trash, and he was directing it at Vince. I can't remember if a play broke down and he just started running, or if he lined up at wide receiver, but he shook this guy really, really bad and it happened in front of everyone that had driven down from their school.

After it happened, he wouldn't look at Vince, but as Vince jogged passed him he said, "It's okay. I know that you use me in the video game when you're at home." Everyone just busted out laughing. That wasn't like Vince to talk about himself like that at all, but that guy had pushed him to it because he had been talking so much trash. That showed how competitive Vince is. It didn't matter that it was only a seven-on-seven practice, he wasn't going to let someone do that to any of our guys.

The other story that I really think of occurred after we won the national championship. We rode the bus back, and we were in the back of the bus doing this little song that we had made up, and everyone was dancing and having a good time. Vince got in front of everyone and told us that no matter what happened with any of us from that moment on, he would always be there for us if we ever needed anything. That was just the kind of guy he is. The thing that I think about today is how he didn't just say that to say it. Every time I've ever called and ever needed to talk to him about anything, he's been there.

FORMER LONGHORN DEFENSIVE BACK GREG BROWN

There was a time when we were playing seven-on-seven in the summertime. I knew Vince Young and I knew of Vince Young, but I really didn't *know* Vince Young, if you know what I mean. I didn't know the Rose Bowl winning Vince Young. So, we're out there playing seven-on-seven and I'm talking smack like I was known to do. I'm out there against his receivers and I was just kind of jamming them up pretty good. This was back when Limas Sweed was a little younger. I was over there jamming him up and talking some good smack at him.

VY came over and played receiver for a down and I was like, "Come on over here Big Slim. You think you can handle me?" I'm just talking a whole lot of trash to him and he was like, "We're going to see. We're going to see." When he comes off the line and I try to jam him, he pretty much grabs my hand and just throws it down real quick. He runs an out and I'm trying to chase him down, but he catches the ball and then he kind of puts the ball in my face and shows it to me. I could not believe I had just let a freaking quarterback do me like that. I couldn't believe it.

I patted him on the butt and said, "Hey, I really underestimated you." I knew he was good and I knew he was Vince Young and all of that, but I'm thinking me going up against a quarterback—no way that's about to happen. He showed me right there that he wasn't just

> **" I could not believe I had just let a freaking quarterback do me like that. "**

a good player, but he was a phenomenal athlete. Now I see him in the NFL and he has Julius Peppers and all of these big-time defensive ends on his heels, and he's just brushing them off and still running and playing. That guy is the *real* deal. I don't feel so bad anymore because he does that to everybody.

RIVALS.COM RECRUITING EXPERT BOBBY BURTON

I was living in Houston back at the time, and I went to see Vince early in his senior season. I'd seen him several times as a sophomore and junior and even through the state seven-on-seven stuff and Elite 11 that summer. But back then I was living in Houston, and when I was in town I'd go see two high school games a night—on Thursday, Friday, and Saturday—in Houston. I'd go see the first half of one game, and then get in the car and go see the second half of another game.

So I go to a game over at Delmar [Stadium] for the first half—it was something like Kashmere against Sam Houston. Not much talent there, so I left a couple of minutes early because I really wanted to get to the next game in time to see how Vince had progressed from last year. So I pushed hard to get over to Butler in time for the Madison game. I think it was the second or third game of the season. And this week, I took my wife with me. When I was in town, she'd come with me, because I was traveling so much back in the day and we were also newly married.

Well, I don't remember every detail, but Vince taught me a lesson that night: never show up just for the second half of a high school game of Vince Young's. We got to the game, used the press credential, walked in . . . and the score was something silly like 50–0 with Madison up.

Halftime was over, and we literally walked in as Madison was kicking off to start the second half. Vince Young was the line-'em-up guy for kickoffs—the guy that raises his arms and then throws them down when the kicker signals he's going to kick off.

That kickoff was the only time I saw Vince play the whole night. On the play, he moved maybe ten yards and didn't seem real interested. My wife goes, "He's a lollygagger." I said, "Yeah, but how did the score get like this?"

So my wife called Vince Young a lollygagger. I still make fun of her about that to this day.

FORMER LONGHORN ASSISTANT COACH AND CURRENT MINNESOTA HEAD COACH TIM BREWSTER

The first thing is I remember was in the spring evaluation period prior to Vince's senior year at Madison. He was obviously a guy that I was recruiting extremely hard, but I had never really seen him in person. There was the excitement that I had from seeing him in person for the first time at that practice in the spring. I showed up to watch him practice and I saw three things. First, I saw him at quarterback, and it was obvious that that's where he was going to play, and I thought he was really good as a quarterback.

Then I see the kid go over to play some wide receiver and I thought he looked like he could be better than Randy Moss. Then at a certain point in practice the kid goes over—and remember that the kid is like six-foot-four or six-foot-five and 200 pounds at that point—but then he goes over to play corner. He's back there and he's moving around at corner like he's a five-foot-ten guy. I was just unbelievably amazed.

I immediately called Mack [Brown] and I told him that I had just watched the greatest high school football player that I had ever seen. Without question, this kid is the most talented high school football player that I have ever seen in my entire life, and I had been at it a while and seen a few good guys. I was really in awe of the guy's athletic ability and his ability to go from quarterback to wide receiver to corner, all in the same practice. To be quite honest with you, to be outstanding at all three positions was just amazing. As usual, Mack's response was, "Well hell, go get him." That was the beginning.

The other story that I'll never forget is when I recruited him and got him to come up on his official visit to Texas. It was a Saturday afternoon and he had come in on the Friday with his mom.

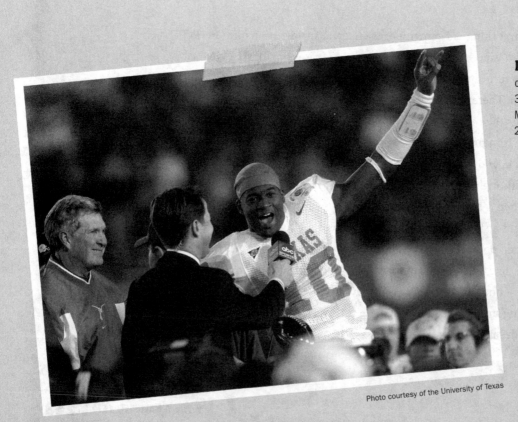

MVP YOUNG celebrates Texas's 38-37 win over Michigan in the 2005 Rose Bowl

Photo courtesy of the University of Texas

We had had a good visit on Friday and then there was a basketball game on Saturday. Vince is obviously a great basketball player and the two of us had a meeting with Rick Barnes before the game. After that, it was about thirty minutes before the game and we were walking on the court to get somewhere. At that time, almost in perfect unison, however many people that were in the Erwin Center that day, they stood up on their feet and chanted, "We want Vince! We want Vince!"

It was one of the most electrifying moments that I've ever been around or been involved with in my life. Very spontaneously, the Longhorn people showed Vince Young a lot of love. When we went back underneath the Drum, the kid had tears running out of his eyes. It was just unbelievable, and he tells me at that point, "Coach Brew, I'm going to be a Longhorn." It was just an unbelievably special moment. Obviously, that was a very special moment for all Longhorns, but that deal there was incredible.

FORMER LONGHORN RECEIVER AND TEAMMATE BRIAN CARTER

This is one of the big things I remember. This was right before we were going to the Rose Bowl. We weren't at the game, but we were at one of the events, and I remember VY going to everyone and asking, "What are you going to do?" The offensive linemen were saying that they would pancake somebody. He'd ask one of our defensive backs what they were about to do and they'd say that they were about to get a pick. He was just going around and asking everybody, and there was just so much excitement, and we just felt so confident.

At one point I thought we might be getting a little bit too cocky. Vince was so serious. He wanted to know what we were going to do to them. He just got us so pumped up.

FORMER LONGHORN DEFENSIVE END AND TEAMMATE TIM CROWDER

The first thing that comes into my head is when we were playing Missouri. We were playing them up there and we were beating them pretty good at halftime. But the refs had given us some bad calls and all that, so we all came into the locker room, and Vince was in there in tears. He was just going crazy. He was like, "The refs are not going to cheat us out of our goals. The refs are not going to cheat us out of this game." I remember thinking, "Man, we're winning like 95–13." He thought the refs were going to try and cheat us out of that game.

That's just how passionate he was, and not just about winning. He was passionate about demanding the best from his team. That's probably the best VY moment I have ever had.

FORMER LONGHORN ALL-AMERICAN SAFETY LANCE GUNN

I think it was back in 2004 and it was fourth and 18 against Kansas, and he pulled it down and ran. The fact that it was almost fourth and 20, nobody is open, and he pulled it down and was able to run for the first down is amazing. Most guys just can't do that. They are not even thinking that they can run to pick up the first down. Most guys are thinking, "I've got to throw it for a first down and I've got to somehow throw it into a tough spot and maybe get lucky." For most quarterbacks that is an incompletion or probably an interception. Just to have the balls to pull the ball down and to be able to pick it up, that's unbelievable.

At the time there was probably one other player on the planet that would do that, and it's Michael Vick. There's only one other person that would actually think to themselves that they could pick that first down up by running. It's like watching Tiger Woods play golf. It's just like un-freaking-believable.

That same year in the Rose Bowl, I remember Michigan had done a few things and put some pressure on Vince to respond. We were sitting up in the stands and I turned to a friend of mine and said, "He needs to pull it down and take it to the house." Literally on the next play, he ripped off like a 60-yard run. That's not supposed to happen. There's just no way that someone should be able to do that almost like it's on command. It's just crazy.

Having played on defense, I can say that the most dangerous thing is a quarterback that can run. The play is never over and busted plays turn out to be 20-yard gains. Most plays last like seven seconds, but with a guy like Vince, most plays feel like they are ten or twelve seconds. You've always got to be on top of your game because every time you are not, you never know what he's going to do, whether it's running with it or passing it.

ESPN AUSTIN 1530-AM
RADIO PERSONALITY ERIN HOGAN

For personal reasons, it has to be the game against Ohio State in Columbus during the national championship year. I'm an Ohio State fan and I was on the sideline for the game. I was there early because it was a prime-time game on ABC at 7:00 p.m. I got there early and just kind of hung out on the sidelines taking in the whole scene. It was a big game and it was the first night game since they had finished off the renovations to the stadium and closed in the north end zone.

I think most people know how the game went. Texas won 25–22, and Vince had brought them back, and he played an unbelievable game against one of the best defenses in college football. My recollection of his greatness wasn't just about the great game he had played and how tough he was. I just remember the Ohio State fans at the beginning of the game and how confident and cocksure they were about winning that game and beating down those boys from Texas. But when Texas won the game, their admiration for him was tremendous. They were mad at their own team because of their own quarterback controversy between Justin Zwick and Troy Smith. But to watch Vince in that environment and knowing that he was always a big-stage guy, their attitude about him changed instantly.

To see that against a team that I root for and to see the fans, who were rightfully much-maligned for how they had acted, turn and respect Vince Young the way they did was pretty amazing. Ohio State fans could tell just how magnetic of a personality he had. They were cursing Jim Tressell and the loss, but there was no doubt that some of the people that I had talked to before the game—they had thought this was going to be easy, and that Vince was overrated—to see Vince lead the way and then to see the Ohio State fans turn and show a new respect and admiration for him, you knew he had something special going for him. You knew you had a guy that was going to turn out to be Vince Young.

FORMER LONGHORN TIGHT END AND TEAMMATE STEVE HOGAN

Vince was a superstar, and we had several superstars on our team, and they were all different. He was always the most respectable toward people on the team that might not have been superstars—like me. I remember one time when my back was starting to hurt, and we had never talked a lot, but he came up and asked how I was doing. He was so charismatic with every person on the team and that's what made him a great leader in my opinion.

He didn't ever big-time anyone. You always felt like you had a personal relationship with him, even if you weren't really good friends with him. Obviously, he had his really good friends on the team, but he was always looking out for everyone. That's the number one thing that I always took away from Vince.

ORANGEBLOODS.COM WRITER SEAN ADAMS

I remember being at the Rose Bowl and after it was over, we made our way back to the hotel. After finally getting something to eat, I sat down and kind of soaked in everything that we had just seen.

In the post-game press conference, Vince wasn't talking about himself, but he was so deflective. He wanted to talk about David

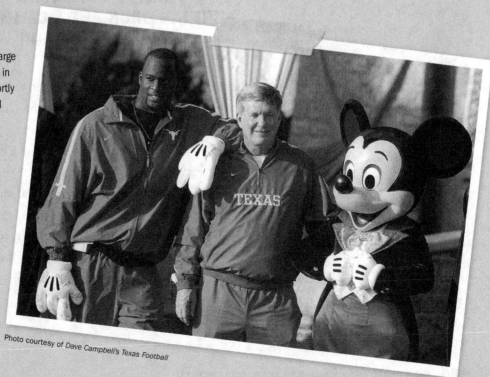

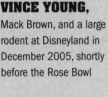

VINCE YOUNG, Mack Brown, and a large rodent at Disneyland in December 2005, shortly before the Rose Bowl

Photo courtesy of Dave Campbell's Texas Football

Thomas and the offensive line. He talked about the receivers that made plays. Finally, he talked about his family. He spoke about the women in his life and then he talked about the Man upstairs, and that's how he phrased it. He said that God could have chosen anyone to quarterback this University of Texas team, but He chose him.

I think it goes back to his mindset and how serious he took that responsibility, which is why even when he's tired he signs autographs. When he was hurt, he was still cordial to the media. Even when they lost, he was cordial to the media because he understood the responsibility of being the starting quarterback at the flagship university in the state of Texas.

FORMER LONGHORN RUNNING BACK AND TEAMMATE ANTHONY JOHNSON

In the Tulane game of his redshirt freshman year, Chris Simms was our starting quarterback, and the game was in New Orleans. We won the game and we ended up winning pretty convincingly. A couple of freshmen like Selvin Young and a couple of others from his class had played a lot in that game. I remember that he came in [to the locker room] and was crying. He was hugging Miss Sally [Brown] and crying real hard because he wanted to play.

That's probably one of my most memorable Vince Young stories. He's just so competitive and he hated not to be able to play. It wasn't that he was being selfish; he just wanted to help the team win. That's just how he always was.

FORMER LONGHORN
WIDE RECEIVER AND TEAMMATE
B. J. JOHNSON

VY stayed with me during his first year that first summer when he got to school. He stayed with me and my roommate Richard High-tower, who is the special teams coach of the Houston Texans. He was staying with us and we used to play Madden all the time. Every time he would lose, he would cry. He wouldn't literally cry, but he would leave the room and go to sleep kind of like a little baby because he didn't want to play any more because he didn't win. We used to mess with him about that all the time.

He used to do that all the time. I can remember when he first started throwing with us, he and Roy [Williams] used to go back and forth at each other like they couldn't stand each other. Roy used to always kid him that he wasn't good enough and that he was going to get moved to receiver and never play quarterback at Texas. Roy was always just playing with him, but VY would take it kind of personal because that's just the kind of competitor that he is. I remember when they would get into little fights and we'd have to break them up. We still get on him about that all the time.

I knew he always had the ability, the toughness, and the heart. I'd have to say it was the run against Oklahoma during his fresh-man year when I knew there was something special about him. We just got tired of running down the field because we didn't know where he was going. He was zig-zagging all over the field. He had like a 50- or 60-yard run that would have been more like 125 yards if he had been running straight ahead. I remember seeing that play and thinking about all of the potential that he had. There were some things like that when you could see that he had some great-ness to him.

FORMER LONGHORN DEFENSIVE TACKLE AND TEAMMATE DEREK LOKEY

My favorite Vince Young story is when we were at Oklahoma State and we were down something like 35–9. It was pretty bad. He told us at halftime that he wouldn't let us down and we all believed in him, and he went out there and led us back from that big deficit.

It was just his demeanor at halftime. We were running into the locker room and he was singing, clapping, and carrying on. The guy had a real positive, up-beat attitude about it. The whole time he was just smiling and having a good time. He didn't say much; it was just his demeanor. He knew he could take control of that ballgame at any point that he wanted and that was kind of a turning point for him as a leader. He went out there and got it done, and the rest is history. For me, that was when he really stepped up as a leader and showed the kind of leadership abilities that he had, as well as his unique ability to take over a game all by himself.

FORMER TEXAS WIDE RECEIVER WANE MCGARITY

It was his will to win—his will to succeed. I think with Vince, really, you saw a leader first-hand. A true leader under center. Major was a great leader, Major was a winner. James Brown was a great winner. I compare James and Vince all the time because James brought that same dynamic. But if you talk about Vincent, I think his junior year where he said, "You know what? This is what we have to do," and everyone followed him. That type of leadership right there and that will to succeed, I admire that about him.

FORMER LONGHORN QUARTERBACK AND TEAMMATE CHANCE MOCK

You know, there are a lot of really funny stories, but to be honest the one that I think about all the time is when I had dislocated my little bone in my heel before my senior year. I couldn't drive because it was my right ankle and Vince would come pick me up and it was totally out of his way. He would pick me up, take me to practice, and then take me back home. When you're in the middle of two-a-days, the days already feel a lot longer. That was something he didn't have to do and I've never forgotten it.

FORMER LONGHORN ALL-AMERICAN DAN NEIL

The biggest thing was that Oklahoma State game up in Stillwater during the national championship year. I was sitting in a bar watching it with my wife. I'm a die-hard Longhorn fan, and I was just disgusted because they had such a good shot at winning the national championship and here they are, they're going to blow it against Oklahoma State of all schools. I watched a little bit of it and just got upset. We went and ate dinner or something and I came back to the TV on the way out and said, "Oh my gosh." Then we had to sit down and finish watching that game.

He would have never had the chance against USC if he hadn't done it that day first. That was just amazing to watch one guy dominate that entire second half.

FORMER LONGHORN CORNERBACK AND TEAMMATE ROD BABERS

It was when I saw him play in high school and he was playing safety. That's when I knew that he was a freak of nature. Even in practice when he first got to Texas he was doing wild and crazy stuff. He was always freakish, even when he was young, in some shape or fashion. I think once his confidence got up to par with his talent, nobody was going to touch him. He's still one of the most confident guys I've ever seen or been around.

I feel like the game I saw when I knew he was different than everyone else is when we played Texas Tech during his junior season. We were ranked No. 2 and they were ranked like No. 10. It was a big game and he came out and just crushed those guys. I remember before the game most of the guys were tense, and then you look at Vince and he's out there slapping people on the butt. He's out there cracking jokes with Coach Brown and getting on Cleve [Bryant]. He was so confident and relaxed that it was contagious. They went out there and crushed those guys and that's why. He's just a special guy and a unique player.

FORMER LONGHORN TRAINER STEPHEN RATLIFF

I was a student manager during the four [Chris] Simms years. Needless to say, one of the toughest losses I was a part of was at Texas Tech in 2002, as it knocked us out of an almost certain Sugar Bowl appearance. For all the seniors, it meant never having a chance to play in a BCS bowl.

Obviously the mood in the locker room after the game was incredibly somber. About thirty minutes after the post-game speech, it was still overall pretty silent in the locker room, but there was some quiet chatter as everyone was showering up and trying to shake off the loss. Then, as I was going about my duties, I looked over where the quarterbacks were and VY still had a towel over his head and hadn't moved. He was taking the loss as hard as any of the seniors because I think he knew how much it meant to Chris and all of the other seniors on the team. Note that this was VY's redshirt year and he hadn't played a snap all season.

At that point I honestly had no idea what kind of player VY would be, because you can only tell so much by watching him run the scout team. However, it hit me then what kind of teammate and

Photo courtesy of Dave Campbell's Texas Football

YOUNG (in backward cap) celebrates on the field with Ramonce Taylor after leading the Longhorns to their first national championship since 1970

team player he already was. As I watched him progress from the stands the next three years, I always remembered that moment and knew he was out there playing for Texas and not for himself. Knowing that, nothing the team accomplished over the next three seasons ever shocked me.

ORANGEBLOODS.COM WRITER JASON SUCHOMEL

It's tough to pick just one moment or characteristic of Vince Young's that stands out. The obvious choice would be the game-winning touchdown in the national championship game, but I think what defines Vince in my mind is more the confidence that he instilled rather than that one particular play. In fact, I remember when I was watching that game and Texas got the ball back, down by five and fifty-six yards away from the end zone, there wasn't a doubt in my mind that Young would lead the Longhorns down for a score.

Before that, when Texas was down by twelve midway through the fourth quarter, I actually thought the Longhorns were sunk. After Vince scored the game-winning touchdown, I remember telling my wife, who I was watching the game with, "I should have known better than to doubt that guy."

> **"I should have known better than to doubt that guy."**

Be it fans, players, or coaches, I don't know that I've ever seen a player at the collegiate level that had such unwavering confidence from those around him. And with all due respect to the other great leaders that have come through the Texas program in my years covering the team, I know I've never seen a player that commanded the respect of his teammates the way VY did. Every single player on that team would have walked through fire for Vince, and they all knew, from top to bottom, that he had their back as well.

FORMER LONGHORN TIGHT END AND TEAMMATE DAVID THOMAS

I think the best story I can think of is when he was a redshirt freshman. When you play at Texas, after your first game, all of the upperclassmen make you dance the next day after we're done lifting weights. That was really the first time I had ever not seen Vince hamming it up. He was a little shy. He was just trying to play it off and everyone was getting after him pretty good. That was the first time I had ever seen him shy, and that wasn't like him at all. Thinking about how he always was, even in practice, he was always a character. He was acting shy then, like he didn't want to dance. We couldn't believe it.

The thing about Vince is that he didn't care if you were an NFL guy or a walk-on that nobody even knew. He would mess with you and he wouldn't let anyone slide if they did something, He would make fun of them or get on them. He didn't let anything go and it didn't matter who you were because he treated everyone the same. He messed around with everybody and had fun with everybody. I think that's what makes him different. He didn't care who you were, what your story was, or what your background was, he just wanted you to work and have fun.

FORMER LONGHORN WIDE RECEIVER AND TEAMMATE SLOAN THOMAS

I caught his first pass. When he came into the huddle, everyone is going crazy for Vince because he was coming into the game for the first time. All he does is look at me and say, "Run. Just run as fast as you can." And he threw it to me. That was the first time when I really knew that this guy was going to be *that* guy.

FORMER LONGHORN DEFENSIVE BACK AND FORMER TEAM ADMINISTRATOR JOE WALKER

He was just a class act guy. It's hard to put it into words, but he was just a person that looked out for everyone on the team. He's just a very humble person and he always had time for everyone. He was always doing things for people, and I'm not talking about on the field, but off the field. For me, I was impressed with him as an athlete and what he could do on the field, but it was more about the kind of person he was and how he acted around people. That's just priceless, at least for me it is. Being around a lot of athletes and a lot of people, some people have their way of thinking about things at times, but he always had time to go out of his way and make everyone feel welcome around him. That's what really made me a fan of Vince Young.

FORMER LONGHORN DEFENSIVE LINEMAN CEDRIC WOODARD

I didn't play with Vince, but I know him pretty well. That championship year was just unbelievable and so was his performance in the Rose Bowl. I think that was the only game I was able to attend that year. I was playing in Seattle and I was able to come down for the game. Vince just seemed so calm during the whole game. It was almost like he was never worried, and it was like he knew they were going to win the national championship. Just being on the sideline during the game, I remember thinking to myself, "That is one cool cat right there." That's probably the moment with him that I remember the most.

Acknowledgments

"Do you want to write a book about Longhorn football?"

When Jim Fletcher first posed that question to me before the start of the 2007 season, I didn't have a quick answer. Although it's certainly something I had pondered over the years, I'll be the first to admit that I wasn't sure I'd be able to cobble together all the pieces that comprise a full-length sports book.

As the owner and publisher of Orangebloods.com, I've written countless feature stories for magazines across the country. But writing a book seemed like an entirely different matter. For someone who was a broadcasting major and had started his career in television news, I can honestly and without reservation say that this kind of intense, long-term project wasn't what I signed up for when I got into the business.

Yet there was something tempting about the prospect of writing a book—it would be a challenge for me in a brand new medium. After doing television, radio, and developing the top Longhorn website, a new frontier seemed exciting.

So I said yes.

Of course, that was the easy part. As I learned in the months leading up to this book's publication, there's a lot more to the process than simply sitting in front of a keyboard and hammering away at some of the greatest stories about one of the preeminent college football programs.

Without the patient, flexible, and always understanding Jack Langer at Regnery Publishing, there wouldn't be a book. When I was lost at one point in the process, he pulled everything together like the good captain that he is, and he trusted me when I told him I'd meet some pretty tight deadlines.

The same thing goes for Jim. I'm really not sure if it's normal to work with someone like me who's a constant headache, but Jim was always running below room temperature whenever any challenging issues arose. Pete Townshend could take lessons on being cool from the guy.

A person to whom I owe several lunch tabs and perhaps a raise is Jason Suchomel, who not only is the managing editor of my baby, Orangebloods.com, but provided vital help down the stretch for which I'm eternally grateful.

Also, special thanks to the other members of my staff at Orangebloods.com—Gerry, Sean, and Blaire, as well as everyone at Rivals.com and ESPN 1530-AM. I know I was a bear for some time as I juggled a thousand balls at once, but I'm convinced that the final product was worth the effort.

Obviously, there wouldn't be a book without the help of the countless former Longhorns who contributed to this project. I hope this book does the lives and stories of these men justice.

Really and truly, I feel that way about the entire Longhorn Nation, especially the community at Orangebloods.com. I am blessed to have so many special people in my life from the Longhorn community—people like Robert and Katy Agnor, who have shown me how much more fulfilling it is to give back rather than to receive.

Finally, I want to take a moment to thank all my loved ones who put up with my scattershot ways for many months. My girlfriend Heather tolerated my manic moods on a daily basis, so she's obviously a keeper. I also benefitted from the patience and understanding of my cousin Ron and my mother. Like a tripod, each of these three people served as a leg to support me, and I hope they will be proud of this tribute to the great Longhorn program that will always remain a major part of my life.

TIMELINE

Longhorns

» **1893:** Longhorn program begins on November 30 with a stunning 18–16 win over unbeaten Dallas University. The team finishes the season with a perfect 4–0 record.

» **1894:** Longhorns win a 38–0 blowout in their first game against Texas A&M

» **1895:** Longhorns defeat Austin YMCA, 24–0, to wrap up the school's third and final victory in the series. YMCA never scored against Texas, dropping three contests by a combined score of 54–0.

» **1900:** Longhorns win 28–2 in their first game against Oklahoma

» **1901:** Longhorns beat A&M, 32–0, in their first Thanksgiving Day game

» **1909:** Dexter Draper era begins in September with a 12–0 win over Southwestern

» **1909:** Dexter Draper era ends in November with a 5–0 loss to the Aggies

» **1910:** A week before Halloween, Texas drains the life out of Transylvania, 48–0

» **1920:** The largest crowd in the history of the state shows up at Clark Field on November 25 to watch the Longhorns cap off an undefeated season by handing the Aggies their first loss in two years

» **1924:** Longhorns play their first game in Memorial Stadium on November 8, losing 28–10 to Baylor

» **1934:** On October 6, the Longhorns win an epic, 7–6, against Notre Dame at South Bend. Bohn Hilliard scores from eight yards out to provide the winning points.

» **1937:** The Scripture Years begin as Dana X. Bible takes over and coaches Texas for ten seasons, going 63–31–3

» **1939:** Trailing Arkansas 13–7 with thirty seconds remaining in the game on October 21, UT fullback R. B. Patrick throws a short pass to Jack Crain, who rumbles sixty-seven yards to tie the score at 13–13. After taking several minutes to clear the field of fans who stormed the field following the touchdown, Crain adds the PAT to give the Longhorns a 14–13 win. The game is dubbed the "Renaissance game" of the Dana X. Bible era at Texas.

» **1940:** Noble Doss accomplishes an "impossible catch" on November 28 in a 7–0 win over arch-rival Texas A&M. The game ends the Aggies' dream of winning back-to-back national championships.

» **1941**: Frustrated at being passed over by the Rose Bowl committee, the No. 4 Longhorns pound Oregon, 71–7, at Memorial Stadium on December 6. Less than twenty-four hours later, the Japanese bomb Pearl Harbor.

» **1943:** In their first bowl game, on New Year's Day, the No. 11 Longhorns upset No. 5 Oregon, 14–7, in the Cotton Bowl behind the strong play of running backs Dale McKay and Jackie Field. Before the game, International News Service reporter Lawton Carver declares, "Texas doesn't belong in the same league with Georgia Tech."

» **1946:** Darrell Royal starts as a freshman at Oklahoma

» **1950:** The No. 7 Longhorns upset No. 1 SMU, 23–20, on November 4. The Longhorns defense limits legendary running back Kyle Rote to –3 yards on seven carries.

» **1950:** One week after beating SMU, the Longhorns defeat Baylor, 27–20, to pave the way for a conference championship

» **1953:** After losing to Tennessee in the 1951 Cotton Bowl, the No. 10 Longhorns get their revenge on January 1 by shutting out the No. 8 Vols, 16–0, in the first televised bowl game in Dallas. The Texas defense limits the Vols to six first downs and –14 rushing yards.

» **1956:** Darrell Royal is hired as head coach

» **1957:** Longhorns post their first win of the Royal era, beating Georgia 26–7

» **1958:** Longhorns defeat OU, 15–14, and go on to win every game in the series until 1966

» **1961:** Senior halfback and future College Hall of Fame inductee James Saxton rushes for 173 yards on sixteen carries to lead the Longhorns to a 27–0 beat-down of SMU on November 4. Coupled with earlier upsets over Michigan State and Ole Miss, the win moves the Longhorns to 7–0 and elevates them to their first No. 1 ranking under Royal.

» **1962:** On New Year's Day, the No. 3 Longhorns beat No. 5 Ole Miss, 12–7, in Texas's first bowl game under Royal

» **1962:** In a match-up of two undefeated and top-rankled teams on October 20, the No. 1 Longhorns edge out No. 7 Arkansas, 7–3, in the first of several memorable games in this decade between the two teams. A 3-yard touchdown run by Tommy Ford caps off a 20-play, 90-yard drive with only thirty-six seconds remaining in the game.

» **1963:** In a battle between the nation's top two teams on October 12, the No. 1 Longhorns crush No. 2 Oklahoma, 28–7, behind the strong play of defenders Scott Appleton and Tommy Nobis

» **1963:** On November 9, with Baylor driving to the Texas 19-yard line and less than a minute to go in the game, Duke Carlisle makes a leaping interception to preserve a 7–0 win and save Texas's national championship hopes

» **1964:** Before Texas's match-up with Navy in the Cotton Bowl on New Year's Day, famed sportswriter Myron Cope remarks, "Tune in your television to the Cotton Bowl and you'll laugh yourself silly....Texas is the biggest fraud ever perpetrated on the football public." The Longhorns go on to crush the Midshipmen, 28–6, to put an exclamation mark on the school's first national championship season.

» **1965:** Facing Alabama and the great Joe Namath on January 1, the No. 5 Longhorns race out to a 21–7 lead and hold on to win, 21–17, in the Cotton Bowl

» **1968:** In a game that's considered the breakthrough for the Wishbone offense, the Longhorns beat Oklahoma, 26–20, in the Cotton Bowl on October 12. With the Longhorns trailing 20–19 with 2:37 remaining in the game, James Street leads the Longhorns on an 85-yard drive capped off by Steve Worster's 7-yard scoring run with thirty-nine seconds left in the game.

» **1969:** In the "Game of the Century," the No. 1 Longhorns take on No. 2 Arkansas in Fayetteville with a national championship on the line in December. Trailing 14–8 in the fourth quarter, quarterback James Street connects with Randy Peschel for a 44-yard pass play on a fourth and three that eventually sets up Jim Bertlesen's 2-yard touchdown. Happy Feller's PAT then gives the Longhorns a stunning 15–14 win. President Richard Nixon congratulates the Longhorns and proclaims them national champions in the locker room after the game.

» **1970:** The Longhorns go to the Cotton Bowl on New Year's Day to face No. 9 Notre Dame, which was ending a self-imposed 44-year ban on bowl games. With the Longhorns trailing 17–14 with 6:52 remaining in the fourth quarter, Texas converts two fourth down plays before Billy Dale crosses the goal line to give the Longhorns a 21–17 win and cement their second national championship.

» **1970:** No. 2 Texas defeats No. 13 UCLA, 20–17, on October 3 at Memorial Stadium thanks to one of the most spectacular plays in the program's history. Quarterback Eddie Phillips connects with Cotton Speyrer on a 45-yard touchdown pass with twelve seconds remaining in the game to give the Longhorns the win, which preserves a school-record 23-game winning streak.

» **1973:** The No. 7 Longhorns cap off a 10–1 season with a 17–13 win over No. 4 Alabama in the Cotton Bowl

» **1974:** Longhorns sign superstar Earl Campbell

» **1976:** Darrell Royal era comes to a close in December with a 29–12 win over Arkansas

» **1977:** After five straight losses to the Sooners, the Longhorns finally get their revenge with a 13–6 win in Dallas on October 8. The Longhorns are led by Heisman Trophy front-runner Earl Campbell, who rushes for 124 yards and a touchdown on twenty-three carries.

» **1977:** Earl Campbell rushes for 222 yards and four touchdowns on November 26 against A&M in a wild 57–28 win

» **1977:** On December 8, Earl Campbell becomes the first Longhorn to win the Heisman Trophy

» **1982:** Texas head coach Fred Akers picks up his first Cotton Bowl Classic win with a 14–12 victory over Bear Bryant's Alabama Crimson Tide on New Year's Day. The key play of the game is a 70-yard touchdown run by quarterback Robert Brewer.

» **1983:** The No. 2 Longhorns take over first place in the Southwest Conference on October 22 with a 15–12 win over No. 9 SMU in a battle between undefeated teams. The win snaps SMU's 21-game unbeaten streak.

» **1983:** On November 26, Texas quarterback Rick McIvor enters the game just before the end of the first half and completes eight of twelve passes for 170 yards and four touchdowns. The Longhorns go on to crush A&M, 45–13, in College Station.

» **1987:** Bret Stafford connects with Tony Jones on an 18-yard touchdown pass with no time remaining on the clock, as the Longhorns upset No. 15 Arkansas, 15–14, in Little Rock on October 17

» **1989:** Freshman quarterback Peter Gardere picks up the first of four victories over the Sooners with a 28–24 win on October 14. The Longhorns lead the game 21–7 at halftime, but find themselves trailing 24–21 in the fourth quarter before Gardere hooks up with Johnny Walker for a 25-yard touchdown pass in the final two minutes.

» **1990:** Oklahoma kicker R. D. Lashar misses a 46-yard field goal in the final minute of the game on October 13, as the unranked Longhorns stun No. 13 Oklahoma, 14–13

» **1990:** In one of the most memorable home games in the history of the Texas program, the Longhorns crush Houston's "unstoppable" offense by intercepting Cougars quarterback David Klingler four times on November 10. Meanwhile, the Longhorn offense rolls up 626 yards as the Cougars get whipped, 45–24.

» **1994:** In his first start at Texas, on October 8, redshirt freshman quarterback James Brown completes seventeen of twenty-two passes for 148 yards and adds a touchdown on the ground to lead the Longhorns to a 17–10 win over Oklahoma. While Brown is the star of the game, the most important play occurs in the final minute when UT defensive tackle Stonie Clark stops Sooner running back James Allen just shy of the end zone on a fourth down play.

» **1995:** Phil Dawson connects on a 50-yard field goal as time expires to lead No. 16 Texas past No. 14 Virginia, 17–16, at Memorial Stadium on October 21

» **1995:** The Longhorns go into Kyle Field on December 2 and end A&M's 31-game home winning streak. Freshman running back Ricky Williams leads the UT offensive attack with 163 yards and two touchdowns in the 16–6 victory, as the Longhorns clinch the final Southwest Conference crown.

» **1996:** In one of the biggest blowouts in the history of the Texas/A&M series, on November 29 the Longhorns roll the Aggies, 51–15, to clinch the inaugural Big 12 South Championship. James Brown passes for 353 yards and four touchdowns, while Ricky Williams adds 145 yards and a touchdown on the ground.

» **1996:** Roll Left—and not much more needs be said. In one of the biggest upsets in the history of the Longhorn program, James Brown leads the team to a 37–27 win over No. 3 Nebraska on December 7, securing the Big 12's first championship for Texas. The key play occurs with 2:40 remaining in the game and the Longhorns clinging to a 30–27 lead. On fourth and inches from the Texas 28-yard line, Brown rolls left and hits tight end Derrick Lewis on a 61-yard play.

» **1998:** Junior running back Ricky Williams announces on January 8 that he will return to Texas for his senior season

» **1998:** In his final game against Oklahoma, on October 10, Ricky Williams changes his jersey number to honor the late Doak Walker and rushes for 139 yards and two touchdowns. The Longhorns take the game, 34–3.

» **1998:** On October 31, in a game signaling the onset of a new era in Longhorn football, an unranked Texas squad beats No. 7 Nebraska, 20–16, in Lincoln to snap the Huskers' 47-game home winning streak. Ricky Williams rushes for 150 yards on thirty-seven carries against the vaunted Blackshirt defense.

» **1998:** In front of a national television audience on November 27, Ricky Williams sets the career NCAA rushing record with a 60-yard touchdown run in the first quarter. Redshirt freshman quarterback Major Applewhite leads a last-minute scoring drive in the fourth quarter to secure a 26–24 win over No. 6 A&M.

» **1998:** On December 12, Ricky Williams becomes the second Longhorn to win the Heisman Trophy

» **1999:** On October 23, before a record crowd of 84,082, the Longhorns overcome a 13–3 halftime deficit to upset No. 3 Nebraska, 24–20, and give Texas its third consecutive win over the powerhouse Cornhuskers. Mike Jones hauls in the winning touchdown pass from Major Applewhite midway through the fourth quarter.

» **2000:** Sophomore quarterback Chris Simms completes eighteen of twenty-four passes for 383 yards and three touchdowns as the No. 12 Longhorns blast No. 22 A&M, 43–17, in Austin on November 24

» **2001:** In what was the biggest comeback in the history of the storied Longhorn program, No. 9 Texas overcomes a 19-point deficit in the second half to beat No. 21 Washington, 47–43, in the Holiday Bowl on December 28. In his final game as a Longhorn, Major Applewhite sets UT bowl records by completing thirty-seven of fifty-five passes for 473 yards and four touchdowns. Freshman linebacker Derrick Johnson is the game's defensive MVP, as he records nine tackles, a sack, and an interception.

» **2001:** With nary a dry eye in the house, on September 8 the Longhorns beat North Carolina, 44–14, at home in a game dedicated to the memory of UT player Cole Pittman, who died earlier in the year in a car accident. Following Texas's final touchdown of the afternoon, back-up quarterback Chance Mock points out to Mack Brown that the Longhorns had scored forty-four points, which reflects Pittman's jersey number. Brown instructs Major Applewhite to take a knee on the PAT to ensure that forty-four remain on the record books forever.

» **2002:** Six years after the Longhorns had snapped Nebraska's 47-game home winning streak, Texas breaks the Huskers' 26-game home winning streak on November 2 with a 27–24 win in Lincoln. Chris Simms passes for a Texas record 419 yards and Roy Williams sets a school record with thirteen catches for 161 yards and two touchdowns.

» **2003:** The Vince Young era begins on October 4 as the redshirt freshman quarterback completes a 52-yard pass to Tony Jeffery and then caps off the game-winning drive with a one-yard touchdown. The Longhorns beat No. 16 Kansas State, 24–20, in Austin.

» **2003:** In one of the wildest games in Texas history, quarterback Chance Mock connects with B. J. Johnson on a touchdown pass with only forty-six seconds remaining in the game, leading to a 43–40 victory over Texas Tech on November 15 in Austin

» 2003: On November 1 Cedric Benson and Vince Young become the first tandem in Longhorn history to rush for 150 yards or more in the same game during a 31–7 win over No. 12 Nebraska in Austin

» 2004: The No. 6 Longhorns overcome a 28-point deficit on November 6 and rally for forty-nine unanswered points, as Texas beats No. 19 Oklahoma State, 56–25, in Austin. Cedric Benson rushes for 141 yards and five touchdowns, while Vince Young accounts for 401 yards of total offense.

» 2004: Vince Young converts a fourth and eighteen play late in the fourth quarter with a 22-yard run and follows it up with a 21-yard touchdown pass to Tony Jeffery with eleven seconds remaining in the game in Lawrence on November 13. The No. 6 Longhorns go on to beat Kansas, 27–23.

» 2005: Vince Young puts on a performance for the ages on New Year's Day, but it takes a last-second field goal from senior kicked Dusty Mangum to give the Longhorns a thrilling 38–37 win over Michigan in the Rose Bowl. Young rushes for 192 yards and scores four touchdowns to cap off one of the most spectacular individual performances in college football history.

» 2005: Limas Sweed catches a 24-yard touchdown from Vince Young in the final minutes of the game, as No. 2 Texas beats No. 4 Ohio State, 25–22, on September 10 in Columbus

» 2005: With their national championship hopes on the line, on October 29 the Longhorns overcome a 19-point first-half deficit and defeat Oklahoma State, 47–28, in Stillwater. Vince Young leads the comeback with 506 yards of total offense, including a career-high 267 yards rushing.

» 2005: Longhorns win their first Big 12 Championship under Mack Brown with a 70–3 throttling of Colorado in the league's championship game in Houston on December 3

» 2006: In what many have dubbed the greatest game in college football history, on January 4 Vince Young puts on a one-man show in leading Texas to a 41–38 win over USC in the BCS Championship at the Rose Bowl in Pasadena. Young sets a Rose Bowl record with 467 yards of total offense, scores three touchdowns, and provides the winning touchdown on a fourth and five from the USC 8-yard line with only nineteen seconds remaining in the game. The win gives the Longhorns their first national championship since 1970.

LIFETIME RECORD

BY YEAR

Year	Record	Year	Record	Year	Record	Year	Record
1893:	4-0	**1922:**	7-2	**1951:**	7-3	**1980:**	7-5
1894:	6-1	**1923:**	8-0-1	**1952:**	9-2	**1981:**	10-1-1
1895:	5-0	**1924:**	5-3-1	**1953:**	7-3	**1982:**	9-3
1896:	4-2-1	**1925:**	6-2-1	**1954:**	4-5-1	**1983:**	11-1
1897:	6-2	**1926:**	5-4	**1955:**	5-5	**1984:**	7-4-1
1898:	5-1	**1927:**	6-2-1	**1956:**	1-9	**1985:**	8-4
1899:	6-2	**1928:**	7-2	**1957:**	6-4-1	**1986:**	5-6
1900:	6-0	**1929:**	5-2-2	**1958:**	7-3	**1987:**	7-5
1901:	8-2-1	**1930:**	8-1-1	**1959:**	9-2	**1988:**	4-7
1902:	6-3-1	**1931:**	6-4	**1960:**	7-3-1	**1989:**	5-6
1903:	5-1-2	**1932:**	8-2	**1961:**	10-1	**1990:**	10-2
1904:	6-2	**1933:**	4-5-2	**1962:**	9-1-1	**1991:**	5-6
1905:	5-4	**1934:**	7-2-1	**1963:**	11-0*	**1992:**	6-5
1906:	9-1	**1935:**	4-6	**1964:**	10-1	**1993:**	5-5-1
1907:	6-1-1	**1936:**	2-6-1	**1965:**	6-4	**1994:**	8-4
1908:	5-4	**1937:**	2-6-1	**1966:**	7-4	**1995:**	10-2-1
1909:	4-3-1	**1938:**	1-8	**1967:**	6-4	**1996:**	8-5
1910:	6-2	**1939:**	5-4	**1968:**	9-1-1	**1997:**	4-7
1911:	5-2	**1940:**	8-2	**1969:**	11-0*	**1998:**	9-3
1912:	7-1	**1941:**	8-1-1	**1970:**	10-1*	**1999:**	9-5
1913:	7-1	**1942:**	9-2	**1971:**	8-3	**2000:**	9-3
1914:	8-0	**1943:**	7-1-1	**1972:**	10-1	**2001:**	11-2
1915:	6-3	**1944:**	5-4	**1973:**	8-3	**2002:**	11-2
1916:	7-2	**1945:**	10-1	**1974:**	8-4	**2003:**	10-3
1917:	4-4	**1946:**	8-2	**1975:**	10-2	**2004:**	11-1
1918:	9-0	**1947:**	10-1	**1976:**	5-5-1	**2005:**	13-0*
1919:	6-3	**1948:**	7-3-1	**1977:**	11-1	**2006:**	10-3
1920:	9-0	**1949:**	6-4	**1978:**	9-3	**2007:**	10-3
1921:	6-1-1	**1950:**	9-2	**1979:**	9-3		

* Denotes national champions

Index

Houston Wheatley High School, 42

Hubert, Wes, 65

Hudson, Jim, 43

Huff, Michael, 217, 230, 237(pic)

Humphrey, Jay, 135

Hunnicutt, Walter S., 228

Huston, Josh, 205

Hutchinson, Kay Bailey, 260

I

Ingraham, Rick, 65

Iowa State University, 133, 134, 214

Ivory, Horace, 68

J

Jack, Jason, 222

Jackson, Alfred, 65, 102

James, Bruce, 48, 50

Janszen, Tully, 160–61

Jarrett, Dwayne, 232, 239

Jennings, Brandon, 136

Jim Thorpe Award, 230

Johnson, Anthony, 260

Johnson, B. J., 260–61

Johnson, Claudia Alt Taylor (Lady Bird), 8

Johnson, Derrick, 197

Johnson, Marquis, 161–63, 165(pic)

Jones, Johnny "Ham," 69(pic), 70, 100

Jones, Johnny "Lam," 69(pic), 70, 89(pic), 92(pic), 97(pic), 103(pic), 106(pic); back injury of, 104–5; cancer battle of, 105–8; college career of, 100–103; drug problem of, 104; high school career of, 87–95; Montreal Summer Olympics (1976) and, 88, 94–95, 96–97; in NFL, 103–5;

recruiting of, 100–101; as track star, 87–95; UT career of, 101–3; Wishbone offense and, 88, 100

Jones, Mike, 194

Jones, Nate, 235

Jones, Ronnie, 51

Jordan, Louis, 18, 18(pic)

Juan in a Million, 94

K

Kansas, University of, 219, 220, 238

Kansas State University, 133

Keasler, Sid, 50

Kelley, Jerry, 43

Kelson, Mike, 49

Kennedy, John F., 45–46

Kersey, Rick, 50

King, Harry, 49

King, James E., 228

King, Kenny, 68

King, Tyson, 109, 121

Koy, Ernie, 40

Koy, Ted, 50, 53, 55, 56, 60, 63

Kristynik, Marvin, 42

Kristynik, Paul, 51

Krueger, Phil, 65

Kyle Field, College Station, Tex., 221

L

Lackey, Bobby, 44

Leaks, Roosevelt, 4–5, 65, 66, 100

Leinart, Matt, 226, 231, 232, 239

Leitko, Travis, 187

Leone, Brandon, 221

Lester, Danny, 51

Lewis, Courtney, 246

Lewis, Derrick, 112, 122, 125

Lewis, Robert, 51

Lincoln Journal-Star, 112

Little, Donnie, 105

Littlefield, Clyde, 21

Lokey, Derek, 261–62

Lombardi Award, 187

Longhorn Nation, 130, 239, 241

Lott, Thomas, 62, 68, 72

Louisiana, University of, Lafayette, 198, 200, 238

Louisiana State University (LSU), 36

Lowrey, Alan, 63, 65

LSU. See Louisiana State University

Luster, Dewey, 35

M

Mabry, Tom, 50

Mackovic, John, 113–15, 119–21, 123, 125, 132

McBride, Charlie, 116

McCallum, Napolean, 138

McClellan, Scott, 260

McCullough, Edorian, 164–66

McGarity, Wayne, 120, 133, 135–36, 144, 146, 262

McGee, Stephen, 219, 220, 221, 222

McKay, Bob, 50, 63, 65

McKinney, Mack, 51

McLane, Paul, 2, 3, 9

McLane, Ray, 2, 3, 9

McLemore, Daniel, 216

McMichael, Steve, 72, 102

McNeal, Reggie, 219, 220, 221

McNulty, Gordon, 50, 53

MacPhall, Lonnie, 101

McReynolds, Walter, 43

McTear, Houston, 95

McWilliams, David, 42

Mangum, Dusty, 196

Manley, Leon, 37, 52, 59

Martin, Marco, 163–64, 188

Maryland, University of, 102

Matthews, Vince, 44

Matt's El Rancho, 32

Mauldin, Stan, 50, 51

Maxwell, Bruce, 50, 55

Mayes, Randy, 181, 182